THE ORDER OF BATTLE
AT TRAFALGAR

THE
ORDER OF BATTLE
AT TRAFALGAR

And Other Essays

JOHN BAYLEY

Weidenfeld & Nicolson
New York

Published by Weidenfeld & Nicolson, New York
A Division of Wheatland Corporation
10 East 53rd Street
New York, NY 10022

Originally published in Great Britain in 1987 by
Collins Harvill.

"The Strengths of His Passivity" © The New York Times Company 1983.
Reprinted with permission.

"The Two Hardys" © NYREV, Inc. 1982. Reprinted with the permission of
the *New York Review of Books*.

"Poems with a Heroine" © NYREV, Inc. 1984. Reprinted with the permission
of the *New York Review of Books*.

"Pasternak, Rilke and Cézanne" (originally entitled "Big Three") © NYREV,
Inc. 1985. Reprinted with the permission of the *New York Review of Books*.

LIBRARY OF CONGRESS CATALOGING-IN-PUBLICATION DATA

Bayley, John, 1925–
The order of battle at Trafalgar, and other
essays.
1. Literature, Modern—History and criticism.
I. Title.
PN710.B34   1987   809   86–29013
ISBN 1–55584–137–6

Manufactured in Great Britain
Designed by Vera Brice
First American Edition 1987

10 9 8 7 6 5 4 3 2 1

Contents

The Order of
Battle at Trafalgar

Some years ago, Lionel Trilling was writing in *Partisan Review* about the "unargued assumption" of our time that the one true object of the intellectual's imaginative life was the modern world and its preoccupations. He expressed a certain nostalgia – even though rather diffidently – for "a quiet place" in which today's intellectual "can be silent, in which he can *know* something – in what year the Parthenon was begun, the order of battle at Trafalgar, how Linear B was deciphered: almost anything that has nothing to do with the talkative and attitudinising present". Things have changed a bit since then of course. I do not know whether the intellectual at the time was at all heedful of Trilling's point, but I suspect that for his successor in the next generation – the present – the status of facts as facts has been still further diminished. *Knowing* something, in the sense Lionel Trilling had in mind, may seem to him more naive than ever.

The climate of structuralism has something to do with this, particularly where the study of literature is concerned. Rejecting "the metaphysic of presence" we study "self-consuming artifacts"; codes and strategies have replaced facts and objects. The past, in literature, no longer consists of events and things. There may be at least one elementary and grim reason for this shift of attitude towards the past, the negating of any cherished sense of it, and this is that so much in the immediate past will hardly bear thinking about. The Germans for many years resolutely refused to think about it at all. The railway timetables that dispatched trains to Auschwitz do not bear contemplating with the same sense of knowledge – the same "fond participation" in Henry James's phrase – as does, say, the order of battle at Trafalgar.

In his Charles Eliot Norton Lectures, published as *The Witness of Poetry*, the Nobel prize-winner Czeslaw Milosz talked about the implications of this, and how Polish poets like Zbigniew Herbert, Alexander Wat, and Anna Swirszczynska, had reacted to it. A poem of Herbert's implicitly rejects the nightmare of memory in favour of contemplating a pebble.

> I feel a heavy remorse
> when I hold it in my hand
>
> and its noble body
> is permeated by false warmth

and he foretells of such stones that

> to the end they will look at us
> with a calm and very clear eye

"The Pebble" does without the past in an honourable sense, not the sense in which the past has been rejected by today's critics on the ground that there can be nothing outside the area they control. Reductive as it may be, the poem does not seek to escape from human events or to deny that they ever take place. "The fact", for Roland Barthes, "can only exist linguistically, as a term of discourse", so that the statement: "Napoleon died at St Helena on May 5th 1821" merely shows that there is an item called "historical truth" in our culture codes. The fact that Poland was occupied by the Germans from 1939 to 1945, and that millions of Poles and Jews died as a result, strikes poets who were close to and intimate with these events in a rather different light.

Herbert and the other poets had come up against the fact – for that is what it seems to be – that certain other facts are not susceptible to being dealt with either by our culture codes or by our capacity for human feelings. They remain outside us, like the pebble in the hand, "permeated by false warmth". Much has been written, often histrionically, about the inability of language to confront Auschwitz, but it is not language which is at fault – language as description

will do all that is asked of it – but our awareness of facts which remain outside the possibility of feeling. Milosz remarks that many
poets tried to bring these events, and their proper feelings about
them, into poetry and as poetry. Such attempts were honourable
but a complete failure. Herbert's pebble, looking at us with a calm
and very clear eye, shows us why this is the case. Poetry, in such
cases, must respect what has happened by acknowledging that it
cannot feel it. Paradoxically it will then be in accord with that other
sense of the past which Lionel Trilling was thinking of. In both
cases the mind reaches out to facts outside itself: in the one case,
facts in which the mind can participate just because they are outside; in the other, those in which it cannot participate for the same
reason. It is the externality of the past, as of the pebble, which makes
art possible in some cases and impossible in others.

The question we have to ask when Barthes tells us that "the fact
can only exist linguistically, as a term of discourse", is "why does
he want to say that?" The answer may be that history and the past,
where so-called facts are, have come to repel him, and that he
wishes to seal off the language of art and our response to it. That
would be in effect a kind of higher escapism, an intellectual elabora-
tion of the theory of art for art's sake. But the more probable
explanation has to do with the necessary division between the past
and ourselves, between works of art and literature and ourselves.
We abolish this division by refusing to admit that the past exists or
that the facts of literature are anywhere but in our own codes of
discourse. The technique is to insist that what is self-evidently true
is therefore comprehensively so. Barthes might have said: "I can
only exist biologically, as a function of cellular activity", and thus
taken for granted that he cannot think, suffer or recognize the
external world for what it is and has been.

Herbert's pebble is irreducible for his consciousness, bringing its
own kind of comfort, giving its own kind of feeling. It is "the feel
of not to feel it", as in Keats's poem "In A Drear-Nighted December", which concerns the difference between natural objects which
have no memory, and therefore feel no pain, and human subjects
which do. Comfort? Certainly; any honest poem is comforting,

because it tells the truth about our feelings, or lack of them, our powers, or lack of them, in the face of externality. The sort of poem which Milosz mentions, one in willed pursuit of "proper" responses to the Holocaust, to the scale and terror of the death camps, has to construct its message in codes which are familiar without being really felt. Faced with Herbert's pebble, on the other hand, we catch a glimmering of what the horror is really all about. The poet did not know he was doing this, did not understand what he was doing. In the phrase of Valéry, he only knew what he had said when he had said it. The sense of the past revealed itself to him in an unexpected way.

Barthes and the structural analysts would scarcely find a way of understanding this, because their methods do not recognize the absolute existence of the past or of the fact outside ourselves. Wittgenstein's reasons for saying "the limits of my language are the limits of my world" were strictly and intently philosophical: his statement has had an unfortunate effect, nonetheless, on the software of literary theory. Dr Johnson broke the Berkleian hypothesis, to his own satisfaction, by kicking a stone, and common sense is always trying to disenmesh itself from literary theory in the same way. Richard Wilbur, like Wittgenstein, may have been expressing a certain kind of truth when he protested:

> Kick on, Sam Johnson, till you break your bones,
> But cloudy, cloudy, is the stuff of stones

but in using stones as a "term of discourse" he was not saying that was the end of the fact of them. For the structural analyst, however, literature and the past have no existence outside his own analysis of them. One result of this is that he cannot understand why a poem cannot be written "about" a concentration camp.

Such a poem would revolt us by its attempt to merge and be with its subject, by its inability to realize that any feeling it concocts is wholly alien to the fact it describes. This is an extreme case of what structural analysis does to literature itself, and to the past and the events on which literature depends. The common critic, like the common reader, has always been conscious that whatever he thought about the works he read, whatever the degree of his fond participation in them, they remained outside himself, their existence was different from his own and would remain unchanged by it. I am now myself trying to say something about the relation of literature and the past, their relation and their externality; trying, like all critics, to make a point. Whatever its validity, however, I know that what I think about it has no significance whatever in contrast with literature itself, and the past in which it lives. The ingenuities of structural analysis — and they can be very ingenious indeed — rest on the premise that the facts in literature are themselves as transparent as the critic's words, into which they merge and are reconstituted.

Again it is necessary to ask the simple question: why do the new analysts want to look at things in this light? The answer too seems simple. They are dissatisfied with the traditional position of critics and teachers as on the sidelines of the real, watching the actual ball game, so to speak, and commenting on it as spectators. They wish to seem, by their processes, to be manufacturing the stuff itself, to manipulate and metamorphose it into endless new shapes, so that it becomes a cloudy constituent of the climate of the modern world. The process needs no facts and truths — the death of Napoleon or the battle of Trafalgar: these have only a relative existence, if any, in the new discourse.

The neo-classic critics and the old rhetoricians were, to be sure, almost equally and confidently dogmatic, and their exercises were often judged not by how much truth they revealed but by how much ingenuity they displayed. Day could be darker than night if the virtuoso produced enough ingenious tropes to prove it so. But the paradox of such ingenuity was that its liveliness depended on a deep belief in the truths and facts available to common sense. It would have been pointless otherwise. Novels today are often written under the influence of the modern critical climate, but it is noticeable that the liveliest ones often resemble old rhetorical practice in that they involuntarily underline the significance of fact even while modishly engaged in calling it in question. Thus in Julian Barnes's novel, *Flaubert's Parrot*, the narrator becomes obsessed with finding the stuffed parrot which Flaubert had on his desk while he wrote *Un Coeur Simple*, a story about a woman who is, among other things, devoted to her parrot. He finds what purports to be the real stuffed parrot in a museum, but then finds a rival parrot in another shrine devoted to Flaubert relics. Flaubert's writings, and what the narrator makes of them, mingle with a sense of unreality presided over by the ambiguous legend of Flaubert, the disappearance of things under close scrutiny, the impossibility of the past itself.

These are the modish notions canvassed by the novel, but the impression it makes on the reader is rather different. The past, the parrot, and Flaubert himself all come most vividly to life, as if to confirm that there *was* a parrot, however now unverifiable, just as there was a real moment (among many others) when Flaubert sat down one afternoon to write *Madame Bovary*, the novel which neither he then, nor its readers now, have ever been quite sure about. The conscious implication of *Flaubert's Parrot* is that since we cannot know everything about the past we cannot know anything; but its actual effect – and its success – is to suggest something different: that the relative confirms the idea of truth instead of dissipating it, that the difficulty of finding out how things were does not disprove those things but authenticates them. It may be that few things happened as they are supposed to, and many things did not happen at all, but why should this be a reason for abandoning traditional conceptions of history, of art, of human character? All three depend upon our sense of the past, and are confirmed by the unknowability of the past. Is it the influence of science, a horror of the past, or a passing fashion of defeatism, which makes us reluctant today to speculate in Lionel Trilling's "quiet place", to assemble the materials of creation and participation?

Our conception of character depends on our conception of history, and can either be seen to be dissolved in the dissolution of history, or actually confirmed by the impossibility of knowing what things and people were like. In the case of Hamlet the uncertainty produced by the brilliance, or perhaps the inadvertency, of Shakespeare's art makes the Prince more of a character, not less of one. He has all the magnificence and the despair, the familiarity and the hauteur, which history suggests about the character of the Renaissance ruler. The contradictions make the man. It is significant that historical novels which try to recreate the past, particularly the distant past, seem unable to make use of the uncertainty which marks the idea of a character at any point in history. Novels about ancient Greece, say, construct a Theseus or an Alcibiades who is held together by the fatal assumption, on the novelist's part, that he must be coherent, recognizable, just like one of us. The element of mystery which determines the possibility of a true character is sacrificed to the attempt to produce a convincing and consistent historical picture – "what it must have been like". This is even more marked in science fiction and fantasy, where the Lord of the Rings, or whoever, is a flat figure without any of the queries and incongruities which history supplies. Such fictions are the abdication of that consciousness of the past which was once second nature to all novelists, who instinctively set their period thirty or forty years before the time they wrote, in order that it might become part of the memory and retrospection of the reader, who was unconsciously creating himself and his own past through the medium of the novel.

That instinct of the novel comes to its full and conscious fruition in Proust, who reconstitutes himself from the past and becomes his own novel in the process. Hamlet is a figure of mystery because he lives in the unknowable past, but this does not stop us from having, like Coleridge, a lot of Hamlet in us. What we do not have in us is a character fixed in a historical role decreed by the writer – Tito Melema, say, in George Eliot's *Romola*. The author spent laborious years getting the background of the novel right, and putting Tito – the man who is a complete self, living only in and for the self – into it. The result is that Tito is neither alive in history nor in the present, nor can we be alive in him. He resembles one of those sad statues on the Albert Memorial in London, in a stony limbo of art which has neither the truth of a photograph album, nor the mystery that continues life and joins past with present.

Trilling's "quiet place" is not quiet in the sense of being fixed and definitive. It is, on the contrary, a place of perpetual speculation, contemplation calmed by an awareness of fact, the fact that lies behind history, art, and human character, and makes them one and indivisible. The line of battle at Trafalgar is well known, amply documented. We know the moment of the day and the look of the calm sea when the *Victory*'s bowsprit surged into the gap between the *Redoubtable* and the *Bucentaure*. All else beyond the fact is mysterious, given over to the possibilities of historical personality. Did Nelson say "Kiss me, Hardy" as he lay dying that evening in the flagship's cockpit? How much it reveals about him if he did, as about his flag-captain, the big bluff invulnerable Captain Hardy, who was not to die for a generation later, full of years and honours. By the end of the century expectations of behaviour had radically altered, and his admirers had elected to forget what seems to have been Nelson's feminine, histrionic, emotional nature. What might a man with a stiff upper lip say as he lay dying, something that sounded like "Kiss me, Hardy"? Perhaps, "Kismet, Hardy"? Nelson had been in the Middle East, after all, and had dealings with the followers of Islam. For the contemporaries of Sherlock Holmes it seemed the kind of thing that a naval or military man might utter, with a slight smile, a notional shrug of the shoulders.

The example is comic, certainly, but at the heart of the comedy is the stuff of true fiction, as it is the stuff of the past. It is because fiction cannot deal in fact that it absorbs us in the nature and reward of fact. In disqualifying the category of fact from text and discourse the modern critic often shows a curious naiveté about its historical relation to fiction. In an essay on how we should read novels today David Lodge notices the moment in Arnold Bennett's *The Old Wives' Tale* when Sophia, foreseeing difficulties in the future, decides to relieve her drunken new husband of his money and secrete it about her own person. His wallet she hides at the back of the cupboard in their hotel bedroom, "where for all I know", writes the author, "it is there to this day". It would be a very naive reader, comments Lodge, who might wonder if the wallet really was still there, in that hotel in the French provincial town. This comment seems to me to miss the point in a potentially disastrous manner.

The reader does not need to be reminded that he is reading fiction: but the author has just shown him how clear, how close, how unmistakable is fiction's relation to fact. How peculiar as well. "There to this day . . ." Sophia and her experience are abruptly brought out of the past where, in an obvious sense, all fiction resides, and into the present. The interchange shows art's simultaneous dependence on its relations with the concepts of past and present, the invented and the real.

Those relations form a criss-cross pattern. Hamlet the character is a literary invention, but he carries his own personal reality both into our sense of history and into our contemporary experience of life. Was he in love with Ophelia? The play gives us no answer: the idea that he might have been increases nonetheless his potential as a fictional character because it is precisely the same kind of possibility which attends our experience of other people in life. Fiction and life are, so to speak, continually changing places, each under the scrutiny that produces art. In theory we can know everything in a fiction, and about a character in fiction, and very little in life, or about the people we meet in life. In practice fiction avails itself of the disablements of life, and under the guidance of a master hand is enriched by them. In *The Princess Casamassima* James gave up the completely rounded fictional form which defined the character of Christina Light in *Roderick Hudson*. As the Princess Casamassima Christina has become, as it were, an "unsatisfactory" character, the sort of person often met with in real experience who calls forth our curiosity without in any way satisfying it. Christina simply continues through her "life". In his later preface to *Roderick Hudson* James was to write that "relations stop nowhere", and that the artist's problem was "to draw, by a geometry of his own, the circle within which they shall happily *appear* to do so". He may have been reflecting, at least in part, on the way in which the circle drawn in the earlier novel was ruptured by the reappearance of Christina in *The Princess Casamassima*. She disappears as the completed concept of a character and comes back in a secondary role, seen differently because she is now free to carry on living in an ordinary untidy way. James has washed his hands of her; she is no longer determined by the resolution of the plot and by a completed role in fictional history. The "fond participation" he was to write of in the New York preface to *The Princess Casamassima* hardly includes her, and this reminds us that characters, although they have to be regarded from the standpoint of art, whether we are reading about them or experiencing them in life, have also their own unshaped existence which we cannot enter, and about this speculation is wasted.

A singular instance of the writer removing a character from the flux of events in order to perpetuate him for the "inward eye" occurs in the original version of the *Lyrical Ballads*. In 1797 Wordsworth saw an old man travelling, and composed a sketch on the subject, subtitled "Animal Tranquillity and Decay". What struck Wordsworth, and makes the crux of his description, is the fact that the old man does not seem conscious of the impression he most makes on others – that of patience and "settled quiet". He doesn't seem to "need" the tranquillity his outward form exhibits, and "the young behold/With envy, what the old man hardly feels". Wordsworth observes appearances with the keenest possible eye, and from them draws conclusions familiar to himself, and with their own sort of comfort for himself and his readers. In the poet's eye the old man does indeed, in some sense, "exist linguistically, as a term of discourse". We are impressed by our own conception of him rather than by the man himself, as is evident from Wordsworth's peroration.

> He is by nature led
> To peace so perfect, that the young behold
> With envy, what the old man hardly feels.

But this view of the matter is completely blown away by the last few lines of the original poem, which Wordsworth dropped in the 1800 edition of the *Lyrical Ballads* and never afterwards restored.

> – I asked him whither he was bound, and what
> The object of his journey; he replied
> "Sir! I am going many miles to take
> "A last leave of my son, a mariner,

"Who from a sea-fight has been brought to Falmouth,
And there is dying in an hospital."

Even the original punctuation, with the speech commas at the beginning of the lines, indicates the totality of the contrast with what
has gone before. The old man shows that he is neither led by nature
to peace so perfect, nor that he is indifferent to the calm about him
which is the envy of the bystander. So far from being subdued to
settled quiet he is concerned with one overriding purpose, to see
his wounded son before he dies, the son who has been present in a
battle at sea.

This collision of fact with appearance was first presented by
Wordsworth with complete fidelity, as if he were unconscious – as
perhaps he was – of the contrast between his view of the old man
and the old man's real preoccupations and place in things. The
poem has stubbed its toe on a fact which has brought it to an end;
but because it is a poem, and a very successful poem, a remarkably
fitting end. There is no incongruity between the old man's speech
and the impression that he made on the poet, but Wordsworth
later became sensitive about such things, and by removing the end
of the poem spoilt the wonderful interplay in it between character,
fact and history, the interplay which was not "subdued" to poetic
discourse but left in what can only be described as its natural state,
the state where our sense of these things is most receptive.

Wordsworth's original poem is both close to Herbert's poem on
the pebble, and opposite to it. It is close in the involuntary way it
opens itself to history and the fact, to what is going on. Both poems
contain a great weight of implication of things the poet knows
about but lets only look over his shoulder. Herbert's pebble knows
nothing of what has been happening, of all miseries since the world
began, and it lets its "noble body" be permeated by the "false
warmth" of the poet's and reader's vision of it, and the comfort it
brings. Poetry cannot take over the pebble, and this is an obscure
earnest of the dire truth that poetry also cannot approach or explain
the recent past and its horrors, the massacres and concentration
camps.

"Old Man Travelling" takes over its subject, the old man, but is then forced to relinquish him when he opens his mouth and speaks, stating things which the poem cannot handle and take over, which can only be dealt with by their removal and suppression in all subsequent editions. His poetry can deal with "old unhappy far-off things", as Wordsworth did in his poem "The Highland Reaper", where subject and vision remained wholly in his mind. But these instances all emphasize the way in which the recalcitrance of the past, its separation from us, confronts art as firmly as does the individual character, and in the same way. Art must both use and respect them; the reader himself feel their presence as separate entities, and speculate on their several realities, as he does in that quiet place where he can learn in what year the Parthenon was begun, and what ships formed the battle line at Trafalgar.

Salmagundi, 1986

The Uncommon Pursuit

Terry Eagleton, *Literary Theory: An Introduction* (Oxford: Blackwell)

Terry Eagleton's justification for theory is that we all practise it. "Keynes once remarked that those economists who dislike theory, or claimed to get along better without it, were simply in the grip of an older theory. This is also true of literary students and critics." But not of readers. Reading a book on economics does not make me an economist, any more than using grammar turns me into a grammarian. At once a gap opens, which Eagleton ignores, between the reader of literature and the "student" of it. Might we not partake best of the reading experience, as of any other, the more we take for granted our relation to the experience itself? To be enthralled by literature, to laugh and cry over it, to wish to know more about what is happening in it, is an equivalent of our instinctual use of language, or of the bicyclist or violinist who has come to be able to do it without knowing how.

The argument that all users of literature are in Eagleton's sense theorists of it is therefore a specious one, however much of a truism it may be that we cannot avoid bringing to an experience of literature all our conditioned modes of understanding, our attitudes and prejudices. But now that literature has been taken over as a subject for theoretical study it moves, as philosophy and the sciences have tended to do, from ontology to epistemology. And beyond. Why do we set about knowing what literature is? Our enquiry should be

> neither ontological nor methodological but *strategic*. This means asking first not *what* the object is or *how* we should approach it, but *why* we should want to engage with it in the first place. The liberal humanist response to this

19

> question, I have suggested, is at once perfectly reasonable
> and, as it stands, entirely useless. Let us try to concretize it
> a little by asking how . . . "discourse theory" or "cultural
> studies" . . . might contribute to making us all better people.

Those last words have a familiar ring, though one not usually
associated with this type of question. For most readers literature is
out there, like the Pyramids. It is not a strategy, or "a matter of
starting from what we want to *do*". New theory, however, pro-
poses to identify literature with the theoretical study of it, and the
purpose of that study. We do not look into literature to find out
how to be better: we find out how to be better by remaking literature as a subject. "The present crisis in the field of literary studies is
at root a crisis in the definition of the subject itself."

It is fashionable nowadays to speak of a crisis in English studies,
as was shown by the recent symposium in *The Times Literary Supplement*. The word and the idea have been transposed from the
scenario vocabulary of journalism, where crisis is always the order
of the day. A real crisis might exist if it could be shown that teachers
had lost the will to share their knowledge and their experience of
reading, and students had lost all interest in what they read. But
for this there is no evidence. The silent majority continues to read
as before, and with the same kind of pleasures and ennuis that have
always attended reading for a degree in English. A minority of
activists are concerned to create a crisis by presenting a picture of
one, and thus simulating a need for revolutionary change.

The political analogy is obvious, and everywhere insisted on by
Eagleton himself. The object of revolution would be the study of
the science of literature, or "literariness", since literature, like
human nature, is a bourgeois concept, dismissed by Eagleton as by
Mao Tse-tung as part of the usual old nonsense about "eternal
verities". "Truth to life", that well-known conservative postulate
– life for its purpose assuming the appearance of a certain stability
and continuity – must also be disposed of. Eagleton quotes Barthes:
"Literature is what gets taught" – it has no existence outside
the teaching of it. The ghost of an old Marxist piety makes an

incongruous appearance here. The separation of literature from the theory and teaching of it is like the "alienation" of the individual in bourgeois society. From now on the two will merge to create a harmonious whole. The crisis involved by their separation will be over.

That at least is the scenario, and it is noticeable that all modern literary theory, not just the Marxist, endorses some kind of unity principle as between literature and the study of it. But suppose that what we like about literature is its distance from us, the fact that it is another world which, as Bacon observed, "gives some show of satisfaction to the mind at those points where the nature of things doth deny it". In that case modern literary theory must write us off as incorrigible.

All revolution must excite, and it is more exciting to feel that we are not just submitting to literature, as to life, but absorbing it and controlling it. All participants enjoy the sense of power, whether in storming the Winter Palace or in reconstructing how we should read books. Eagleton is careful to work up a sense of excitement, and on that basis he has made a lively and useful guidebook to the new methods. It is also full of scholarly distinctions and perceptions. He rightly insists, for example, that the true precursors of today's theory were the Russian and East European formalists of the revolutionary era. The beetle-browed hatchet-men of RAPP and the cultural KGB proclaimed socialist realism as a convenient doctrine for the masses, but the intellectual message of literary Marxism was contained in the formalists' doctrines. In what Eagleton calls "a practical scientific spirit" they enquired into the engineering of the literary work, the "material reality" of the text. Since them, and the forerunners of semiotics like Saussure, literary theory has seemed to rest soundly on a scientific basis, self-evidently superior to any previous kinds of "subjectivist approach".

In practice, of course, and as Eagleton again rightly implies, such literary theorists are as much theologians as the cruder sort of Marxist, for where literature is concerned theory and theology cannot be separated. Mystics like Leavis, whose swords sleep not in their hands, have no time for theory, but they are ideologists too.

We all are, insists Eagleton. In his survey of the development of an Honours School of English, he draws attention to its origins in the routine cultural *Angst* of the nineteenth century: "English" has always been in the forefront of a national idea of some sort, an official or unofficial concern with our cultural heritage, from Matthew Arnold onwards. Identified, too, with a class outlook: upper-middle to start with, then middle-middle, today some more or less auto-constructed form of emancipated proletarian. Each has tended to read English literature on its own class basis; Leavis's Lawrence, for instance, is an essentially middle-class phenomenon, and Leavis's key-word "life" suggests the aspirations and values of a society not all that different from C. S. Lewis's fairy-tale religious one.

Indeed the ambiance of "English" has always been a kind of substitute for the religious one; "a *pacifying* influence" says Eagleton; a new opiate for the student masses. It could, however, pose as a church militant. George Gordon, an early Oxford professor, claimed in his inaugural lecture that "England is sick . . . English literature must save it". Auden, with his Oxford third and his pleasure in Anglo-Saxon, must have responded to that, and he showed how marvellous poetry could be made out of turning the whole thing into a charade, for which Leavis never forgave him. Partly for class reasons Eng. Lit. in England has tended to remain ideologically biased, while France and America go for pure theory. Part of Eagleton's purpose is to claim that ideology and theory must and should enhance each other and become one, so that the scenario in which hermeneutics, deconstruction and reception theory are going forward is also that which makes "action urgent and its purpose clear".

Of course he exaggerates, like all evangelists, the extent to which we and our literature really live by disputation and the voice of the spirit. He cannot drink beer without a stratagem, and much of his book is taken up with proving that all readers are propagandists for their particular set of beliefs and that all writers in the past were so too. Again there is a truism here which distorts by insistence, the same sort of truism as those about language which make up the semiotic approach. In practice, though, the Eagletonian rigour seems partly assumed. He has always smuggled practical perception in his theoretical baggage and slipped out from inside his ideologist's imago. He is not wholly serious in peddling Shakespeare the class enemy, or Richardson the militant feminist, which is why what he writes about them can be illuminating. But dedicated students cannot be expected to share these divisive skills. True, we all interpret the works of the past in our own way. But to encourage its deliberate takeover for ideological purposes is also to encourage in the young a shortsightedness insensate beyond Philistinism.

It also encourages the wholly communal approach. Though the silent majority prefer to do it on their own, students can often be oppressed by the fact that books have to be read that way. Hence the activist's wish to raise morale by full-scale communalization, to put the student inside the subject, rather than leaving him outside literature. By being all together on the inside, no longer alienated by reading books unrelated to ourselves, as if the past were a foreign country where they do things differently, we shall also come to adopt the right political attitudes. Literature must go if it cannot be used, for its independent existence is a threat to the righteous state and the caring society. That at least is the parable with which Eagleton concludes his book.

> *We* know that the lion is stronger than the lion-tamer, and
> so does the lion-tamer. The problem is that the lion does
> not know it. It is not out of the question that the death of
> literature may help the lion to awaken.

What is the lion? The people of England, who have been prevented by their own literature – imposed on them by the upper classes – from expressing and becoming conscious of themselves. And now that increasing numbers of them are reading Eng. Lit. they can be delivered from the burden of the literature itself.

In a remarkably short space of time the ideological wheel has come full circle. Instead of saving England, English literature must now be abolished if England is to be saved. Theory, like a laser beam, will burn out all that dead tissue. We shall have a new scenario, a harmonious workshop of theory and practice, as if we were taking part in a film by Godard. We shall indeed have literariness without literature, the feel of the thing without its actuality.

In practice I suspect this will only take place among the elect, the new élite which communes depend on even more than traditional establishments. The rest of us need not worry too much. For the cultural scenario evolving today and in the discernible future seems in fact very different from the Eagletonian model, one much more like Malraux's "Musée Imaginaire". There is more culture around today for more people than ever before – an excellent theory in itself – and it is conveniently presented and packaged so that people can look and read as and where they choose. For Eagleton these conveniences are a way of keeping us quiet, got up by capitalism and the media. But accessibility does not destroy the reality of art, and it may be this very presentness and diversity of literature and culture which upset the puritan activists of theory. Plausibly enough, open-plan art and culture-viewing seem to them to send the populace to sleep instead of waking it up. Theory braces, culture relaxes. So gruff exclusiveness becomes a duty and an image, as is shown by the present-day *New Statesman*, once the most hospitably relaxed and cultivated of the weeklies.

It must be admitted, though, that there is nothing Philistine about Eagleton's erudition and presentation. On the contrary, as he guides us round the chic stalls of contemporary critical fashion they begin to look like a more intellectual version of the displays got up by the advertising and publishing media. The museum of theory is always open, exhibiting the counterparts of all the other cultural artefacts available today. Feminism, psychoanalysis, phenomenology, structuralism and post-structuralism – we can take our choice, but what they have in common is a similarity of mechanism, offering the student a fashionable substitute for identifying with the human identity of a book, for "the object of the science of literature is not literature but literariness". Among other things, Roman Jakobson's famous statement shows why modern criticism has got the modern literature it deserves.

Literariness is a substitute for experience, the bugbear of modern theory. But unless we read books in search of experience we never get outside the workshop of theory. Literature, like religion, has also depended on Coleridge's "suspension of disbelief", another dead doornail today, for belief in an author's story or in his characters has now no place in theory. This means we also forgo the author; modern criticism has no wish to "get to know" him, in the sense that T. S. Eliot said that the pleasure of reading Kipling was "getting to know a mind very different from my own". The personality of an author is not the same as his literariness.

On the other hand much modern theory often sounds like an attempt to express by quasi-scientific formula what the reader is doing as part of a human transaction. Deconstruction, we are now told, shows how the language of literature escapes the sense which tries to contain it, and also "rejects the literary/non-literary opposition as an absolute distinction". What reader who has not been brainwashed by formalism and structuralism ever supposed otherwise? But theory now requires to sound theoretical in order to undo theory, and jargon can only be discredited by counter-jargon, as was amusingly shown by Edward Said's massive and learned study *The World, the Text, and the Critic*. Today's talk about discourse and strategy, praxis and reification, curiously resembles that ancient craze in art criticism, which once seemed so exciting, for "significant form". In *Art and Anarchy* Edgar Wind finally put paid to it in the plainest language by pointing out that we cannot *see* a picture if we ignore or misunderstand the significance of its human subject, the lasting human reality which a Renaissance painter, say, was able to conjure out of passing forms and conventions.

In matters of literary and cultural taste toleration is so important that it is tempting to see today's literary theory as a number of useful if temporary devices for making us sit up and take notice. Where critical aids are concerned we should be treating of assets only. But the fashion for dehumanization has gone too far, and, as Eagleton's book unintentionally shows, now verges on the farcical. What is strange is that it should all be done in the name of "ordinary" people, with their ordinary non-élite interests. Eagleton seems conscious of this. One can stand almost any jargon but that of bogus humanism, and he constantly employs it, in phrases like "what it means to be a person". Yet no author here is treated as a person, in the fullest sense of art, with whom we learn to commune, whose world we can share. So far have things gone that a simple exclamation of pleasure from a perceptive critic about an author he knows and loves – for example in John Jones's newly published book on Dostoevsky – seems today like the past retrieved, the writer rediscovered. Most of the theories Eagleton expounds may soon seem outlandish curiosities, cooked up by teachers of literature who need to feel professional, in the sense that philosophers or scientists do, or powerful, like politicians.

The Times Literary Supplement, 1983

Formalist Games and
Real Life

It all starts with Shklovsky's famous query about Pushkin's verse novel *Evgeny Onegin*. "Is Pushkin telling us the story of his hero and heroine, or is he having a game .with this story?" To the formalist critics and their successors, structuralists and deconstructionists, literature can only consist in having a game with linguistic properties and characteristics, which determine the game's outcome, as Shklovsky said that the perception of a work's form determines its meaning. The attraction of the approach is twofold. It provides a comprehensive general theory of literature which seems to leave nothing out; and it rescues the student from the morass of subjective and appreciative responses and judgements, putting a weapon in his hand which, like the magic sword in fairy tale, will enable him to deal with every situation. By learning the rules of the game he is bound to win it.

It all depends on the way you look at it. Indeed in some ways such criticism is like the science or philosophy that told us we did not see colour but the appearance of colour, caused by minute particles subjected to a refractive process, etc. Obviously true when explained, but to the common perceiver is it so important? Should it determine the nature of all his subsequent perceptions? We experience literature, as we experience life, by taking it for granted: it is indeed obvious when pointed out that literature consists of an arbitrary code of words and signs. It is obvious, when Wittgenstein points it out, that the limits of my language are the limits of my world.

But this perception can either liberate or define. Wittgenstein, like Blake, is liberating, but his successors want to get the whole

27

thing sorted, wrapped up and parcelled. The structuralists did too, until they saw the dangers. The attractions of structuralism, as of logical positivism, are obvious; the Vienna Circle had an obvious influence on the Prague Circle of linguists and literary theoreticians, like Jakobson and Tomashevsky. Significant that in its popularized form logical positivism claimed to have provided all the answers, or to have shown that the traditional questions had no meaning. Philosophy is a question of using language in the right way; criticism is a question of understanding the ways in which literature must use the coding of language. In both cases points long disputed can be shown to be irrelevant. In one of his essays on Henry James, for instance, Todorov remarks that critics of *The Turn of the Screw* "have formed two distinct schools: those who consider the estate of Bly to be in fact haunted by evil spirits, and those who explain everything by the neurosis of the governess who tells the story. Of course it is not necessary to choose between the two contrary solutions; the rule of the genre implies that the ambiguity be maintained." No problem. And no "human interest". The psychology of the governess, and of the author, with all that could or might entail, can be set aside once we have understood the nature of the game the author is playing.

This sterilizing of the critical field is something which many teachers of literature perennially hanker for. It gives them an incisive authority, like that possessed by the classic and neo-classic schools; it overcomes that sense of *helplessness* in face of the ordinary uninstructed response which is the teacher's nightmare. Such a sense of helpless exasperation is graphically conveyed in a story of Malcolm Bradbury's about a university teacher (himself more or less) who gives WEA classes. The story is humorous, but the author's underlying attitude is not. His hero deeply resents the messy imperfection of discussion, the lack of contact in undirected exchange. One sympathizes very much. But such messy imperfection is the price that criticism pays for remaining in touch with the real world as well as with the world of the work of art. The common reader usually has no idea of separating the two, and no desire to do so. For him the insides of books are not linguistic codes but things like those in his own life, real or imagined, real angers, joys, and disgraces, taking place in damp streets, stately homes, blue lagoons, etc. That is obvious, as is the fact that authoritative critical procedure founders on the reader's disinclination to give up the world of things for the world of codes. He may be seeing through the medium of language, but what matters to him is not how he sees it but what he sees.

Ideally, however, we speak of assets only. A new approach, a new technique of reading is genuinely educational; it enlarges the possibilities of appreciation and understanding. Todorov's book *The Poetics of Prose* certainly does that, and he himself is the most humane, chatty and accessible of the new-style critics. But the dichotomy remains. What is "poetics"? It is not a matter of "poetry or literature but 'poeticity' and 'literariness'". I recall writing a review of Frank Kermode's book *The Sense of an Ending*. That was about poeticity and literariness. I remarked that for some readers poetry and literature made things *more* like things, not less like them. Wordsworth's poem was about a particular fine morning, and meeting a leech-gatherer, and joy and dejection and religious example. But for Kermode it was a poem about poeticity. The two approaches are not necessarily incompatible, but poeticity is easier to handle critically than poetry, and it can be taught.

Though Todorov is of Russian origin, which makes him fully at home with the Russian formalists, his intellectual elegance and air of metaphysical precision is more French than the French (it is important to remember in this context that the French academic tradition has never distinguished between philosophical studies and critical *explication*, which in higher education go hand in hand with a naturalness never attempted in England since modern literature became with us a subject of academic study). And for the French it was a logical and easy step to structuralist methods from the formulation of such a respected *intellectuel* as Valéry: "Literature is, and cannot be anything but, a kind of extension and application of certain properties of language."

Poetics is about literariness, and its opposite is what Todorov calls "projection", the kind of criticism which treats literature as a record of experiences, discussable in terms of the experiences we have in life. These can have no part, as Jonathan Culler's introduction reminds us, in a *general* theory of literature, that chimera which has floated so long before the eyes of the critics, and in the New World before the eyes of Northrop Frye, honoured as a pioneer by the new men. As with all philosophical systems, life – or in this case literature – continues to carry on unperturbed beside the perfect model, but this does not bother the critics, who maintain, and correctly from their own standpoint, that it is not the business of criticism to interpret works of art, to use literature as a commentary about life. That can only lead to an assertion of prejudice and preference, the anarchy of the WEA class.

Like logical positivism, structuralism works perfectly in terms of its own premise, the closed circle inside which any general theory of literature has perforce to work. Barthes and the deconstructors restored subjectivism, and a new free-for-all for those who sought new pleasures and perceptions in the text. The experiential and the reflective, the aesthetic and the moral – everything that we use language *for* – thus came back into criticism through the window after being kicked out of the door. Criticism also reacquired values, mostly of a dogmatic and theological kind, which helped to mask the fact that it was back at its old business of speculation and inter- pretation, or "projection", the endless and rewarding flux out of which no definitive conclusions can ever be drawn.

Todorov, however, remained true to formalism, though his knowledge of English and Anglo-Saxon methods gives it a certain gaiety – the temper of his discourse would be appreciated by our Victorian critic E. S. Dallas, who thought of criticism as the "gay science" (in the days before the *double entendre*). The comedy can at times be unconscious. "Up to a certain moment, we possessed no more than observations, sometimes penetrating and invariably chaotic, as to the organization of one narrative or another. Then came Vladimir Propp." The syntax of that is inherently gay, even if unintentionally so. All new critics have to be showmen, bringing fresh wonders to the reading public, and Barthes often reads like a simultaneous parody of science fiction and nineties prose. Todorov introduces the man who establishes the structure of narrative, through the study of one hundred Russian fairy tales, in rather the same spirit. The solution has at last been found. No need for criticism to remain in the state of being "sometimes penetrating and invariably chaotic". But the conclusion of Todorov's essay "How to Read" is oddly equivocal.

> No doubt there is an *untheorisable* element in literature, as Michel Deguy calls it, if theory presupposes scientific language. One function of literature is the subversion of this very language; hence it is extremely rash to claim we can read it exhaustively with the help of the very language it calls in question. To do so is equivalent to postulating the failure of literature. At the same time this dilemma is much too inclusive for us to be able to escape it: confronted with a poem we can only resign ourselves to the impoverishment caused by a different language, or else (a factitious solution) write another poem. Factititious because this second text will be a new work which still awaits its reading: an entire autonomy deprives criticism of its *raison d'être*, just as a submission to ordinary language affects it with a certain sterility. There remains, of course, a third solution which is silence: we cannot speak of that.

"Specifications" and "options" are the lifeblood of formalism, and there is again a certain comedy in the fact that Michel Deguy's remarkable discovery has itself to be fitted into an appropriate slot, instead of just taken for granted. Derrida or Barthes would never allow themselves to be confined within the stark limits of such options, but on the other hand they are apt to freewheel into doggerel and mumbo-jumbo. Todorov's self-imposed rigour is always incisive and clear. Formalism is historically related to Marxism, which tolerated it to a surprising degree (Shklovsky survived many literary pogroms and is still honoured in the Soviet Union). Both systems concentrate on a general theory, literary or historical, and on finding a "correct" solution in terms of it.

The "perfection" of a successful work of art can be a misleading concept, for the best tend to have bits and pieces of personal untidiness or irrelevance left hanging out of them. Still, it is a natural concept, while the idea of a perfect piece of criticism – perfect in the sense that it exactly and comprehensively defines the nature of the work it treats – is not natural at all. Formalism aspires towards such a comprehensiveness, and its claim to do so reveals itself in the opening sentence of one of Todorov's chapters – "Literature must be treated as literature". This is a way of saying that criticism must be treated as criticism, that it must not hang out, must contain no commentary or reflection of a social or moral or historical sort. But the trouble is that works of literature contain plenty of such material which has not changed its nature from the context, which cannot be "treated as literature". When Todorov writes about Henry James's stories, in two of his most interesting chapters, he concentrates on the ones that present a problem, a ghost or a secret, the treatment of which constitutes the art of the story. He ignores the stories which explore a society, a personality, the phenomena of a given time and place, though these are surely among the most interesting as well as the most masterly of James's productions.

Such selectivity is obviously necessary to this criticism, which prefers as it were a dry field – fairy stories, primitive narrative, Arabian Nights and *romans policiers* – on which Todorov is always both illuminating and entertaining. In these cases we have indeed a game with the materials, and the point is to spot what rules the author reveals by his observance or departure from them, conscious or unconscious. (Post-structuralist criticism has worked in this way on the James Bond stories.) It is important to admit that this approach sharpens the mind and has on occasion produced excellent results; and also to remember how stereotyped was the approach against which it originally protested. Trubetskoy, one of the founders of structural linguistics, was particularly indignant at the old treatment of medieval literature as a source of information on local colour and conditions. But one stereotype is apt to succeed another: one wishes it were possible to have the game and the social comment as well – Eugene and Tatiana's story as something to be played with, and also something to be moved by, something which contains new revelations of life and meaning.

In practice of course it is; and formalist criticism is prepared to let in life under the disguise of literature – in fact it has no choice. Todorov isolates with characteristic precision the narrative dynamism of the *Arabian Nights*: the assumption that nothing in life is more important than curiosity.

> The characters of this book are obsessed by stories; the cry of the *Arabian Nights* is not "Your money or your life!" but "Your story or your life!" . . . faced with the choice between happiness or curiosity, the dervish chooses curiosity. Just as Sinbad, for all his misfortunes, sets out again after each voyage: he wants life to tell him stories, one narrative after the other . . . if its characters had preferred happiness, the book would not exist.

The critic thus involuntarily reveals in the *Arabian Nights* a moral outlook as consistent and omnipresent as that in George Eliot's novels. Todorov then reverses, as it were, the process by which normal judgement and perception arrive in formalistic disguise. A formal "Law" of the work, we are told, is that any reaction to one story is postponed by the commencement of the next, with the result that the "supplement" of the reader's response – tears, laughter, indignation, pity, etc. – is indefinitely postponed. Any possible response of the reader is consumed within the next narrative. "We may weep when reading *Manon Lescaut*, but not when reading the *Arabian Nights*." But this attempt to regularize the response of the reader, to license his emotional reaction to one text rather than another, tacitly admits that such a reaction may at times be appropriate, actually part of the formal specification. And it is surely a little risky to lay down that a proper perception of a work's form will indicate whether we may laugh or cry at it.

About Henry James Todorov is particularly brilliant, but once again the upshot of the formal moves is an unexpected checkmate in the open field of moral comment. At first sight those stories chosen as obviously suited to the game are the ones Todorov calls "metaliterary tales, devoted to the constructive principle of the tale". The form here is a quest but an odd one, *"the quest for an absolute and absent cause"*. Italics signify the importance of this, for absence determines everything: all that is present is the search for an absence. "The cause is what, by its absence, brings the text into being. The essential is absent, the absence is essential."

This splendidly defines the structure of a number of stories James wrote around the turn of the century, among them *The Turn of the Screw*, *The Jolly Corner*, *In the Cage*, *The Altar of the Dead*, and *The Beast in the Jungle*. In the last, the most formalistically ingenious, the cause is revealed as being absence itself, the perpetual non-event to which Marcher's life is condemned, and which becomes a story when he finds what it is. The heroine of *In the Cage* never discovers what is going on as a result of the telegrams she takes down in her little office; the society pair who send them remain permanently mysterious in their doings, but this mystery is what gives her consciousness, that indispensable Jamesian *conscience* which is the breath of life. "If nothing was more impossible than the fact, nothing, on the other hand, was more intense than the vision." The essence does not become present, but it fills the tale, for which it constitutes reality. The tale ends when what is no longer speculative supervenes: the operator giving up the puzzle, leaving her job, and getting married.

The most perfect absences are of course ghosts, whom James habitually refers to as presences. Todorov makes a persuasive distinction (enlarged at length in his book *The Fantastic: A Structural Approach to a Literary Genre*) between fantasy in James's stories, and the uncanny or marvellous. The fantastic is the product of uncertainty, and lasts as long as it lasts. Once the author, or the reader, opts for a solution, he is in the world of the marvellous, and in most cases – such as *The Turn of the Screw* – the specification of the story refuses a solution. At times, as in *Sir Edward Orme* (1891) the story allows the marvellous by explaining itself unequivocally: the ghost disappears when the heroine marries the narrator and its motivation is revealed – it was jilted by the heroine's mother and has come to see that the same thing does not occur again. (Though Todorov does not say so, there is a significant contrast between the distinction of absence in such tales, and the banality of presence.)

But the best point Todorov brings out is essentially a moral perception, to which the form may help to draw attention but which is certainly independent of it. Marcher in *The Beast in the Jungle* and Spencer Brydon in *The Jolly Corner* are both preoccupied with *being* themselves: their sense of their fate is what determines their wholly self-absorbed identity. They assume their absence to be their essence. But the irony is that the story which determines their being also shows that they don't exist, can't exist except in relation to another person – the long-suffering woman to whom they have confided nothing but their sense of themselves. Brydon feels that his *alter ego*, the ghost in the New York house, will be a more essential self precisely because it is a self that never existed: he is appalled to discover that this other has no resemblance to him, an identity that "fitted his at *no* point". This search for the self is fruitless because as a discoverable entity it cannot exist. Brydon comes to with his head in Alice Staverton's lap, and with the knowledge, obscurely conveyed in James's serpentine syntax, that *he* does not exist but only *have*; *I* have no meaning, only *you*. Todorov teases out beautifully, and offers without comment, a moral which is certainly there, and which would be appropriate to the *Pilgrim's Progress* or a pop song.

The question then remains, is such a moral inside the story's specification or not? Is it part of the game? Are we authorized to take it to heart as we are to weep when we read *Manon Lescaut*? Surely such a moral cannot be self-contained, like the ambiguity of *The Turn of the Screw* about which we are not required to make up our minds? These tiresome queries are quite rightly ignored by Todorov, who goes on his way like a sensible critic without squaring his perceptions with his system. Indeed in the last sentence of the essay he seems to drop it altogether: ". . . For the individual to be heard, the critic must fall silent. That is why, discussing *The Jolly Corner*, I have said nothing of the pages which form its centre and which constitute one of the peaks of Henry James's art. I let them speak for themselves." An implication of formalist theory is unmanifested here but significantly present, like a Jamesian ghost, and it seems to me the most salutary thing suggested by this school. Writers play games but readers do not, or do not have to, would be a way of putting it. The weakness of formalism is its assumption that the reader must obey the rules invented by the nature of the work. Its strength, though, is the realization that the writer is not feeling with the reader, and showing him by direct example what to feel. Mixing up the writer's feelings with the reader's is the cause of much sloppy criticism, especially Shakespeare criticism. The same critic who wrote of Pushkin's attitude to his story, and its hero and heroine, dryly observed that his readers took it for granted that he was as moved by the story as they were. He pretended to be but that was part of his art, the game that the artist was playing. No sensible person supposes that Shakespeare shed tears as he worked on *Lear*, or after he finished it.

The most far-reaching implications of formalism, therefore, are connected with the relations of the reader and writer, and of the expectations in both parties that came about as a result of the general climate of romanticism. Formalist and structuralist hypotheses are anti-romantic, in that they desired to break the real or concocted bond of intimacy between writer and reader – the source of most of the confusion that bedevilled critical theory. Thus, for example, there is no point in asking: was Sterne sincere in *Tristram Shandy*? The enduring value of this approach is not that it presents us with a watertight general theory of literature but that it shows something important about different kinds of writers. It would be true to say, for instance, that the claim to be feeling and thinking while writing what the reader will be feeling and thinking while reading is an actual claim in the stylistic specification of George Eliot or Margaret Drabble; and one which the reader who becomes aware of it may either like or dislike. Conversely, it is probably true that the abandonment of Dickens or Charlotte Brontë, as of Byron or Chateaubriand, has an idiosyncratic zest and absorption which communicates itself to the reader. They are not exactly playing their game but doing their thing, and the reader drawn into it would not be grateful for the implication that they were doing it with high motives for human welfare in mind. James, too, is so absorbed in the fine issues of his tale that he can leave out any "idea" or moral, for the reflective reader or for the critic like Todorov to define and to draw. As a rule the more palpably "serious" the writer, and the more he assures us he is not playing a game, the more we tend to distrust him, because of what James himself called "the drop to directness which is thereby the voice of insincerity". Many modern novelists – the more flamboyantly "serious" ones – might benefit from a stiff dose of formalist doctrine, but on the other hand those who have taken it to heart often produce fiction which bears all the hallmarks of having been written to illustrate a critical theory.

The Poetics of Prose is full of rewards and insights, particularly when flexibility is ensured by intelligence and theory allowed to develop its own natural contradictions. Todorov is no autocrat. The formalists in general were not only less dogmatic than their successors but less insistent on imposing their method and vocabulary on a student body. They were aware of the limitations of their approach, of its comparatively specialized application, and above all of the fact that it raised – like any critical technique – queries and problems that spread outward and could not be disposed of inside a closed system. Todorov's affection for Henry James would make him well aware of the relevance to the critic as well as to the artist of that pronouncement of James which, with that alteration, might well be written in large letters over the doors of any institution where literature is studied: "Really, universally, relations stop nowhere, and *the problem of the critic* is to draw, by a geometry of his own, the circle within which they shall happily appear to do so." Todorov draws it very happily indeed.

Essays in Criticism, 1981

Full-Grown Infants

Helen Vendler, *The Odes of John Keats* (Cambridge, Mass.:
Belknap Press/Harvard University Press);
Dorothy Van Ghent, *Keats: The Myth of the Hero*,
edited by Geoffrey Cane Robinson
(Princeton: Princeton University Press);
J. S. Hill (editor), *Keats: Narrative Poems* (London: Macmillan)

At the beginning of *The Possessed* we learn that Stepan Verkhovensky had written, in the late 1820s "when people were constantly
composing in that style", a lyrical-dramatic poem "with a chorus
of women, followed by a chorus of men, then a chorus of incor-
poreal powers of some sort and at the end of all a chorus of
spirits not yet living but very eager to come to life". Such a
production was certainly typical of European poetry at a time
when personification was being pressed into the service of ideological and idealistic themes, and remained a sort of generic
stand-by, used by good and bad poets alike, a favourite with
"national" poets like Petöfi, Conrad's father Apollo Korzeniowski,
or the Romanian Eminescu, a sign too of the poet's aspirations to
produce something "great".

The Ode form, traditional but adapted to any new emotional
effervescence, old-fashioned but always capable of being in vogue,
was as useful for this purpose to Wordsworth as it had been to
Gray, as handy for Pushkin in the third decade of the nineteenth
century as it had been to Derzhavin in the eighteenth century. It
went with allegory, and its potential was as responsive to discipline
as to instability. In his later manner Yeats was still writing what are
virtually Odes, and the late Paul de Man has explored the ways in
which Yeats remained a persistently allegorical poet. The drafts of

the Byzantium poems display the inherent comicality of allegory squeezed into dynamically physical terms, recalling Hopkins's amused comment on a very early poem of Yeats which described a man and a sphinx alone on a rock in mid-ocean: "How did they get there? What did they have to eat? etc."

Yeats's craftsmanship as a "last romantic" could overcome these incongruities, compelling them to serve the deeper purposes of the poem instead of displaying themselves on its surface. Shelley, his first great love, had also evolved a style which could float over the groundwork of allegory and etherealize its awkwardness. Keats's genius took exactly the opposite course. He explored, exploited and felt his way into the Ode form by drawing attention to the war of the physical and the figurative that went on in it; by emphasizing, however involuntarily, how its shape and diction lent themselves to a kind of felicitous bathos of touch and space.

This shows in the "Ode on Indolence", unpublished by Keats but the seminal poem, as Blackstone observed, for the Odes that followed. Its opening stanza is an instance of "all that information (primitive sense) necessary to a poem" to which Keats refers in the last letter he wrote. The kind of information he had in mind would reveal "the knowledge of contrast" already implicit in the figures who appear to him.

> One morn before me were three figures seen,
> With bowed necks, and joined hands, side-faced;

Awkwardness is a part of the accuracy, and it is significant that in the first line Keats should exhibit that absolute lack of self-importance so characteristic of the Odes, and so different from the tone essential in Wordsworth ("To me alone there came a thought of grief / A timely utterance gave that thought relief . . .") and in Shelley's Odes. Keats is very much there: in spite of the passive tense the vision is not impersonalized, just as it will not be in the "Ode to Autumn", but it is personal in the kind of sense that Shakespeare's sonnets are; not calmly or excitedly insistent on the novelty of his experiences, as Wordsworth needed to be.

It is typical of Keats that his figures emphasize their actuality in being compared to the figures on a vase, because the vase itself is joined to human movement and domestic manipulation.

> They pass'd, like figures on a marble urn,
> When shifted round to see the other side;
> They came again; as when the urn once more
> Is shifted round, the first seen shades return . . .

The word *shifted*, and its repetition, epitomizes awkwardness, the necessary awkwardness in stepping as well as in handling. Helen Vendler observes in *The Odes of John Keats* that Keats was never so clumsy again as to transfer figures from vase to vision and back, but Keats's "development" in the Odes is precisely a matter of learning to perfect this sort of clumsiness. The end of it is the inspired manipulation of the figure of Autumn. It can also waft the nightingale's song, even though it has been put into decorative Ode language as a "plaintive anthem", past the near meadows, over the still stream, up the hillside, and into the next valley glades. Anthems cannot move as live birds can, and as Keats's imagination can see and feel them.

There is irony in the fact that sculpture in Keats's time, particularly funerary sculpture, often engaged in the same kind of three-dimensional mobility which is so effective in the language of the Odes. Barham, in the *Ingoldsby Legends*, describes in deadpan style the strenuous activities in progress among the tombs of national heroes in St Paul's, and the scene

> Where the man and the Angel have got Sir John Moore
> And are quietly letting him down through the floor . . .

With its genius for intermingling the figurative and the literal, Keats's language is able to undertake kinds of mobile composition which were quite beyond the reach of the Regency sculptor's chisel. But that is where its relationship lies, as much as, or more than, with the spirit of an Attic frieze. Autumn, sitting careless on a granary floor, her hair soft-lifted by the winnowing wind, could not be a subject for Canova, as Eros and Psyche were, or so many Shelleyan tableaux, but only because she belongs so much to the realm of Keatsian linguistic intensities. The winnowing wind is, in a synaesthetic sense, a purely statuesque concept, and was no doubt the reason why Keats had to remove a line ("While bright the sun strikes through the husky barn") whose dust-laden warmth could have cancelled out its cool fluidity. Personified Autumn, sex mysteriously known but not revealed, comes and goes with the same fluid movement throughout the poem, as if its measured language could imagine her extinction in the earth as well as her multiple presence in human form.

The purpose of the Grecian urn is to heighten contrast between the statuesque and human movement. Barham himself might have asked the question "Who are these coming?" – and emphasis on the perfected stillness of art is only made possible by the incongruous presence of human bustle. Progress is made; maidens become overwrought and the weed is trodden, while at the same time the marble figures are immobilized in their strenuous enactment of desire or flight. Beauty and truth – the eternally statuesque and the necessarily in motion – are not so much synonymous as poetically and essentially coexistent. The untouched urn, the still unravished bride of quietness, is also "a friend to man", like a helpmate or a dog. Such coincidences, a Shakespearian fusion of the one with the other, are the continuous business of the Odes, of the nightingale as both bird and legend, indifferent as the one and, as the other, comforting as all art can be. The poet both dreams and wakes, confirming the fact by asking which he does; and art itself can be all or nothing, the thing that most moves us and the thing that in our real distress gives no help at all.

These Keatsian coincidences, felt through in a form so dualistically compelling that it comes to seem the essence of the Ode itself, extend to every dimension of his language. The unforgettable dragon's tail, "still hard with agony", of the first cancelled stanza of "Melancholy", calls up its Keatsian opposite, hard with pleasure, while at the same time suggesting a Gothic horror of fixity and finality repudiated by the Ode's movement into joy and sadness, the sadness that can only be comprehended by joy. Completion by rhythmic alternative is expressed by the choir of gnats in Autumn, borne aloft or sinking as the light wind lives or dies. It is the Keatsian equivalent of the bellows and the fan which set on and cool Cleopatra's ardour, and the pun on rising and falling at the end of Shakespeare's Sonnet 151. As Helen Vendler observes, the "full-grown lambs" of Autumn are the equivalent of "full-grown infants", a striking Keatsian coincidence which for me embodies not only things dying and things new born but the single identity in this poetry of the infantile and the mature, achieved fruition with ardent attempt, what is "good" and "bad" in the context of Keats's poetry, in fact.

In "The Eve of St Agnes" Madeline is both child and woman, the rose that can become a bud again, and Porphyro is both "puzzled urchin" looking up into the nurse Angela's face and stereotype seducer "brushing the cobwebs with his lofty plume". Identity in contrast is, as the formalists would say, the master trope of this wonderful narration, from the tiger in the moth wing, chill and warmth, the young and the old, consummation and vanishing, to the fact that the poem itself is both fanciful and true, a beautifully concocted and derivative confection and a profound vision of life. This in itself contradicts the implication of Helen Vendler's study: that the Odes are something apart, a progress to perfection above and beyond the rest of the poems. It also validates both essays on "The Eve of St Agnes" in the excellent Casebook, *Keats: Narrative Poems*, one by Earl Wassermann on the poem as a metaphysical construct, "a series of concentric circles"; the other, by Jack Stillinger, on "The Hoodwinking of Madeline", and the role in the poem of scepticism, deception and "the ordinary cruelty of life". The essays stand in avowed opposition to one another, Stillinger disputing the "metaphysical critics" for whom the poem is a dramatization of Keatsian ideas about spiritual progression, the chamber of maiden thought and the world as a vale of soul-making.

What may strike the reader is the obvious parallel between such opposing interpretations of the poem and different ways of reading Shakespeare's plays. The "behaviour" of Porphyro, as both romantic dreamer and practical seducer, is in one sense as realistically indeterminable as Hamlet's. Despite appearances, the poem is also a surprisingly advanced romantic construct, entering the psychological territory of Kleist's *Die Marquise von O*. Keats had never heard of Kleist, but of all their contemporaries both made, in their own characteristic ways, the most deeply intelligent use of the Shakespearian example. Both, too, were in the grip of personal obsessions, Keats with the image of Fanny Brawne as both innocent dreamer and loose flirt: Madeline's sexual awareness is as latently ambiguous as Ophelia's. In her chapter on "The Ravished Bride" in *Keats: The Myth of the Hero* Dorothy Van Ghent explores at length, and very effectively, the folklore and symbolism in the poem. But the trouble, as with Shakespeare, is that interpretation of Keats necessarily denatures its subject by its very coherence and consistency, its reversal of the strategies of negative capability. Stillinger gives the game away by remarking "Whether *The Eve of St Agnes* is a good poem depends in large part on the reader's willingness to find in it a consistency and unity that may not in fact be there."

That seems to me the wrong proposition. The critic can always find consistency, as both Stillinger and Wassermann do, as Dorothy Van Ghent and Helen Vendler also do in their lengthier enquiries into patterns of quest and hero, query and fulfilment. But as with Shakespeare's plays the question is not one of unity but of identity. The identity in contrast in "The Eve of St Agnes", as in the Odes, is clear enough to the appreciative reader, even if such a reader is not fully conscious of what it entails in terms of Keats's stylistic personality. In all his major poems there is a naturally dramatic relation between fancy and reality, the two becoming one in the consummation of the poem while not losing their pressing sense of distinction for the poet. "Fancy," he wrote, "is indeed less than a present palpable reality." At the same time Keats knew that his poem existed, like Adam's dream, to turn the imagined into truth. As a whole, *Hyperion*, like *Endymion*, has no true Keatsian identity because Keats has sought – and sought in vain – to give them the kind of overt consistency and unity which the critics are looking for. Truth and dreaming remain schematic, as they do in the lively projection of Lamia.

In "The Eve of St Agnes", as in the Odes, they do not. The fact is attested by the rival interpretations. Stillinger's has the great merit not only of sharpening the identity contrast, though he would not put it quite that way, but of emphasizing the down-to-earth cynicism which Keats was consciously seeking to put into the poem, to make it less "smokeable". Keats's relation to the Byronic stance is always worth emphasizing. He wished to write a poem "for men", a poem that would finish " 'twixt a sigh and laugh", like the Beadsman in the amended closing couplet, a poem more like Chaucer than Ariosto. Fortunately he did not succeed, but the identity contrast between the rapt romantic poet and the restlessly eager young man having "evil thoughts" about women (touching phrase!) remains a fascinatingly human one. Both are in the poem. Keats as poet not only imagines in Shakespearian fashion an Iago and Imogen but enjoys identifying with them as we do not see Shakespeare doing, identifying with Porphyro as guileful seducer and as innocently ardent future husband, with Madeline's empty dress and with Madeline as charmed maid who should never become a woman and have cancer, though the poem shows she will and may. The hoodwinked Madeline is not condemned by Keats, as Stillinger says, for being a dreamer like the knight-at-arms, avoiding in her fancies both pleasure and pain and awakening on the cold hill's side. Keats shares her fancies, as he does those of Bertha in "The Eve of St Mark", but he also shares the ordinary truth of their being, intensified into the spell of his reality.

In a British Academy "Master Mind" lecture on Pindar (January 1982; published in the *Proceedings* of the BA), Hugh Lloyd-Jones commented on the variations in the patterns of his Odes and the instinct for particularity which shows Pindar's mastery of the form. Keats too makes of the normal properties of the Ode something completely characteristic of his own genius. He literalizes the abstract structure of the Ode, enlivening it in sometimes clumsy but entirely personal ways, as well as emphasizing its conventional mass and movement. Movement of all kinds is as important in the Odes as in the "St Agnes' Eve" narrative: propositions and queries are moved and shifted like vases, and tranquil certainty seems coincident with instability at each moment. In no other poetry do we ourselves seem both more and less in the text; so that in the "Ode to a Nightingale", for example, we may have the very intense feeling of what it would be like to read it in misery and find no comfort in it, and the feeling that Keats in composition might have been feeling the same.

This is indeed Vendler's starting point. She quotes Valéry: "When a poem compels one to read it with passion the reader feels he is *momentarily its author*." From this he knows too that the poem has come off. Such a reader, for Valéry, is like a virtuoso conducting a performance, bringing a score to life by himself becoming its expression and enacting its meaning. Valéry was a poet, and his example could be dangerous for the critic, whose vice, as Auden dryly noted, can be "to treat a work of art as his own discovered document". But Keats can make poets of us all, even of the critic, and Vendler's study of the Odes is as sympathetic, as fundamentally Keatsian, as it is persuasive. It contains the fullest and most searching expansion of these six poems – "the tale of a brief seven months in Keats's artistic life . . . from March to September 1819" – that has yet appeared.

Quoting Valéry's "The virtuoso makes the word flesh . . . gives life and real presence to what was merely a piece of writing at the mercy of all and sundry", she modestly comments that "how a work is made flesh in commentary is not so clear as in the case of performance". The metaphor is equivocal, for commentary cannot approach the palpability of the poem, even when "many forms of enquiry – thematic, linguistic, historical, psychological and struc-tural – are brought to bear on it at once". Vendler has also written the best and longest study of Wallace Stevens's longer poems and she tells us that she is reading Keats's Odes "under Stevens's implicit tutelage", and in the light of Stevens's comment that "one poem proves another and the whole".

Keats, whenever he returned to the form of the ode, re-called his previous efforts and used every new ode as a way of commenting on earlier ones . . . Each ode both deconstructs its predecessors and consolidates them. Each is a disavowal of a previous "solution"; but none could achieve its own momentary stability without the support of the antecedently constructed style which we now call "Keatsian". Keats was practising a form of intrinsic self-criticism [and] . . . examined, in a sustained and deliberate and steadily more ambitious way, his own acute questions about the conditions for creativity, the forms art can take, the hierarchy of the fine arts (including the art of poetry) . . . the relation of art to the order of nature, and the relation of art to human life and death.

This could also be a description of Wallace Stevens's poetry, a better description in fact, for obvious reasons, because Stevens is consciously and coherently doing what the critic says he is, and doing it the critic's way. But Keats has not – most emphatically not – sold out to the principle of the supreme fiction: his poetry resists in every fibre of its being the logic of its own verbal status. That indeed is the crucial reason for the structure of the Odes and our response to them as if "made flesh". It is their form that makes them physical, a physicality specifically denied by the forms of Stevens's poetry, and also in Keats's own "commentary" poems, such as "Sleep and Poetry", or the letter to Reynolds. The Ode form solved for Keats the coincidence of dramatic immediacy with solid sculptural stasis, of poet with personification, of question and uncertainty with resolution and reply. It could take care of the assertiveness that poses in the more relaxed poems, in their rodomontade and extrinsic self-criticism; even take care of the fact that Keats's poetry is not fictional but human in every line, bursting with the kind of unresolved longings and puzzlings that Byron could pour out in the lines on hearing his wife was ill, which Keats himself poured out in his letters. His Odes and his letters are coincident in their complete formal contrast.

Although Vendler is magnificently, even exhaustively, thorough in her exegesis of the Odes she takes no note of this intrinsic humour, surely a vital aspect of what she rightly refers to as Keats's intrinsic self-criticism. Dryden and Gray and Collins strike one as exhibiting from outside their skill in handling a boisterous medium, like an expert groom with an overfed horse, or a craftsman showing his skill in a plastic art. Such bravura allows itself an external humour, but there is a more inward and more touching comedy in the way Keats loads the form with its full aesthetic pomposity: his own rapt attentive self does not then seem to handle the medium but to be present among its manifestations, identified with them like the urn, the nightingale, the figure of Autumn. Vendler is exceedingly short with Paul Fry for his facetiousness about the properties of Autumn in *The Poet's Calling in the English Ode*, but though his tone may jar on the new criticism it would not have jarred with Keats, whose seriousness was not of the modern critical kind. Though Dorothy Van Ghent is equally grave, equally conscientious in her pursuit of meaning, her picture of Keats as hero of successive myths and quests makes implicit allowance for the incongruities involved.

Nonetheless, Vendler's treatment of the Odes, the kernel of Keats's poetic achievement, is so masterly that it will certainly become the standard by which others are judged. She is particularly good on "Autumn", exploring among many other things its relation with Spenser's Mutability cantos, and she finds a singularly touching parallel for the choir of gnats, wailing like orphans, in Wordsworth's comment on himself and his young orphaned siblings, "trooping together as we might". As Allott and Woodruff have shown, the gnats "who form themselves into choirs that alternately rise and fall" derive from Keats's reading of an *Introduction to Entomology* of 1817. Art feeds on books, and Gray's droning beetle appears in many an eighteenth-century poetic context before it finds a final unlikely lodgement in a canto of Pushkin's *Evgeny Onegin*. But art also feeds on life. Gray really heard the swallow twitter (Vendler misses that one) and so did Thomson; and Keats listened to it too, as he must have listened to the hedge cricket that evening, a small whisper by the side of the stubble field that can still be heard on a Hampshire chalk upland in a mild September. Steeped in literature as it is, the Ode makes its "information (primitive sense)" as authentic to the reader as if it were the poetic completion of a real experience.

Completion in what sense? Reading the Odes in terms of a progress to self-knowledge, self-acceptance, of art's reconcilement to life and thought's to sensation, Vendler sees "Autumn" also in terms of an acceptance of death, fruition as the rounding by a sleep from which there will be no awakening. "Cast in the form of a dialogue of the mind with itself", *The Fall of Hyperion* for her looks forward to Autumn, the sexually ambiguous figure of Moneta (drawn from Spenser's figure of Nature from whose face it could not be seen "whether she man or woman inly were") leading to the appearances of Autumn with gender also unspecified, but in ways more subtle and more calm. The gathering swallows – "gather'd" was Keats's first version – suggests a drawing together to mortality, the paradox in the poem's ending being that the summer's death is most deeply apprehended as a finality, felt by art in the face of nature but with her acquiescence too, since a year, like a life, has gone for good.

All readers no doubt feel something like this, a deep sense of the very lightly mysterious, the music of the Ode as Keats's *Tempest*. Certainly the master trope of "Autumn" is to coincide the deepest implication of such meaning with airy lightness and insouciance, "rich in the simple worship of a day". Nothing could be less like *Hyperion* than that. And the more systematic and co-ordinated critical penetration becomes, the more easily the Ode evades it. Helen Vendler's envisaging of the choir of gnats as in some sense souls trooping together on death's banks brings us back to those choruses of spirits in the lyric-dramatic poem composed by the elder Verkhovensky. Yet how important it is that they are *small* gnats, *real* gnats! Keats's poetry never minds the symbolic or portentous any more than the facetious: its greatest art in the end, as well as its greatest livingness, is in not taking itself seriously, which is why the overt and official seriousness of *Hyperion* became a kind of death. Or we could say that the seriousness of Keats's art in the Odes is never the same thing as the seriousness of the critic's performance of it.

The Times Literary Supplement, 1984

Larkin and the
Romantic Tradition

Harold Bloom has written that "a poem can be about experience, or emotion, or whatever, only by initially encountering another poem".* The same idea was expressed by the Russian poet Brodsky in his comment that "no one absorbs the past as thoroughly as a poet, if only out of fear of inventing the already invented".† Brodsky, as one might expect, puts the matter from the poet's point of view, and Bloom from that of the critic. What is certainly true is that poets absorb the past, consciously or unconsciously, in ways most suited to the bent of their own temperament.

This can produce effects of subtle incongruity, even inadvertence. Keats's absorption of the past included Dryden as well as Shakespeare and Spenser, and "Lamia" shows his joy in Dryden's vigorous couplets and the cynical-sentimental *roulades* and flourishes of his narrative fancy. "The Eve of St Agnes" is Spenserian in form, Shakespearian in diction, the two precedents blending in the intensity of Keats's own romantic imagination. But Dryden too makes an unexpected appearance, causing an incongruous swirl in the gliding dream of the narration, as at the moment when the lovers are about to embrace and appear to proceed to sexual union.

> Give me that voice again, my Porphyro,
> Those looks immortal, those complainings dear!
> Oh leave me not in this eternal woe,
> For if thou diest, my Love, I know not where to go.

---

* Harold Bloom, *The Anxiety of Influence* (New York: Oxford University Press).
† Joseph Brodsky's introduction to *Poems* by Anna Akhmatova, selected and translated by Lyn Coffin (New York: W. W. Norton).

Keats's working brain was almost certainly recalling a well-known song in a very different key, from Dryden's "Marriage à la Mode".

> She cry'd, Oh my dear, I am robb'd of my bliss;
> 'Tis unkind to your Love, and unfaithfully done,
> To leave me behind you, and die all alone.

Keats is handling a totally unstable mixture, with the kneeling Porphyro acting the part of Chaucer's Troilus – himself a sound Drydenian precursor – and Madeline unconsciously uttering the sentiments of a lady begging her gentleman to postpone, in the interest of their mutality, his sexual climax. Porphyro, indeed, seems inspired by the old enticements that look out of Madeline's words. "Beyond a mortal man impassion'd far / At these voluptuous accents he arose . . ." Keats may have sensed the situation he was in, for his brother's uncancelled holograph removed from Madeline her two "voluptuous" lines, replacing them with appropriately dreamlike romantic action, that sleepwalker's motion of the poem which both allies and contrasts with the world outside. "See while she speaks his arms encroaching slow / Have zon'd her, heart to heart – loud, loud the dark winds blow." That stabilizes the onward move to the metaphor of their union – about which Keats was characteristically to remark that he would be ashamed of any young man in the circumstances who left the girl in the state in which he found her – though it does not alter those incongruous literary precedents and influences which the remark itself suggests.

But the romantic imagination, at its most devout and inspired, is never at a loss in such circumstances. It can make them its own, turn the challenge of incongruous reality to its own advantage. The dream of love and the midnight storm are heightened by the suggestions of Chaucerian and Drydenian fabliau, the whole taking on a poignancy peculiar to Keats. The vision becomes the more romantic the more it insists on reality.

> Let the mad poets say whate'er they please
> Of the sweets of Faeries, Peris, Goddesses,

> There is not such a treat among them all,
> Haunters of cavern, lake, and waterfall,
> As a real woman, lineal indeed
> From Pyrrha's pebbles or old Adam's seed.

When Keats talks of a real woman his vision of her is at its most fervently romantic.

The poet since Keats whose temperament is most attuned in the same way is Philip Larkin. For him too romanticism is the most intense aspect of a common reality, an elsewhere conjured up by soberly precise insistence on the banality of the here and now. Keats's "real woman" – real because so much imagined – becomes for Larkin "that unfocused she / No match lit up nor drag ever brought near . . ." As Keats with Dryden, so Larkin transforms for his own vision "that not impossible she" of the cavalier poets. Romance lives at the edge of the colloquial glimpse, the forcefully and unexpectedly crude observation. Keats's ribald comment on the hero ʾand heroine of his poem is carried, as it were, inside Larkin's poem ("Essential Beauty") and into its haunted visions of joy, its absences and oblivions. Social banalities intrude on the same terms. Does the poet care to attend a sherry party?

> In a pig's arse, friend.
> Day comes to an end.
> The gas fire breathes, the trees are darkly swayed.

That "unfocused she" can also be a girl in a photograph album, "a real girl in a real place, / In every sense empirically true", and the girl on the poster advertising a seaside resort.

> *Come to sunny Prestatyn*
> Laughed the girl on the poster,
> Kneeling up on the sand . . .

Obscene disfigurement is inflicted on her image by the travelling public, and finally "a great transverse tear / Left only a hand and some blue. / Now *Fight Cancer* is there". Yet her image is inviolable and remains one of unattainable romance. The degradation of daily circumstances does not alter her transcendent nature, or that of the poem. "She was too good for this life"; but when seen through the lens of Larkin's romantic art ordinary living appears itself just that.

Larkin's absorption of the past is itself a device for turning it into the present. All the *topoi* of early nineteenth-century romanticism – the remote enchantment, the unattainable vision, the distant princess, "La Belle Dame Sans Merci" – are realized in his accurate account of today's decencies and deprivations, the sense of "our falling short". Keats's "Queen of far-away" is used by the poet in his meticulous inventory of "The Large Cool Store" with its "stands of Modes For Night / Machine-embroidered, thin as blouses, / Lemon, sapphire, moss-green, rose . . ." For Larkin romance is not just still bringing up the 9.15; it beckons at the end of every human vista in the shape of death, sex, or just emptiness, the comfort of absence. The more emancipated and enlightened our lifestyle is seen as becoming ("When I see a couple of kids / And guess he's fucking her and she's / Taking pills or wearing a diaphragm") the more seductively vacant appears the image of distance.

> Rather than words comes the thought of high windows:
> The sun-comprehending glass,
> And beyond it, the deep-blue air, that shows
> Nothing, and is nowhere, and is endless.

The "inexpressible" is, ironically, conjured up by the totally unromantic and up-to-date routines of living. They lead, in Larkin's poetry, to the same long perspective of silence and light which is seen beyond all living. The inexpressible and far away are associated not only with death and unmeaning but with the goal of art, as "The Eve of St Agnes" ends with the dream in which it began, the return of distance and romance long past. The title of Larkin's poem "Here", the opening poem of *The Whitsun Weddings*, is again faintly ironic. "Here" is the town of Hull, where

> residents from raw estates, brought down
> The dead straight miles by stealing flat-faced trolleys,
> Push through plate-glass swing doors to their desires –

Cheap suits, red kitchen-ware, sharp shoes, iced lollies,
Electric mixers, toasters, washers, driers –

These are the Larkinian equivalent of the rich details in "The Eve
of St Agnes", and the same perspective of art carries us away
from them to where "Loneliness clarifies" and "silence stands like
heat". The silence, associated with light and water, which waits
behind all Larkin's art, attends us to the end of the land, "Facing
the sun, untalkative, out of reach".

Larkin adapts the romantic narrative to his own art – his first
novel *Jill* retells the story of "Lamia", and *A Girl in Winter*,
originally called *The Kingdom of Winter*, is organized with the
same beauty as "The Eve of St Agnes" and ends with the same
dying fall. An early poem, "Wedding-wind", uses the "elfin storm
from faeryland" which blew for Keats's lovers, and subtly combines monologue with romantic narrative. The girl on her wedding
night, "the night of the high wind", finds it the expression of her
happiness, which the poem presents ambiguously.

> Can it be borne, this bodying-forth by wind
> Of joy my actions turn on, like a thread
> Carrying beads? Shall I be let to sleep
> Now this perpetual morning shares my bed?

The perpetual morning in the bed argues not only the end of rest
but the end of that sense of art, the needful part of life which
embodies and frames oblivion, looks forward to darkness and
silence. The enchanted world of romance has ended with marriage,
which pushes the participant to the side of life and out of art, taking
away the contemplation of death on which this art depends, and
substituting for it (to quote "The Whitsun Weddings") "all the
power / That being changed can give".

Larkin dramatizes in "Wedding-wind" the situation explored
analytically in another poem of the same collection, "Dry-point".
It is a striking example of Larkin's use of the odd effect found in
Keats and other romantics, the buried sexual innuendo which
seems to go against the poem and be ignored by it, as if the raptness
of the poem had a purity of concentration like innocence, which

did not notice such things. Many of Larkin's most effective words and phrases have this sort of deliberate opacity about them, a charge of meaning that declines knowingness, like the memorable last stanza of "Next, please".

> Only one ship is seeking us, a black-
> Sailed unfamiliar, towing at her back
> A huge and birdless silence. In her wake
> No waters breed or break.

The theme of the poem and its central image are as graphically simple as in a lyric of Heine or Housman, yet the inside of the poem is more mysterious than any of theirs. The word "birdless" shows why: its refusal to carry any double sense – the sense of "bird" as "girl" – which in a clever modern poem would be proffered as, so to speak, standard practice, helps to fill the end of the poem with the almost palpable blankness that it tells us of. Larkin's most discerning critic, Barbara Everett,* has pointed out his unexpected debt to what he once dismissively referred to as "foreign" poetry – Baudelaire, Gautier, Mallarmé, and the techniques of continental symbolism. But they were themselves the direct heirs of romanticism, and Larkin by temperament is a straightforward romantic of the older school – the school that includes both Housman and Keats – who has introduced it in a later kind of feeling for words and for poetic effect, "the imagination of silence" as a disciple of Mallarmé called it. It is the silence of elsewhere, the place we cannot live in, as the poem "Days" tells us, but which the words of this poetry continually and unobtrusively suggest. These poems are not only crystal clear but superlatively recessive; as Barbara Everett remarks, they do not *say one thing*; but, both in seeming to and not seeming to, they summon an intensity that takes us straight back to the simplest and most poignant romantic themes.

---

* To date the two most illuminating essays on the inner world of Larkin's poetry are by Barbara Everett. "Philip Larkin: after symbolism" (*Essays in Criticism*, July 1980) suggests his oblique affiliations with continental symbolism, and subtly indicates the almost Wittgensteinian pose involved in his statement that his poems "are too simple to profit from criticism", "Larkin's Edens" (*English*, vol. XXXI No. 139, 1982) explores in perceptive detail the nature of the "ideal" world glimpsed in so many of the poems.

In "Dry-point", however, something else is happening, which makes direct comparison with the Keatsian ability to bring discrepant modes of feeling from other poets together and make the result uniquely and successfully his own. The conceit of the poem is elaborate, and in the sort of poetry it draws on, from Donne to Empson, would be immensely knowing. Sexual desire is imaged as a bubble endlessly expanding to bursting point and then growing again. It forces concentration – "bestial, intent, real" – until "The wet spark comes, the bright blown walls collapse".

> But what sad scapes we cannot turn from then:
> What ashen hills! What sailed shrunken lakes!

Sex as romance ends at its climax, as Keats reveals in "La Belle Dame Sans Merci". Larkin transposes its fleeting magic into a world of industrial landscapes and processes ("Birmingham magic all discredited") and then swerves away – too consciously here perhaps – into the image of an alternative – "that bare and sun-scrubbed room" – "that padlocked cube of light" – where the remorseless procession of sexual anticipation and anti-climax cannot occur. Deprivation and absence are formalized as they are at the conclusion of the "Ode on a Grecian Urn". Keats's gods, men and maidens inhabit there the eternity of romantic expectation and desire, forever beautiful and true because forever unfulfilled.

Larkin's art needs the same premise, and plays its own wholly individual variations. Its deeply erotic romanticism makes fully explicit the humour (all humour being a substitute for despair) which is immanent in Keats or Housman. In his capacity as voyeur Larkin can partake, through his art, in a far more deep and mystic fashion of the idea of marriage – the dozen marriages getting under way in "The Whitsun Weddings" – than if he participated in its inessential dailiness. "Reasons for attendance" makes the point with pungent simplicity. The poet hears "the beat of happiness", "sensing the smoke and sweat, / The wonderful feel of girls". The word there almost parodies the big sense of *feel* in high romantic terminology: Byron's "high mountains are a feeling", and Keats's "the feel of not to feel it", which Larkin is clinically observing in this poem. The decision for elsewhere, the world outside, is made deliberately in the cause of art, and should work: "If no one has misjudged himself. Or lied." The poem is an ironic variation on the same theme as Yeats's poem "The Road At My Door". And in the same way "Essential Beauty" is Larkin's full-length version of the "Ode on a Grecian Urn", the world of advertisements representing the "little town" whose "streets for evermore will silent be". Theirs is a world we miss, feel we just miss, but which, like love and death, is perfect only in art,

newly clear,
Smiling, and recognising, and going dark.

Critical Quarterly, 1984

The Strengths of
His Passivity

Ivan Turgenev, *First Love and A Fire at Sea*,
translated by Isaiah Berlin (New York: Viking Press);
Turgenev's Letters, edited and translated by David Lowe
(2 vols.) (Ann Arbor: Ardis)

A game might be played about the great Russian authors: with which of them do we feel most at home? Feeling at home with them is important, for it explains their extraordinary popularity with English-speaking readers from the time translations of their work first appeared. The Victorian intellectuals deeply respected Goethe and the German philosophers and admired Balzac and Victor Hugo, but Tolstoy and Turgenev, and later on Dostoevsky as well, they really took to their hearts. Of course, their enthusiasm was for the charm of the unknown, which suddenly seemed wonderfully accessible and familiar. But that enthusiasm was based on an often remarkable ignorance. In the course of a rhapsodic review of the French translation of *Anna Karenina*, Matthew Arnold broke off to remark patronizingly that "the crown of literature is of course great poetry" and the Russians had not produced a great poet. Presumably he had never heard of Pushkin.

But Arnold certainly knew all about Turgenev, who was taken up in England as much as or more than in cosmopolitan Germany and France; he was invited out shooting on great estates and was given an honorary degree at Oxford. The English (and Henry James) saw him as one of themselves. Not only was he obviously a gentleman, but his art – to borrow the perhaps unintentionally ironic verdict of the literary historian Prince Mirsky – "answered to the demands of everyone". The right admired its sensitivity and aesthetic beauty and the left its liberal tendencies, which they saw as embodying their own radical and revolutionary programme. But the danger of pleasing everyone is that in the end you please no one; that happened to Turgenev, even in his own lifetime. More than any other factor, perhaps, it has contributed to the gradual eclipse of his once great reputation.

One feels·that Turgenev's novels should have increased in stature by virtue of their wise and civilized impartiality, while those of Tolstoy and Dostoevsky should appear more and more clearly as having been written by opinionated fanatics. But art does not work that way. Turgenev's humanity now looks like weakness. As his best biographer, Leonard Schapiro, has observed, "Much of Turgenev's life and work can be explained in terms of a longing and admiration for the kind of all-consuming will he himself lacked". Probably he never recovered from the capricious domination of his mother, a rich, embittered and often sadistic woman, who flogged the serfs on her large estate and sometimes treated her son as if he were one of them. Though he had one or two affairs with servant girls, and produced an illegitimate daughter whom he looked after but who remained a constant source of worry to him, Turgenev never achieved a mature relationship with a woman. All his later life he clung to Pauline Viardot, the masterful Parisian opera singer who, together with her husband, provided him with a ready-made home and family.

There seems to be a connection between weakness of will in an author and the length at which he can most successfully work. Turgenev admired Tolstoy's stories but abominated *War and Peace*. The repetitive patterns in his own novels – indecisive men and pure, strong-hearted women – make them predictable and boring before they end; but weakness comes into its own in the forms Turgenev was best at – the sketch, the story and the personal letter. *A Sportsman's Sketches*, which is supposed to have contributed to the emancipation of the serf, still holds its own as a work of singular freshness and charm; Turgenev's mother said its prose reminded her·of the scent of wild strawberries.

But the tale that exploits most effectively Turgenev's gifts of pathos and humour, insight and self-awareness – the strengths of his own passivity, so to speak – is *First Love*. It is a masterpiece that shows the curious literalism of Turgenev's talent. He is best when eschewing all fancy stuff and describing exactly what happened, as he does in *First Love*, in *A Sportsman's Sketches*, in the miniature memoir *A Fire at Sea* and in his extraordinary eyewitness account of the death by guillotine of a French murderer, *The Execution of Tropmann*. His famous style seems built for international consumption; he wrote in French as easily as in Russian, and he was fluent in German and competent in English, though the letters he wrote to English friends demonstrate a rather peculiar vocabulary. But appearances are misleading. Turgenev's Russian style, far from going easily into other languages, is exceedingly difficult to translate: the ordinary sort of faithful rendering, which will do nicely for Tolstoy or Dostoevsky, quite fails to do him justice. The translator must understand, from inside, the wonderful supple intimacy of his Russian and evolve a comparable kind of ease in English idiom. This Isaiah Berlin has triumphantly managed, producing the best translation available of Turgenev's most effective tale.

Turgenev was more honest with himself than the other great Russian writers, and in his prose this transparent honesty combines with a profound sympathy for romantic delusion. In *First Love*, the young Vladimir falls in love, with Zinaida because he knows about love from reading Schiller and sentimental fiction. But the literary springs of his feeling do not in the least affect the passionate and spontaneous nature of the emotion. When she mockingly tells him to jump off his seat on a high wall if he really loves her, he finds himself falling as if pushed from behind. Going to bed, he lays his head down carefully, afraid of upsetting the precarious joy that fills his entire being.

Zinaida herself is by far the most realistic of Turgenev's heroines, and her passion for the boy's father has a kind of earthiness and substantiality that is wholly convincing. Turgenev knew how to render the erotic. The white blind that Vladimir sees suddenly and softly descend over the dark transparency of Zinaida's window is more suggestive than any account of doings in bed. Zinaida's mother, a slatternly old princess, and the hero's father, with his withdrawn and dangerous attractiveness, are memorable portraits from life. The events of the tale are certainly taken from the writer's own adolescence, his father having been a noted roué who married his mother for her money and died young.

The origins of *A Fire at Sea*, another little masterpiece, are more curious. When he was nineteen, Turgenev obtained his mother's permission to visit Germany; he departed for Lübeck on a steamer that caught fire a few miles from its destination and was run ashore and burned out. Gossip began to find its way back to Russia that Turgenev had behaved in a comic and cowardly fashion, running distractedly up and down the deck and promising 10,000 roubles to any sailor who would save him, since he was his mother's only son and too young to die. Turgenev was never allowed to forget that story. Dostoevsky mentions it with glee in his venomous caricature of Turgenev as Karmazinov in *The Possessed*.

Turgenev's own attitude was a curious one; he seems to have defended himself, as he often did in contexts of political and literary controversy, by acting the buffoon, deliberately drawing attention to his own absurdity. (In this spirit, he once imitated a cancan dancer in the presence of the censorious Tolstoy, who noted curtly in his journal: "Turgenev – the cancan – sad.") That, at any rate, seems to have been Turgenev's intention when he gave some amateur theatricals on his big estate at Spasskoye and brought the house down by acting a scene in which a fire broke out and yelling at the top of his voice: "Save me! I am my mother's only son."

As Isaiah Berlin says, such behaviour was characteristic of "his incurably ironic sense of his own person and conduct, which he often used as a defensive weapon to blunt the edge of the hostility and mockery he constantly excited in his native land". People in general, and especially Russian authors, don't forgive you for not taking yourself seriously enough. When he was dying of cancer of the spine – and, let it be said, dying heroically – Turgenev set down in French his own account of the fire at sea, showing that his talent for words had lost none of its magic. (He remembers the Danish

sailors, with their "cold energetic faces".) In Mr Berlin's words,
"The memory of a moment of weakness that must have preyed on
him for more than 40 years was exorcized, turned into literature,
rendered innocuous and delightful. His conduct becomes that of
an innocent, confused, romantically inclined young man, neither
hero nor coward, slightly cynical, slightly absurd, but above all
amiable, sympathetic and human." Conrad's Lord Jim in reverse,
as it were. But in a sense it is a judgement on Turgenev's art that it
does transform everything into the innocuous and delightful.

That is one reason for the charm of his correspondence. David
Lowe has provided an admirable and scholarly two volume edition
of the letters, including more than 200 translated for the first time.
Though Turgenev's letters are not in the same class for literary
interest as Flaubert's, some of the best and warmest are to the French
novelist; that the pair got on so well together says much for Turgenev's charm. With his friend Pavel Vasilievich Annenkov he
kept up a running commentary on the current literary scene in
France, Germany and Russia; and his few letters to Dostoevsky
have the peculiar fascination of two utterly opposed temperaments
generously agreeing (in Turgenev's case, at least) to look beyond
their own limitations. Both writers took part in the famous Pushkin
Commemoration of 1880, in which Turgenev made a sensible and
rational speech in praise of Russia's poet, doubting nonetheless that
he was a "world poet", whereas Dostoevsky inspired his audience
to hysteria with his claim that Pushkin was Russia's ultimate gift
to Europe, "re-creating Shakespeare, Goethe, and all the others".
Turgenev's uninfectious common sense was coldly received, after
that, by a Slavophile Moscow audience.

Some of the most touching and revealing letters are those to the
illegitimate daughter, Paulinette – a name derived fondly but with
singular tastelessness from Pauline Viardot, the love of Turgenev's
life, whom he first helped into what proved a disastrous marriage
and then supported in her cantankerous solitude. Mr Facing-Both-
Ways as he was, he possessed an unadvertised personal heroism. It
comes out in a letter he wrote on his deathbed to Tolstoy, imploring
that "great writer of the Russian land" not to forsake art but to

write more novels and stories. From a writer to another who had always sneered at him, and from a writer who was dying by painful inches, that represented an uncovenanted nobility of spirit. But it was not at all untypical of Turgenev.

New York Times Book Review, 1983

The War
Between the Diaries

Tolstoy's Diaries, edited and translated by R. F. Christian
(2 vols.) (London: Athlone Press);
The Diaries of Sofia Tolstoy, translated by Cathy Porter
(London: Jonathan Cape)

Tolstoy was much preoccupied with questions of identity. His brutally penetrating intelligence, as well as the instinctive self-confidence of an aristocrat, were always running incredulously up against the fact of existence, and the certainty of non-existence. What and who was he at different moments of the day? One of his earliest attempts at writing is a history of twenty-four hours, a record of his various selves during that period. His early diaries have the same feel to them. This is not like the stream of consciousness, but something far more urgent, emotional and volatile. "My God! Where am I? Where am I going? And what am I now?" That is almost exactly like Natasha's exclamation at the death of Prince Andrew, which the translators weaken by paraphrase, finding its literalness too disconcerting. It should be: "Where is he and who is he now?"

Who is he now? Tolstoy's sense of identity was so strong that it would obviously survive death. But because so strong it was also so fearful and so tormented – joyous too, but never taking itself for granted for a moment. Solipsism is an index of immortality. Tolstoy's intellectual realization that he was going to die, dramatized in *A Confession* but vividly present in the pages of his earliest diary, engaged all his life in the most literal of struggles with the conviction that nothing of the sort could possibly happen. It is the first of the paradoxes of his life and writing, and the one that underlies all the rest. The Jewish philosopher Lev Shestov, his most perceptive critic, dryly remarked that Tolstoy struggled against solipsism all his life, because he didn't know what to do with "this impertinent thing", but that eventually he gave in to it, as one does give in to the thing in one's life that really matters. At the age of twenty-nine he was already writing: "Thoughts of approaching death torment me. I look at myself in the mirror for days on end." The last entry in the diary, not long before pneumonia caused him to lose consciousness, runs: "Here is my plan. *Fais ce que dois, advienne que pourra.* And all is for the good of others and above all for me."

Above all for me. The magnificent obsession conjures into positive and nightmare being – as if it were the witch Babi-Yaga rushing through the forests in her hut on fowls' legs – what is for most people the normal neutral background of life. Tolstoy's sense of himself was so strong that it must be the most important thing in the world, to which he incessantly called everyone's attention. So strong, too, that it communicates itself to the rest of us. That "who is he now?" underlies every word he wrote and every character he created. Stiva and Vronsky, and the mare Frou-Frou, and the horse Kholstomer in the short story, are possessed of the same inner life, that presence of interior being which Tolstoy can suggest like no other writer. So "who is he now?" seems the one question worth asking when somebody dies. He must still have being, for nothing makes sense otherwise.

Tolstoy, aged twenty-eight, was travelling in Switzerland when he jotted in his habitual telegraphic manner the query about where he was and what he was. It is perhaps significant that he had just had an encounter, later described in his story "Lucerne", with an itinerant singer whom he had invited into his hotel for a drink. The waiters sneered at the man and put the couple in a room by themselves, away from the hotel guests. Earlier, Tolstoy had been incensed by the fact that the public had listened to the singing, but then turned away without giving the performer any money. The singer himself proved to be "a commonplace, pathetic person". But the incident shows how Tolstoy's sense of himself, almost mystical later on that evening as he looked out of his hotel-room window on "darkness, broken clouds, and light", was particularly responsive to encounters of this sort. Towards the end of *Anna Karenina* Levin has a similar encounter with a peasant, which suddenly reveals all that matters to him. Solipsism, unexpectedly, is both intensified by other people and intensely responsive to them. Tolstoy's social instincts were always generous and immediate, but what mattered to the artist and writer was the encounter itself, and its effect on the ego. There are highly memorable ones in *War and Peace*: Prince Andrew on the retreat to Moscow, for example, meeting the two little girls in the garden who are stealing plums, and Pierre's encounter with the party of Russian soldiers after the battle of Borodino.

His diaries have been well used by every biographer, but a proper English version has not appeared before, and Professor Christian has done an excellent job on this selection of them, as he did a few years ago on Tolstoy's letters. The second volume, from 1895 to 1910, when the man has become an adjunct of the legend, is mostly rather boring except to Tolstoy addicts. The most striking thing, to the reader who is familiar with his life and works, but who now reads the diaries consecutively for the first time, is the way in which his ambition to be a great writer had always come first. Though biography gives the impression of him blundering around, and trying first this and then that, the diaries unobtrusively emphasize the overpowering will to be a great writer, a "general of literature", and the efforts to write in all situations. They only really begin when Tolstoy goes as a cadet to the Caucasus in 1851. This was a sudden impulse – his elder brother Nikolai, who was already an officer in the army, was returning there. All his life Tolstoy enjoyed making sudden decisions, like the one at the end of his life when he left home and died at Astapovo railway station, but the idea of going to the Caucasus was one that any other ambitious young Russian writer might have had. Since Pushkin and Lermontov it had been the prime place to seek romantic experience and copy.

The second impression the early diaries give one, apart from Tolstoy's firm ambition to become famous through authorship, is how easy it was for him to lead the kind of life that made this possible. Dostoevsky, not the most unenvious genius in the world, used to complain that he would be able to write a real masterpiece if only he had the time and the resources that Tolstoy and Turgenev had. In fact, of course, Dostoevsky wrote best under great pressure – debt or prison or the firing squad were challenges that brought his most characteristically brilliant responses – but he himself probably did not see matters in that light. Like him, and like Pushkin, the young Tolstoy gambled heavily and got into debt, actually having to sell the big house on his estate at Yasnaya Polyana after one crushing loss at cards in the Caucasus. But however often this occurred ("*16 April. Staro gladkovskaya* . . . Lost 100 silver roubles effortlessly to Sulimovsky"), it was not really a serious matter. Tolstoy got up in the morning full of remorse and doggedly proceeded with trying to write *Childhood*, or *The Cossacks*, or one of his brilliant stories of army life in the Caucasus.

In fact, his army routine was the most leisurely affair possible, consisting almost entirely in talking and trying to compose stories, shooting hares and pheasants, having affairs with Cossack girls, and getting treated for gonorrhoea at the local spa. Neither then nor later in the Crimea, at Sevastopol, did military duty interfere in any way with such things. Though he does not seem to have exploited his name and aristocratic rank, there is no doubt that a privileged position was tacitly allowed him by senior commanders. Everything conspired to help him become a writer. There is a parallel here with the military experiences of his admirer and self-proclaimed rival, Hemingway, who spent less than a week at the Italian front as a Red Cross welfare officer, distributing oranges and chocolates. Having had the luck to be wounded by a shell at the end of that time, Hemingway subsequently invented for himself and in his writings, a whole saga and mystique of heroic military service, the real facts only becoming known after his death.

Tolstoy's service was not like that, for though the diarist often accuses himself of being a coward, he behaved bravely enough on the few occasions when he was in actual danger. Like Hemingway, though, he was both obsessed with the need for a macho image and at the same time privately disgusted with the need and the idea. *War and Peace* is far more frank and open about all this than Hemingway could ever be. Nonetheless, the resemblance goes further than the marked self-division in both writers, and the popularity of Hemingway – seen as a sort of disciple of Tolstoy – in Russia. Both men were quite unable to get on in the marriage relation, because – as Sofia Tolstoy was to write in her diary – "he doesn't want me to have any life of my own". Hemingway's wives made the same point, and no doubt it is and was a frequent complaint against husbands who have no claim to be great writers. Yet in all cases, even the most commonplace, it arises from the husband's obsessive fear that his wife has seen through his childlike macho image, and is secretly mocking it. Hence the abuse and distrust of wives, and the desire that they should have no private or secret life of their own.

In her diary for 1898 Sofia Tolstoy recorded an evening in which her husband and his sister were reminiscing about their childhood:

> It was such fun. Mashenka told us about the trip they had all made to Pirogovo when Lyovochka Tolstoy, then a boy of about fifteen, decided to run behind the carriage for the first five versts to *impress* everyone. The horses were trotting along but Lyovochka didn't fall behind, and when they stopped the carriage he was gasping so heavily that Mashenka burst into tears.
>
> Another time he wanted to *impress* some young ladies (they were staying in Kazan at the time, in the village of Panovo, their uncle Yushkov's estate) and he threw himself fully clothed into the pond. But he couldn't swim back to the bank, so he tried to touch the bottom, found he was out of his depth, and would have drowned if it hadn't been for some peasant women haymaking in the fields nearby, who saved him with their rakes.
>
> Yes, he always wants to *impress* and *impress* – he has been like that all his life. Well, he certainly has impressed the world, as no one else!

Rambling, full of vague detail and the teasing malice of its emphases,

Sofia's journal is very different in tone from that of her husband. For one thing, her voice can be heard, and its mixture of tones is quite subtle. She wants to take Leo down a peg, of course, and to show to herself and posterity what it is like living with this childish great man. She is possessive about him: but she is also full of the vitality which Tolstoy once so much admired in her and her sister Tanya, and portrayed in the character of Natasha in *War and Peace*. At such moments there is visible in her diary, though not in his, the cheerfulness that must have kept breaking in all the time. "It was such fun . . ." Like many powerful men who need to "impress", Tolstoy also needed to be laughed with, even – by a loving wife – to be laughed at. With his wife and sister, and in the bosom of his family, he probably entered with amusement even into stories of how he had been saved from drowning by the rakes of the women haymakers.

Being taken down a peg, openly or secretly, was probably the least of his matrimonial troubles. Sofia must have possessed from an early age all the latent intolerableness which is apt to go with great physical vitality. As her husband was to remark of certain sorts of powerful and sensational novel, you see the point and then you become bored. Sofia must rapidly have developed into the most formidable of all bores: not the monotonous sort who merely send you to sleep, but the kind who demand from their *vis-à-vis* an equal display of gratuitous energy. Like Natasha in *War and Peace* she had flashing self-regard without any corresponding powers of self-analysis; immense subjective drive without any objective talent. Indeed, perhaps the most cunning achievement of Tolstoy's essentially cunning talent is to portray in *War and Peace* a wonderful heroine who seems to exemplify and gather to herself so much of the open space, power and joyous movement of the book, but who is really a monster.

Her monstrousness is just ripening into maturity as the book ends. Pierre her husband will receive the full force of it in that speculative future which stretches out at the end of many great novels, and *War and Peace* most of all. An additional irony is that Tolstoy toyed with the idea of making Pierre a Decembrist, who after the abortive liberals' plot against the Tsar in St Petersburg would be sent into exile in Siberia. Many of the Decembrists' wives voluntarily accompanied their husbands to Siberia, and heroically endured great hardships. Natasha would have been tailor-made for this role. Disaster and challenge would have brought out the very best in her. And the same sort of destiny would have done the same for Sofia Tolstoy. As it was, she had nothing to do but endure her husband, incessantly bear his children, copy his manuscripts till three in the morning, put up with his Christian principles and with the fact that in spite of them he always expected and got the best of everything for himself. Siberia would have been a more acceptable alternative.

The Christianity must have been the hardest to bear.

> What sort of *Christian* life is this, I should like to know? He hasn't a drop of love for his children, for me, or for anyone but himself. I may be a heathen, but I love the children, and unfortunately I still love him too, cold Christian that he is, and now my heart is torn in two with doubts: should I go to Moscow or not? How can I possibly please everyone? Because as God is my witness I am happy only when I am making others happy.

That is touching, and one believes every word of it. But it also has the involuntary humour sometimes displayed by those who have absolutely no sense of humour at all. Being made happy by Sofia can have been no easy task, and no wonder her children, as well as her husband, came to flinch from it. In the meantime "Lyovochka is being quiet and friendly at the moment – and extremely *amorous*". She notes that he has begun reading English novels, which is a sure sign that he will soon be starting to write a novel of his own. In 1891, at the age of forty-seven, she is expressing what is in many ways a conventional Victorian view of herself and her sexual destiny. She longs for all *that* to be over and done with. "All my life I have dreamed sentimental dreams, aspired to a perfect union, a *spiritual* communion, not *that*. And now my life is over and most of the good in me is dead, at any rate my ideals are dead."

Yet on the same morning she had felt differently.

> Horribly dissatisfied with myself. Lyovochka woke me
> this morning with passionate kisses . . . afterwards I picked
> up a French novel, Bourget's *Un Coeur de Femme*, and read
> in bed till 11.30, something I normally never do. I have
> succumbed to the most unforgivable debauchery – and at
> my age too! I am so sad and ashamed of myself! I feel sinful
> and wretched, and can do nothing about it although I do
> try.

All *that* evidently still has its attractions. She was in a muddle, and
the muddle, together with all her loves and fears, prejudices and
passions, goes instantly into the diary.

Tolstoy was a good father when the children were young, but
as they grew older only the daughters had any appeal for him.
"My sons, of whom I seem to have about a hundred", were
"impossibly obtuse", filled "for all time with impregnable self-
satisfaction". The diaries are continually noting self-satisfaction in
others, with censoriousness but also sometimes with a kind of envy,
as if the tormented genius who sought always to find out the
Hedgehog's secret, "the one big thing", secretly knew that what
he saw and rejected in others was indeed the proper and human
way to get through life. His art knows it. *War and Peace* celebrates
the rightness, indeed the necessity, of human self-satisfaction, as if
Tolstoy knew that his own brand of dissatisfied egoism – a very
different thing – was not likely to produce the harmonious outlines
of a Russian idyll.

He identified the "stupidity" of his children with that of the
mother, which was natural enough, a ploy used by many parents
in the marital struggle, though usually more good-naturedly.
Tolstoy wanted to rub it in. One of his sons has "the same castrated
mind that his mother has. If you too should ever read this, forgive
me: it hurts me terribly." Probably the son Seryozha read it in
time, but his mother was reading such things in her husband's diary
almost every day. At the same time there may have been some
comfort and reassurance for her in the comically universal,

Thurber-like nature of Tolstoy's complaints and self-pity. Naturally his family "don't see and don't know my sufferings". What
wife hasn't heard that her spouse is "depressed . . . a worthless,
pathetic, unnecessary creature"? What wife or husband doesn't
know that "I'm the only person who isn't mad in a house full of
mad people, run by mad people"?

Self-knowledge, difficult enough for anyone at any time, and
especially for Tolstoy's Lear-like genius, was made possible for
both of them by the war between the diaries. While Tolstoy was
presenting himself as a suffering martyr, his wife noted how everything in the house was done for his benefit, how he, who had run
a school at Yasnaya Polyana in order to "impress" people, would
not take the slightest interest in his own children's education. It is
significant, too, that Tolstoy's novels, multitudinously true and
perceptive as they are about the nature of family life, contain no
real hint of what was going on; just as his early stories of the *Childhood* sequence never contained the sort of facts about himself which
his sister remembered and shared with his wife. Honesty with each
other, parodied by the ritual of reading each other's diaries, and by
Tolstoy's insistence that his young fiancée should know all about
his early sexual adventures, made it all the more impossible for
them to be honest with themselves, was a kind of substitute for such
self-knowledge.

So indeed was the kind of honesty which Tolstoy could always
deploy in his writing. As with D. H. Lawrence, everything that
went in was true but a good deal was left out. Both can only appear
to their own advantage in their autobiographical novels, however
much a Pierre or a Levin is presented as comical, a Paul Morel or
Rupert Birkin as priggish. Both were deeply inspired and supported
by their wives, yet if he had lived long enough Lawrence might
well have left Frieda, as Tolstoy left his Sofia. The last ingratitude
is the need to leave the person who has helped you become what
you are. Lawrence at least had the good fortune and the intelligence
to be genuinely classless: he never had to struggle, as Tolstoy did,
with the clutches of a way of life which would not give him up,
and which he could only defy in himself and his family by the

absurdest of gestures, like cobbling his own boots, which he did very badly. Lawrence, for all his frailty, was physically a far more efficient person, for whom it was natural to do all the chores.

> Mowed. Stitched boots. Can't remember what I did. The girls love me. Masha clings to me. Letter from Chertkov and an officer.

Like so much in both diaries that sort of entry is touchingly commonplace. Everyone "forgets what I did", and wants wives and daughters to love them. Happiness in families is all the same, as stated in the opening sentence of *Anna Karenina*, but the unhappiness of the Tolstoys certainly had some rather special features. There was Chertkov for one thing, an insinuating aristocrat and former guards officer who had seen the light and become one of Tolstoy's most dedicated disciples. Sofia couldn't stand him and in this her instinct was surely right: he was a home-breaker of the most disagreeably high-minded kind. Sofia even goes so far as to suggest in her diary that there is between him and her husband a homosexual attachment. Here she was clearly wrong, but pardonably so when one considers that she was dealing with a man who was trying to get all the family assets, copyrights and literary properties into his own hands. He haunts the pages of her diary before her husband left home to die.

In the early entries, when he was stationed in the Caucasus, Tolstoy is predictably frank about his sexual feelings, about both men and women. Lust he regarded as an illness, attendant on seeing a desirable woman, and to be got rid of as soon as possible by having her. Disgust of course afterwards. "I have never been in love with women," he remarks at that stage. He finds it embarrassing to look at men he is – or has been – in love with, as with a company commander whom he regards as a good solid homely type, backbone of the Russian army. But in general he believes he has fallen in love with men for some sort of excitement or delicious fear, "the fear of offending or not pleasing the object of one's love".

> I fell in love with men before I had any idea of the possibility of *pederasty*, but even when I knew about it the idea

of the possibility of coitus never occurred to me. A strange case of inexplicable sympathy was Gautier. Although I had absolutely no relations with him except for buying books, I used to be thrown into a fever when he entered the room. My love for Islavin spoilt the whole eight months of my life in Petersburg for me. Although not consciously, I never bothered about anything else except how to please him . . . I always loved the sort of people who were cool towards me, and only took me for what I was worth . . . There is the case of Dyakov . . . I shall never forget the night when we were travelling from Pirogovo, and wrapped up under a travelling rug, I wanted to kiss him and cry. There was sensuality in that feeling, but why it took that course it's impossible to decide, because, as I said, my imagination never painted any lubricious pictures; on the contrary, I have a terrible aversion to all that.

This is straightforward enough. Shakespeare and Stendhal probably had the same sort of feelings, and Tolstoy had them on the same scale as he had everything else. But it is easy to see why his wife hated Chertkov so much. Nothing could be more infuriating than a man like that whom your husband was always trying to please, though he never made an effort to please you. No doubt with Chertkov, a guardsman and aristocrat with whose upbringing he felt in deep if unconscious accord, Tolstoy may have experienced in some way "the fear of offending or not pleasing the object of one's love". Even though Chertkov was his disciple, Tolstoy saw in him an idealized version of himself, free from his own humiliating family entanglements.

It is an odd paradox that Tolstoy's novels seem so "English" – as he wanted them to be – but his family life and temperament were as "Russian" as could be: mad, grotesque, touching, funny as anything in Dostoevsky. Boring too. You see the point and it begins to bore you. Unlike her husband, Sofia was a bore in herself, but her diaries are more vivacious than his, more zestful and surprising. Part of the pleasure is to see her getting her own back while at the same time cosseting her husband, who was that not unfamiliar type, a red-blooded hypochondriac. Both were also masochists on a truly Dostoevskian scale, and Sofia seems to have enjoyed nothing more than copying out her husband's diaries. "There is no such thing as love, *only the physical need for intercourse and the practical need for a life companion*. I only wish I had read that remark 29 years ago, then I would never have married him." (Tolstoy, one notes, rejected romantic "love" as emphatically as D. H. Lawrence was to do, as something fit only for women.)

> Self-admiration runs through all his diaries. It is strikingly obvious that people exist for him only if they directly concern him . . . He would like to destroy his old diaries, as he wants to appear before his children and the public as a patriarchal figure. Still the same old vanity!

Copying the diaries was no doubt a way of preserving her spouse's feet of clay for posterity. It grieved her terribly when he shouted at her, as he did most days, that he must leave this "hell": and yet few days passed without a reconciliation, tears, kisses, and hugs of love. Like many marital opponents, they needed each other in spite of everything, and it is likely that the final departure would only have been temporary if Tolstoy had survived. After his death Sofia's writing loses its zest and becomes exculpatory and tedious. Cathy Porter has done an excellent translation of the complete diaries, adding as appendices Sofia's notes on her girlhood and the early part of her marriage. Detailed family trees enhance the quality of the book's production.

London Review of Books, 1985

Shatost

Robin Feuer Miller, *Dostoevsky and "The Idiot"*:
Author, Narrator and Reader (Cambridge, Mass.: Harvard University Press);
John Jones, *Dostoevsky* (Oxford: Oxford University Press);
New Essays on Dostoyevsky, edited by Malcolm Jones
and Garth Terry (Cambridge: Cambridge University Press);
Robert Louis Jackson, *The Art of Dostoevsky*:
Deliriums and Nocturnes
(Princeton: Princeton University Press)

Most novels, if they come off, are orgies of self-congratulation, shared between the writer and the reader, who unconsciously understand both what is going on and what is needed. To enjoy a novel is by extension to enjoy oneself, and novelists in their various ways accommodate the process. Although the rules are always changing, both sides know the game. And as the form becomes more self-conscious, the writer – Henry James is the obvious example – indicates both inside and outside his novel how the reader will divide the work with him and share the spoils. In this partnership we become lucid and wise. Even the most unlikely circumstances are arranged for our self-satisfaction.

In *War and Peace* Tolstoy goes so far as to make self-satisfaction the key not only to the reader's enjoyment but to the satisfactory discharge of living in general. In Conrad's "The Shadow Line", or *Lord Jim*, even in *Heart of Darkness*, everything is intensely satisfactory, the language, the sense of things, the reality, or rather the thereness, of objects and people. The novel did not invent such reality, but has developed its conjuration into a fine art. Think of Scott, virtually the founder of the great classic novel, and his unemphatic and impenetrable ability to seem to order and control experience, to give a self to history and to men and women in

75

history. From this point of view, Scott at one end of the century and James Joyce at the other are blood brothers, *Ulysses* a fine old-fashioned novel that could almost be in the Scott canon. Like Scott, like Conrad (whose insistent phrase it is), Joyce "makes you see", sharpens still further the artificial focus of language that gives a selfhood to places and people.

But some novels undermine this majestic and (as it sometimes seems) almost involuntary process of creation, and the chief of them are Dostoevsky's. Instead of giving a self to things, a naming of parts, an artifice of order and being, they take it all away. This has nothing to do with "form", in which Dostoevsky believed as fervently as Henry James ("*Form, Form,*" he keeps exhorting himself in his notebooks). But nothing *seems* invented or arranged in his novels and no one objectively exists. Things are "said" to happen, supposed to exist. Language, the unending dishevelled calculating intelligence of Dostoevsky's prose, dissolves the picture instead of creating it. This, if you like, is more like most living, a closer representation of actual consciousness, which cannot perform art's godlike feat of immortalizing days and events, objects and people. In life, we could say, things only seem to happen, whereas in fiction they really do. The novel has come to feel guilty about this art (the guilt may even be the symptom of a terminal disease), and novelists have tried hard – and in the case of someone like Virginia Woolf all too obviously – to avoid creating the novel's all too solid artificial worlds.

Dostoevsky does not appear to try; his genius just seems to make it happen that way. But in fact he tried very hard indeed. No novelist is more theoretical; none examined with more critical acumen the subtle ways in which he could produce the effects he desired. These he referred to as "the deeper realism", in contrast to such realists as Balzac and Zola, whose worlds are fashioned with as much solid artifice as those of Scott, Joyce or Proust. The deeper realism has the properties physicists now associate with matter itself: it causes everything to waver, slip, collapse and re-form. "Reality strives towards fragmentation," says one of his narrators. In terms of the deeper realism, we have to be somewhere but have nowhere to go. Writers like Beckett have framed and stylized what in Dostoevsky appears to be an absolutely natural, unending and frameless state of affairs. We all live under the floor of a non-existent house. In *The Possessed* this *shatost* – radical instability – is most pervasive in terms of method, consciousness, society. One of its characters is called Shatov.

But Dostoevsky developed the method very early, in his very first novel. Many novels come into existence in order to show the falsity of their predecessors, and he exploits in secret subterranean fashion, more effectively than any other novelist, the kinds of parody that make their original look untrue. *Poor People* is this kind of parody of Gogol's *The Overcoat*. (We have all come from under it, Dostoevsky is supposed to have said: if true, a typically ambiguous statement.) Makar Devushkin, in *Poor People*, comes into existence in order to reveal the solid-all-through artificiality of Gogol's Akaky Basmachkin. The reader enjoys Akaky just because he could only exist in a novel. His immortally vague trailing speech patterns, his invariable supper of a piece of beef with onions and sometimes a cockroach that had happened to find its way into it, his sitting down after it to the copying work which he loves and has brought back from the office – above all, the overcoat itself, the dreaming of it, the planning, the making, the tailor who makes it: all these are of the same order of being as the armour wrought for Achilles, or the pig's kidney that Bloom cooks and eats for his breakfast.

Gogol's inspiration is obviously akin to that of Dickens, but it is more consciously artful and detailed, as it is more deliberately unkempt. As with Dickens, though, there is a connection between the way invention works and the relation of the author to it: Gogol, like Dickens, is creator, showman, and commentator on his world. It was this relation that the young Dostoevsky set out to subvert, promising himself and the critics that the youthful author's "ugly mug" would be nowhere visible in *Poor People*, a novel mostly in letters. (That form, too, Dostoevsky utterly subverts, making the novel a predecessor of his *Notes from under the Floor*.) Pathos is not pathos in Makar Devushkin as it is in Akaky, fixed as he is in Gogol's imperial eye, a character who is introduced, *seen*, and taken away. The very authoritative Russian critic Bakhtin said of the Dostoevsky character that "we do not see him, we hear him". He appears to be talking to us behind the back of the author. By not seeing the character and the tokens of his existence (over-coats, noses, kidneys) we feel him as a disembodied, independent consciousness. There is nothing to be seen under the floor, but there are many impressions to receive, none definitive, none beginning, none ending. Bakhtin calls Dostoevsky's an "imperfective" world, in which Makar Devushkin, for instance, really does seem a con-tinuously, an anonymously, an unendingly *poor* person. Almost every nineteenth-century novelist was successfully illustrated, the drawings acting as another and complementary way of seeing the characters. Illustrations to Dostoevsky would not even begin to be unsuitable: they would be utterly beside the point.

About such a genius as Dostoevsky's, dualistic, "imperfective", but also wide and multifarious, infinitely capable of surprisingness, there is always more to say. In that sense he is Shakespearian: his powers give power to others. Though the canon is already formi-dable, these new studies all add to it in different ways and suggest something new going on. For newness, of a unique kind, is per-petually immanent in Dostoevsky, always on the verge of breaking out, needing the new reader to be excited by it (as Belinsky was by *Poor People*) and the reader already experienced to be caught in a fresh fever of speculative excitement and admiration. No writer is so seldom dull, but at the same time no great creative writer is more essentially abstract.

And yet what does "abstract" mean here? Dostoevsky has none of Gogol's overcoats, or Turgenev's or Tolstoy's houses and dinners and landscapes, but his novels are full of a stifling smell of living and littered with the detritus of objects that constitute daily reality. What is the function of such things? To undermine the all-too-solid surrogate world of the "novel", just as he borrows Gogolian dishevelment and takes the Gogolian life out of it, or borrows and transforms the love sentiments of a novel in letters, or changes the Gothic into the contingently banal, the Devil into a furtive and seedy bourgeois, or the romantic spectre of the *Doppelgänger* (as Bakhtin pointed out) into something wholly pervasive, limply commonplace. His prose is a remorseless solvent of what normally constitutes literary distinctiveness. Dr Miller has some penetrating things to say about this, and about how the meandering accumulations of Dostoevsky's descriptions – and his humour above all – "depend on the reader's acquaintance with the form of the novel of manners or the domestic novel" – indeed any novel. Take the Epanchin family in *The Idiot*. All seems normal at first, or rather normally abnormal, as in any vigorous and lively novel. The Epanchin girls are "tall young ladies, with amazing shoulders, powerful bosoms, and strong almost masculine arms". They like to eat, as does their mother, the wife of a general, and Dostoevsky's account of their eating habits rambles on until it suddenly gets out of hand and reveals that it is not really focused on girls or on eating at all. "Besides tea, coffee, cheese, honey, butter, the special fritters adored by the general's wife, cutlets and so forth, a rich hot soup was even served."

The dangling emphasis of that "even" gives the game away. This is not like the big eating in *Dead Souls*. In going too far, that soup deprives the reader of normal expectations. The Epanchin family is not being satirized or undercut. Far from it – that would be normal. The reader is being manipulated into a new kind of awareness, a response far more metaphysical than sex or eating or the satisfactions of the novel. One could write an essay on uneaten food in Dostoevsky, culminating in the cold veal left untouched by Svidrigailov before his suicide. And the atmosphere of eroticism in which every novelist, even in the days of respectability, reposed as on a sofa, is utterly absent. Only Kafka equals Dostoevsky here. Both use objects and people for the same purpose – to bury them in the mind, in obsessions, preoccupations, boredoms, so that they become part of the furniture of consciousness rather than that of the external world. Kafka works on a small scale, but Dostoevsky is glittering, majestic, Olympian. With the laughter and disorder of the gods flattened on to the swarming, unending versts of Russia. No wonder there is so much to say about him.

Not that the overkill, the heaping-up of subject matter into the life of feeling and idea, always comes off; if it did, he would not be so extraordinary a writer; he towers in imperfection as well as imperfectively. While Dr Miller has much that is of interest to say about *The Idiot*, she does not quite persuade one that it comes off, indeed she does not really try, because like many scholars today she is more concerned with showing how the thing works than with judging if it works well. A rereading of the famous scene at the end when Rogozhin and Myshkin keep watch over Nastasia Filippovna's body, whose naked foot protrudes from the sheet while a fly buzzes over the Jeyes fluid, makes one feel that Dostoevsky did not always turn parody into new reality and the Gothic into his own version of the electrically banal. John Jones may be right to write off *The Idiot* in his study and leave it out of discussion. Even its humour is disproportionate, and it is peculiarly difficult to separate in it the essential from the inessential, the blind alley (Myshkin) from the continuing way. Yet just because of this it is in some ways the most characteristic as it is the most ramified of all the novels, the one with the most varied aspects to explore, as was shown in Michael Holquist's *Dostoevsky and the Novel* and by Richard Peace's remarkable examination, in *Dostoevsky: The Major Novels*, of its catacomb of religious symbolism and clash of hidden dogmas. It is a quarry for quite separate lines and kinds of study, like a work of the Renaissance.

Like a play of that time, as George Steiner pointed out, is the swift development in Dostoevsky of themes which sweep us on to further excitements and possibilities before they themselves have been used up or made clear. The French structuralist critic René Girard has a good metaphor for the process: "In Proust the game proceeds slowly; the novelist constantly interrupts the players to remind them of previous hands and to anticipate those to come. In Dostoevsky, on the contrary, the cards are laid down very rapidly and the novelist lets the game proceed from beginning to end without interfering. The reader must be able to remember everything himself." Freedom in Dostoevsky is the freedom to be confused, and there is a close relation between his method and the consciousness that "if God does not exist, all is permitted". The author has apparently ceased to function as God. The character and the reader have together taken over from him, in a relationship that is bound to be uneasy and claustrophobic. The double again – Dostoevsky's most consistent obsession.

Girard is quoted in a useful piece on "Formalist and Structuralist Approaches" by Christopher Pike, one of the contributions to *New Essays on Dostoyevsky*. (Why is there still no unanimity about how we spell him? – the variations seem a suitable emblem for *shatost*.) There is no doubt that he is the biggest influence both on the "new novel" and the new critical terminology – the two are much the same – and Ann Shukman points out how close his process is to the French idea of *texte pluriel*, also endorsing Bakhtin's verdict that literature in the usual sense disintegrates in Dostoevsky, falling, in Pike's phrase, into a kind of "noble ruin" suggesting new worlds to come which will have to be described and explored in other ways. There are several notable essays in the collection, from which one might single out R. M. Davison on the role of Stavrogin in *The Possessed*, and Sergei Hackel on Father Zosima's discourse in *The Brothers Karamazov*.

Striking, though, and perhaps rather depressing, is the almost purely technical nature of this modern criticism, even more unsuited to how we actually respond to Dostoevsky than it is to most authors. It is natural that Soviet experts should seek to emasculate him by purely technical enquiry (an address by Valery Kirpotin confined him safely in "a multiplicity of objectively existent psychologies affecting each other"): but that is no reason why we should seek safety in jargon from an author whose primary strength is to enthral us, to make us love and hate, laugh and cry. I recall, as many must do, a first reading of *The Possessed*, hating Pyotr Verkhovensky so much, and feeling so sorry for Shatov, that it coloured my mind for days. It is this that makes John Jones's approach so refreshing. He exclaims, wonders, chuckles, buttonholes and insinuates, just as Dostoevsky's people do. The blurb describes his book as "passionate and tender", a rather startling claim by a University Press, but one that is, in a sense, fully justified by the text.

Although he does not mention them, Jones's approach marks a return to the *ad hominem* style of the old-type Russian critics, such as Mikhailovsky and Merezhkovsky, Rozanov and Shestov. Merezhkovsky called Dostoevsky "the seer of the spirit", as opposed to Tolstoy, "the seer of the flesh"; Mikhailovsky held that his great genius was essentially cruel, fuelled by malice, envy and ill-will. That, it could be argued, is in any case what the human spirit is all about. Another forceful critic, Dostoevsky's one-time friend Strakhov, turned against him and wrote a venomous piece identifying him with all his most repellent characters, the Svidrigailovs, Stavrogins and underfloor men, rapists of little girls in bath-houses. It is natural that one should feel love or hate, or both, for this author, as for his characters, but Strakhov's reductive line leads nowhere and Jones is right to ignore it. Jones's meditation is rhapsodic, often emotional – he expresses admiration for Middleton Murry's pioneering study, brewed up at a time when Constance Garnett's translations were being rapturously received by the English intelligentsia – but it is a scholar's approach to the novels, not to their author.

Professor Jackson's study is more nicely balanced between, as it were, the human and the critical; and it is particularly strong on the relation of Dostoevsky's novels to the literature of the time, complementing in that respect the massive literary biographies of Grossman and Frank. Inside the novels the characters have a genius for depriving all other literature and literary figures of what one of them calls *zhivaya zhizn* ("living life"): the notorious instance is the treatment by the narrator of Karmazinov/Turgenev in *The Possessed*. And this is the real point of Mikhailovsky's charge of cruelty. In fact, Dostoevsky himself admired, even revered, other writers, just as his own admittedly somewhat distracted home life was full of love and generosity: but his personal genius reaches to the extreme of human dualism, which was analysed by the Russian-Jewish philosopher Shestov, of whom Jackson makes good use. In some respects the subtlest of Dostoevsky's admirers, Shestov dissects the ways in which both he and Tolstoy draw their immense creative vitality as artists from modes of being which, as spokesmen and sages, they passionately repudiated. In Tolstoy's case, that mode is the way of life of the Russian nobleman; in Dostoevsky's, the consciousness of the underfloor man. For Shestov, as for Nietzsche, the greatness of the human spirit lay not in its aspirations but its actuality, in what it was, not in what it thought it ought to be.

Shestov puts a finger on the spot, and yet the dualism itself remains more important than the conclusions he draws from it. It is precisely as artists that Tolstoy and Dostoevsky need to draw on both sides of their natures. Their incomparably vivid sense of actual life – *zhivaya zhizn* – would be nothing without their longing for a new life – *voskresenie* – regeneration and resurrection. Jones himself suggests this when he remarks that "it is a condition of Dostoevsky's art to arouse our longing for the settled and the normal and the beautiful". To arouse our longing, in fact, and ironically, for the world of the *novel*. This is an unexpected asset of the "deeper realism": to make us feel and live life as the folk in an ordinary novel can't.

It is his endings, as Jackson points out, that show Dostoevsky at his most conventionally novelish (*Notes from under the Floor* does not have one, and *The Brothers Karamazov* has an end rather than an ending). Jones plays this down, probably rightly, suggesting that such tedious old portents as the "great sinner", who sins his way to God, are more an affair of Dostoevsky's notebooks (thank goodness Shakespeare didn't keep a notebook) and of his commentators than the stuff of the novels themselves. I myself would feel that Dostoevsky took a trick here from Pushkin, whom he revered and of whose "secret" he often spoke. In all his kaleidoscope writings – poems, plays, stories – Pushkin seems to have developed the art of cutting off an end without an ending, leaving the reader to ponder the implications and do the rest of the work. Tolstoy did something rather similar. In the wide Russian context it seems an appropriate way of losing conventional literature while retaining art.

Both Jackson and Jones are interesting on *The House of the Dead*, which, in a curious way, and perhaps because it is "true", is Dostoevsky's most framed and artificial work. The horrors of

Auschwitz or of the Gulag are ten times worse than anything he saw in the convict prison, or even dreamed of, and they have been chronicled by Solzhenitsyn, and still more graphically by Varlaam Shalamov in *Kolyma Tales* – some of the most powerful stories to come out of the Soviet Union. But grim as these records are (and they, too, have been got up into works of art), they cannot hold a candle to Dostoevsky's masterpiece in its capacity both to inflict sheer overwhelming oppression on the reader and to free him with instants of redemption and joy. The reason, of course, is that we stand outside these Soviet stories, while Dostoevsky has the secret of involving us wholly in the life and atmosphere of the prison. It is a singular paradox, because we can see and feel that Solzhenitsyn and Shalamov suffered all the horrors with their fellow sufferers, while Dostoevsky, or rather his narrator, remains a strangely disembodied voice – as it were, from under the prison floor. His secret, in fact, is *not* to say, or even imply: "I am the man, I suffered, I was there." Shestov goes so far as to observe, with some justification, that his narrator distances himself from the convicts, telling himself to go on living, for he will be out in four years' time.

The more disembodied he is the more he involves us. This seems to be Dostoevsky's secret, and any claim, even a merely implicit one, to participation and fellow-suffering, would have amounted to what he called "false inspiration". He uses the term about *Crime and Punishment*, where he must not himself be too close to the nightmare of the Petersburg whose atmosphere – "summer, dust, mortar" – he so stiflingly conveys. Jones calls it "a feat of illusionist sorcery" and "the most accessible and exciting novel in the world", but weirdly couples it as a masterpiece with Conrad's *The Nigger of the Narcissus*. Surely there, as in all Conrad's work, we are in the presence of the *novel*, in the most marvellous of ways (never more so that in the first half of his "Dostoevskian" novel, *Under Western Eyes*), and we are *seeing* and being *shown*? On the other hand, all the swarming impressions in *Crime and Punishment* (Henry James could not bear to finish it) oppress us as they do the characters themselves; their nightmares become our own; in this sense, the work is indeed "accessible". On the texture of the novel, however, Jones is continuously absorbing, reading it like the lines of a Shakespeare play. He has given us here some of the best close criticism of Dostoevsky now available.

Being Two
is Half the Fun

Jeremy Hawthorn, *Multiple Personality and the Disintegration of Literary Character* (London: Edward Arnold);
Karl Miller, *Doubles: Studies in Literary History* (Oxford: Oxford University Press);
C. J. Koch, *The Doubleman* (London: Chatto & Windus)

"The principal thing was to get away." So Conrad wrote in *A Personal Memoir*, and there is a characteristic division between the sobriety of the utterance, its air of principled and ample reflection, and the wild idea of getting out, of doing a bunk. It is one of the many divisions examined in *Doubles*, which explores in compelling proliferation the implications of duality in all the forms in which it has touched, inspired and shaped the writer. For imaginative literature not only depends upon but *is* duality. Novels need doubles to dream them up, and readers to find and recognize their own separate elements in the pages.

The sense of character is itself a sense of duality: amazement at the difference between the way we seem to ourselves and the way the world appears to find us. We pretend to be "men" and "women" in order the more diversely to be ourselves. By an obvious paradox awareness of identity is a natural response to the separations of experience; by our consciousness of being Hume's "bundle of sensations" we become ourselves, *homo duplex*, unified because multiple. To lead several lives and to be several people is thus the normal state – even the ideal state – and if there were such a thing as natural justice to our species and society it would protest against any attempt to force us into singularity on ideological or social grounds. Many novels, usually bad ones, recognize this in reverse today by giving out as text or theme that the hero, or more probably heroine, is trying to find out who he or she "really is". Real people never try.

At least not in that way. For the inherently sane, who are interesting to each other as human beings, it is normal to explore the ways in which consciousness multiplies itself. Normal and indeed fascinating. Both Karl Miller and Jeremy Hawthorn consider as one of their classic texts Conrad's short story "The Secret Sharer". Suggested by the concealment of a fugitive which actually took place on board the clipper ship *Cutty Sark*, the tale is of a young mate accused of murder who swims to the narrator's ship in the gulf of Siam (where the twins come from) and is harboured by him and put off for shore when the chance comes. The two young men have fascinated critics and psychologists alike, and many a theory has been woven round the story. Its strength in fact is in its simplicity as a tale, and the author's saving lack of emphasis on any meaning it might have, for him or for us. It is full of matter, and the matter is chiefly romance. Conrad is deeply there, but in ways which – as always in his best work – show the contradictions of his being most subtly and most dramatically.

In *The Double in Literature* Robert Rogers pointed out that the young captain narrator "symbolically summoned his double" by rope ladder dangling over the side, as if in a tale by Hoffmann, whom Conrad mentions elsewhere, and that the story conjures up the contrasting sides of Conrad's, or Everyman's, character: notably the wish to stay and make a sober orderly success of things, and the urge to get out and do what one damn well likes. But the captain's double is also, as Hawthorn says, the secret and ideal conception of Conrad's personality, the sort of fellow we would all like to be. Taking the reductive view needful to psychoanalytic theory, Joan Steiner argued that the double was, quite simply, the captain's unconscious come aboard, and that when the double is lowered into the water, and passes "out of sight into uncharted regions", this signifies what she calls "the resubmergence of the captain's unconscious and the reintegration of his personality". Too tidy by half, surely, and above all too tidy for good art, as is Hawthorn's reading of the story as an elaborate study in hallucination? Miller puts the finger on what is perhaps the most significant aspect of the tale – the fact that both young men "are united at the close in an exercise of freedom which does not bode well – though Conrad seems to think differently – for the future of the ship".

Trust the tale not the teller? But, more important, the "subtle unsoundness" which Marlow detected in Lord Jim is not only a part of Conrad himself but an essential part of the way literature and duality work together. Never mind about the ship at the end, and the way the captain, to do service to his double, risks his first command: what matters to Conrad and to us is the success of art, and the final irresponsibility of art. Dualities, as Miller intuits, are necessary to art because necessary to our nature: by and in the division of our beings we are all in some degree artists. Moreover dualities, like art itself, are incompatible with solutions, the key to the puzzle that is craved by one – the most responsible – aspect of our multiple selves. Conrad, it seems to me, understood all this as an artist when he began his story with a trim and haunting paragraph describing the strange incomprehensible structures in the calm shallow sea off the Siamese coast. Fishtraps? Perhaps: but they and the beings who put them there are outside experience or curiosity. They are not referred to again, but they have their place, like the towns and caves in *A Passage to India*, to remind us that separations are of the order of existence.

Like *Dr Jekyll and Mr Hyde*, "The Secret Sharer" is one of the classic texts about duality and doubles. But, as Miller's book shows, the theme is often the more revealing the more it is traced into unexpected and less obvious places. Madame Bovary, for instance, is a far deeper, more comprehensive and more compromised study in doubleness than, say, Dostoevsky's Mr Golyadkin in *The Double*. Miller's book has an atmosphere at once like Scott and like Proust, full of marvels, full of shrewdness and of humour, its perspective all-embracing. For one thing, it redefines and reinstates the concept of escapism. Hawthorn's shorter book is more avowedly clinical in its approach, often equally brilliant in its *aperçus*. Both authors discuss the case of Sylvia Plath, who for Hawthorn had the problem that being a woman – personified in the heroine of *The Bell Jar* – "she is not granted the luxury of a *double* life". But Madame Bovary has one – indeed, three lives and more. Plath's problem was certainly connected with this disability but took a different form. Like many fictional heroines, she was trying to find out who she was, but her talents made this a matter of choice: should she be virgin, mother, whore, hostess, tragic poet, etc.? Instead of encouraging pluralism of roles, these various possibilities imposed on her the necessity for unity, and death is the great unifier, indeed the only one.

Hawthorn suggests that men are natural hypocrites who can enjoy being double. Their poetry, like their sex lives, was for Hardy, for Frost or for Auden a thing apart, whereas for Plath it had to be her whole existence. My use of the Byronic tag –

> Man's love is of man's life a thing apart,
> 'Tis woman's whole existence –

shows that recognition of the problem is not new, but Sylvia Plath's life and art put it in a form that has fascinated modern readers. No wonder Miller's essay on her is entitled "Who is Sylvia?" It does indeed seem true that she could not bear the thought of natural male dissimulation – obsession with father shows that – and the way in which a male artist is a natural double with his art, both sanctifying and discrediting it. One of Miller's most suggestive chapters is on Robert Frost, and his talent for stealing away from himself into poetry; for his poetry to steal away from itself; for the poet to steal back into his own sort of wise odiousness. Sidling to and fro, with a finger on the side of the nose – that is the image of the poet Frost that has finally emerged, and it is an enhancingly satisfying one because it shows how dualities can be handled by art: art, that two-faced word, being in all senses a matter of dissimulation. More poignant, and equally effective for her art, was Sylvia Plath's refusal to find it so. *Aut simplex aut nihil* was her motto, and in one sense it is odd to find her featured so prominently in two studies of duality.

But whereas Miller revels in duality, so to speak, and by loving it makes it show all it can do, Hawthorn is against it. This undeclared and perhaps almost unconscious bias in favour of unity becomes explicit in his conclusion. Though nothing human is alien to him, his purpose is therapeutic. "Case-histories and literary analyses" alike suggest to him that "the pressure of the truly human is towards the fighting out of contradictions and the establishment of internal consistency both within society and within the individual". And he points out that the idea of an undivided society is linked with the ideal of the undivided individual: "only by establishing a society that is undivided, in a world that is undivided, can there be human individuals free from hypocrisy and duplicity." Good sentiments, and yet they have a chilling sound, not entirely due to the rather wooden way in which such pious hopes have to be expressed. The idea of unity in any field – political, psychological or artistic – may have its own drawbacks, even its own dangers. The age-old wish for unity and happy integration, for a golden time way back from the present, or to be realized in the immediate future, does not necessarily relate to anything that makes for actual human happiness. Besides, growing up in New Guinea turns out to be just as difficult and duplicitous a process as growing up in Market Harborough. What might more modestly be achieved is the reconciliation of individuals and societies with their own kinds of inner and outer disparity. Sylvia Plath might have been happier could she have felt like the sensible agony aunt on a woman's magazine, who advised anxious readers not to worry a bit if their views on sex and their fantasies about it did not match. But the separations that keep some people, and some artists, sane – like Wemmick and Jaggers in *Great Expectations* leading their different lives in home and office – were not possible for Plath as a poet, any more than they had been for Emily Dickinson. Their art, in Hawthorn's unexpected words, was "not granted the luxury of a double life".

In fact, I suspect that in art as in living we *have* made progress in the conscious recognition and acceptance of the dualities within us. Modern works which emphasize them do so in a fairly frivolous spirit, which may be good for society but bad for their achievement in art. The best doubles – Dickens is the prime case – are in some degree somnambulists, whose powers depend on working in obscurity and breaking out in unfamiliar fashion on the page. Miller writes on Martin Amis as "the latest of Anglo-America's dualistic artists" for whom "the world wavers", as we read in *Money*, and "people are doubling". Maybe so, but taken in this spirit the process becomes banal, in the novel or out of it.

Over-knowingness on the part of the author, and perhaps his audience too, is indeed liable to be the trouble with doubles. As Tolstoy pointed out, *à propos* of a particular kind of sensationalist literature, "you see what the author would be at and it bores you". Miller comprehensively indicates the modish side of doubleness, and its genesis in the Romantic movement, whose theoretical mechanics was largely supplied by the Germans: Tieck, who coined the phrase "romantic irony" for the artistic apprehension of human duality; John Paul Richter, who invented the term *"Doppelgänger"*; Schlegel, for whom, as for Coleridge, Shakespeare was a Proteus, and who wrote that dualism "is rooted so deeply in our consciousness that even when we are, or at least think ourselves, alone, we still think as two, and are constrained as it were to recognize our inmost profoundest being as essentially dramatic". A natural process which when exploited is easily turned into an artistic trick. Borges writes a story called "Borges and I", whose last sentence is "I do not know which of us has written this page." When accosted in the street by a stranger who asks, "You are Borges, no?" he replies: "At times."

This is merely tiresome, it seems to me, as is the appearance of the wild entrepreneur John Self and the sober writer Martin Amis in Martin Amis's *Money*. The real power of the thing is lost by sophisticated literary exploitation. A recent novel by C. J. Koch, *The Doubleman*, scores by showing a more simplistic and old-fashioned attitude. But arguably, even some classics of the genre, like Hogg's *Confessions of a Justified Sinner* or Stevenson's *Dr Jekyll and Mr Hyde*, suffer from our getting the point too soon, seeing what the author would be at. This is where Dickens scores so heavily, and Emily Brontë. Who shall say whether Quilp and Little

Nell are really one and the same person, two aspects of Dickens himself, the ogre and the orphan? Dickens loved to be both victim and executioner, as he would probably have been revealed in *Edwin Drood*, in which, as Wallace Robson has brilliantly surmised, the figure of Mr Datchery might well have turned out to be "Dickens" himself, the writer making his last bow. The masterly structure of *Wuthering Heights* conceals the fact that the author *is* Heathcliff, as the heroine Catherine proclaims she is. In her strange poem about the different coloured streams that "tumble in an inky sea" Emily Brontë shows herself well enough aware of the sources of her most radical fantasy: but every other virtue of her novel contributes to a ramified sobriety that need never own up. Owning up was left to sister Charlotte, who obtains the luxury of a double life by portraying herself as Jane Eyre and Lucy Snowe, air and snow with a torrid tropic burning within them.

Ranging exuberantly over the widest possible spectrum, Miller's study notes that fictions like Hermann Hesse's *Steppenwolf* of 1927, which "speak up" for duality and multiplicity, are apt to do so too "solemnly and self-consciously". More effective as art are the ones that steal upon us, as their duplicitous components steal apart from each other. Miller perceives that the word "steal", like the word "bound" ("with one bound Jim was free") contain their own dualities. Fictions steal from themselves, like the lovers at the end of "The Eve of St Agnes", that most dualistic of poems. Keats both knew and did not know that his richly romantic tale was also a classic story of seduction and betrayal. He worships in it the images of purity and beauty of eager-eyed romance, but he knew very well what Porphyro would be about. The style itself steals from itself. Porphyro is "impassion'd" by Madeline's "voluptuous accents". "For if thou diest, my Love, I know not where to go." Keats's other self is at home in the early practicality of Dryden's "Marriage à la Mode", where song is very much to the point:

> 'Tis unkind to your Love, and unfaithfully done
> To leave me behind you and die all alone.

"Die" is as fissile as "steal" and "bound". Keats is both a robust young man fighting butcher boys and frequenting prostitutes, and a pale romantic luxuriating in the glamour of castles and damsels, love and beauty. Both need each other and both are in the poem.

One of Miller's happiest *démarches* is on "Keatses", the metamorphoses of the Keats image that haunted the nineteenth century and its writing. One hitherto undetected Keats double is Dickens himself, the small orphan of the blacking factory, who was to write of his childhood, "Small Cain that I was, except that I had never done harm to anyone", and who was actually tipped half a crown at the factory by the father of Keats's friend, Charles Wentworth Dilke. Keats and Dickens were both Cockneys, both alienated from and formed by what Keats described in his first published poem as "the jumbled heap of murky buildings"; and in *Little Dorrit* Dickens invents John Chivery, a Keats figure both amusing and admirable who is also one of Dickens's doubles:

> Young John was small of stature, with rather weak legs and very weak light hair. One of his eyes (perhaps the eye that used to peep through the keyhole) was also weak, and looked larger than the other, as if it couldn't collect itself. Young John was gentle likewise. But he was great of soul. Poetical, expansive, faithful.

Typical of Dickens to make the eyes themselves doubles, one the weak wide-eyed voyeur. Miller thinks Dickens had Keats in mind and is re-creating him, with the authority that comes from recognizing a side of oneself. Both unite in the epitaph that Young John, disappointed in love, invents for himself.

STRANGER!
respect the tomb of
John Chivery, Junior,
Who died at an advanced age
Not necessary to mention.
He encountered his rival in a distressed state,
and felt inclined
TO HAVE A ROUND WITH HIM:
but, for the sake of the loved one,
conquered those feelings of bitterness, and became
MAGNANIMOUS.

Keats advised Shelley to "curb his magnanimity", but it was a word dear to Keats as to Dickens, expressive of new and wholly secular political and moral hopes. (A French ship of the line called the *Magnanime* fought at Trafalgar.) Had Keats died at an advanced age he would certainly have been magnanimous, though he might have been no longer a poet.

The nineteenth century saw the heyday of the double. In his book on literary metamorphosis, *The Gaping Pig*, Irving Massey commented on the separation of self and status, present in Gogol's story "The Nose", and of key importance in Dostoevsky. Most Soviet fiction, for obvious reasons, suppresses and ignores duality, and is impoverished in consequence. Leaping with one bound into strikingly different cases, Miller ranges from Hogg and Scott, via Poe and Chekhov and Dostoevsky, to Eaton Stannard Barrett's *The Heroine*, which came out in 1813, midway between Jane Austen's writing of *Northanger Abbey* and its posthumous publication. *The Heroine* beautifully burlesques literary treatments of the girl divided between romance and every day, and, as Miller shows, beckons to the Edith Wharton heroine at the end of the century, the Edith Wharton of whom it was said, "Wherever there is romance it is the proof that you are outside yourself and leaving yourself behind" – a remark of Percy Lubbock's which in its delphic ambiguity might be taken as the motto of doubleness.

Duality in America, land of orphans, assumes a more clinical aspect. It also happens on a suitably vast scale. Flora Scheiber's book *Sybil* (1973) is about a woman with sixteen distinct personalities, and Doris Lessing felt it forced you "to look at yourself and the people around you in a new way", as well it might. William James and Weir Mitchell, who looked after Edith Wharton during a breakdown, had earlier investigated the multiple self, or "alternating personality", as James calls it in *The Principles of Psychology*, and he thought it of significance in relation to the hypothetical survival of consciousness after death.

From art's point of view clinical multiplicity is not very rewarding. Neither perhaps is the mass exploitation of the artist's selves, even though it can lead to such masterpieces as the Berryman *Dream*

Songs, heavily influenced by the duality of the Yeatsian masks. Yeats, though, like his fellow Celt William Sharp, took a more naively dramatic view of doubleness. Sharp sometimes called himself Fiona Macleod, inscribing his book *The Winged Destiny* with the words: "William Sharp from his comrade Fiona Macleod." Sharp was a robustly heterosexual Anglo-Scottish type, happily married, who nonetheless felt the need as an artist to function sometimes in what Miller calls "Celtic drag". It fascinated his contemporaries and no doubt increased the circulation of his books. It also leads us back to the implications of "getting away". The authority and point of art narrative seem to require a "real self", from which others diverge down the long perspectives of possibility, like the hypothetical self which Henry James's hero meets in "The Jolly Corner". At the same time, escapism is a misnomer, for we are not getting away from the real, but entering another version of it. Art begins on the inside of life, where dualities are the norm. As the talented Soviet novelist Yury Trifonov rather surprisingly put it: "Reality has no exclusive external status. It is wherever your thoughts happen to be."

London Review of Books, 1985

The Two Hardys

Michael Millgate, *Thomas Hardy: A Biography* (New York: Random House);
Kristin Brady, *The Short Stories of Thomas Hardy*
(New York: St Martin's Press);
The Collected Letters of Thomas Hardy, Volume 3, 1902–1908,
edited by Richard Little Purdy and Michael Millgate
(Oxford: Oxford University Press)

Hardy at one time seemed the very spirit of subversion and pessimism, the author whose last novel, *Jude the Obscure,* was burned by a bishop – in despair "presumably" – as Hardy observed – "at not being able to burn me". As late as 1905, when he went to receive an honorary degree at Aberdeen University, he was forcibly attacked in the Scottish press. To his friend Sir George Douglas he wrote that Swinburne had shown him a cutting which stated: "Swinburne planted, & Hardy watered, & Satan giveth the increase." A year later he wrote to Millicent Fawcett, stating his principles in terms that still sound an echo today.

> I think the tendency of the woman's vote will be to break up the present pernicious conventions in respect of manners, customs, religion, illegitimacy, the stereotyped household (that it must be the unit of society), the father of a woman's child (that it is anybody's business but the woman's own. . .), sport (that so-called educated men should be encouraged to harass & kill for pleasure feeble creatures by mean stratagems), slaughter-houses . . .& other matters which I got into hot water for touching on many years ago.

Hardy's first novel, *The Poor Man and the Lady,* was turned down for being, in a jejune way, too radical; forty years later his views seem almost those of a *bien pensant*, and his personality had begun to produce in literary circles a general respect and reverence, almost veneration. Siegfried Sassoon praised his calm and saintly personality; Charles Morgan wrote of the hidden fires that seemed to glow beneath his gentle homely exterior. Even Virginia Woolf was impressed by her meeting with him. That view held until roughly a decade ago, Hardy's stock having continued to rise steadily in the meantime, when prolonged and elaborate biographical investigation at last began to bear fruit.

It has long been accepted that Hardy was somewhat close, self-protective: that he had written his own biography under the name of his second wife, giving a mildly romantic version of his origins and early life, and a respectably innocuous one of his domestic and social career as an increasingly famous man of letters. That was all very well, a deception in the interest of privacy and modesty that was positively endearing, and how charmingly innocent of the old man to suppose his simple stratagem could stand up to modern methods of investigation. It was blown at once, of course, but oddly enough that only increased a general sense of Hardy's quaint kind of unwordly integrity.

Not for long, however. When Robert Gittings's masterly two-volume biography appeared (*Young Thomas Hardy* and *Thomas Hardy's Later Years*) it presented a very different image of Hardy, and was at once accepted as definitive by critics who prefer to think the great not only have feet of clay but are constructed of that substance throughout. The picture seemed all the more accurate because Gittings, a scholarly biographer who had taken immense pains, eschewed the wilder speculations about a dark and possibly incestuous secret in Hardy's life, and dismissed the story that his cousin Tryphena Sparks may have secretly borne him a male child.

Such sins as these might be tolerated, even admired. The Hardy who emerges from Gittings's narrative would not have been man enough for them. He is a mean man, of frigid purposes and slow reptile determinations, snobbish, selfish, uncompassionate and unfeeling, calculating in high society, obsequious to great ladies, nasty to servants, heartless to his wives. Gittings's Hardy was also

a voyeur who preferred a girl glimpsed on top of a motorbus to a
real one living beside him at his Dorchester villa; even a sadist
whose most memorable encounter was with a lady poisoner at a
public hanging that he attended in his early teens. Very handsome
and shapely she looked, all in black silk, turning slowly around and
around in the rain. Hardy was particularly impressed by the way in
which the cloth hood over her face grew wet, and the features
showed through. The episode throws a rather different light on the
epigraph from Shakespeare with which Hardy prefaced *Tess*:
"Poor wounded name! my bosom, as a bed / Shall lodge thee."
Gittings also seemed to take *au pied de la lettre* the cruel remark
which a no doubt much-tried Emma aimed at her husband on the
occasion of the notorious Crippen trial in 1910. From Hardy's
appearance, she is alleged to have said, he might well be taken for
the murderer.

To Gittings it did not seem to occur that Hardy might, so to
speak, have enjoyed the joke. Might he not have taken a sardonic
pleasure not only in the morbidity with which he was regularly
taxed by earnest critics and public spokesmen but also in the knowledge that he was himself a man of very ordinary tastes, tastes of a
kind that in respectable society people keep strictly to themselves.
His poems were the outlet of his feelings, and indeed of his self-
knowledge. The man who in his actions and in the impression he
left on others comes to dominate the Gittings biography as the true
Hardy could never have written those touching lines at the end of
"After a Journey", one of the poems that poured out of him after
Emma's sudden death in 1912, in which Hardy imagined himself
returning to the wild Cornish coast where he had first met her.

> Trust me, I mind not, though Life lours,
>   The bringing me here; nay, bring me here again!
>   I am just the same as when
> Our days were a joy, and our paths through flowers.

"Just the same" – not worse, not better, the habitual self as when
Emma used to "muse and eye me" in the days of courtship at Beeny
Cliff. Hardy's passionate pronouncement has the marvellous

honesty of art, the assertion of the self as its own kind of self-knowledge, as in Shakespeare's sonnet.

> No, I am that I am, and they that level
> At my offences reckon up their own. . . .

In both cases the art that so triumphantly blows away secretiveness could only have been produced by a secretive man.

And that paradox is particularly marked in Hardy's case. Gittings quoted Edward Clodd's comment, probably based on something said to him by the second Mrs Hardy, that Hardy was "a great writer but not a great man". But that is not so much deadly as affectionate: one does not want one's friends to be "great men", and Clodd, a banker by trade, had clearly become very attached to Hardy, attached in the same quasi-maternal way that the second Mrs Hardy herself was. They teased each other, Clodd sending Hardy a cutting from a local paper about a Thomas Hardy who had just been sent to trial for stunning one of his relatives with a bust of Gladstone. The touchy, vain, and morbidly sensitive author manifested in the Gittings biography would hardly have put up with this sort of thing from the hearty and rather philistine Clodd, any more than he could have written the lines at the end of "After a Journey" about the neglected wife whom her often almost equally neglected successor used dryly to refer to as "the late espoused saint".

Apart from his scholarship and its lively narrative style, Gittings's biography was salutary in that it compelled Hardy lovers to confront (if they had not already privately done so) the contrast between the calculating egotist of Max Gate and the wistfully, vulnerably, and totally sincere poet and novelist. Sincerity, as Aldous Huxley observed, is mainly a matter of talent, but temperament comes into it too. Hardy the poet just does not know how to be bogus: his forthcomingness always rings true. To illustrate this it would not be unfair to quote in apposition to "After a Journey" the last stanza of Richard Aldington's poem "After Two Years", praised by Herbert Read (whose very phrase is an unwitting kiss of death) as "one of the most perfect lyrics in the English language".

> She is as gold
> Lovely and far more cold.
> Do thou pray with me,
> For if I win grace
> To kiss twice her face
> God has done well to me.

Aldington may well have been a nicer man than Hardy, a more passionate lover, a more devoted husband, but all one can say of such a poem is that one does not believe a word of it. The gambits and devices of intimacy ("Do thou pray"), of modesty and understatement ("God has done well") would not deceive a child. The poem appears false throughout, and its technical accomplishment merely compounds the falsity. It strikes one as not even intended to be believed in, while every line of Hardy's poetry compels belief, not excluding that line – "I never cared for life, life cared for me" – to which W. H. Auden took such violent exception on just these grounds. "*Never* cared for life? – Well, *really*, Mr Hardy!" But yes, Hardy the poet never did care for life in this sense, however much he may have cared for moments of living, moments that have been "great things, great things to me". The general life has to be put up with, by making "limited opportunities endurable". However apparently disingenuous, Hardy's art can never lie in the teeth of its own technique.

It is nonetheless true that Hardy was in some sense a split personality, a divided man, and that this takes the form to which we have been accustomed by modern studies and analyses of the Victorian mind and personality. Gittings was doing to Hardy, though with a much greater authority of research, what Lytton Strachey had done many years before to the eminent Victorians, Arnold and Cardinal Manning and General Gordon. The division there was that those men of power and charisma were something else inside, or so it was claimed, something which subverted and contradicted the Victorian ideal of the great man. That would not do in Hardy's case, for he had never made the implicit claims of Arnold or Tennyson, or set up a corresponding façade to theirs. But Gittings was able to suggest that Hardy was not even in reality "up to" the measure of his own negativism and pessimism and the great scenes of tragedy and disillusionment he had created in the novels.

In fact, the true division was perhaps a very simple one, with nothing Victorian about it. Like D. H. Lawrence, Hardy was exceptionally close to parents of markedly different temperament. Lawrence possessed all his mother's fierce repressive puritanism, as well as his father's zest for living. Hardy's father had a passive, contemplative nature, his mother a canny initiative and an iron will. Their eldest son inherited both tendencies, in all the measure of a genius. And as Lawrence's stories reveal more directly than his novels the two biological sides of his nature, Hardy's too have the same tendency. They encapsulate in miniature, and in an elemental way not found in his poems or novels, both the bleak, close determination of his being, and its tender, vulnerable passivity. The characters in the best of the stories tend, significantly, to represent one side or the other, misfortune resulting from collision between the two.

Thus in "The Son's Veto" it is the mother who is tender, open, and lovingly docile while her clerical son is a mean-minded tyrant who refuses to let her find happiness in marriage to a tradesman, since a connection with him would lower his own social status. These transposed contrasts reveal Hardy's understanding of the lurking hardness in family situations, in individuals' capacity for concealment, and the pathos of the needs they conceal: Ned Hipcroft in "The Fiddler of the Reels", though manly in behaviour and appearance, is not really interested in sex and acquiesces in his wife's relation with the fiddler; but is passionately – even pitilessly – concerned to keep and to father the fiddler's child Carry. In "On the Western Circuit", one of Hardy's best stories, the childless and neglected wife "falls in love" with the young barrister who has seduced her servant, on whose behalf she has written to him engaging love letters; but she secretly and almost unconsciously wishes to keep the servant girl for herself in a quasi-lesbian relation, and to mother her expected child. To add a specially Hardyan twist the barrister is in love with the letters, not with the woman who wrote them or the girl he has seduced. Most writers of good short stories, like Maupassant and Somerset Maugham, exhibit in them in a virtuoso way both the authors' toughness and their worldly-wise understanding. Hardy conceals his under the guise of a homely tale.

Nonetheless the stories reveal with remarkable accuracy the two sides of Hardy's nature, so closely bound up not only with his parents but with social class. The close exclusive kinship of his mother's family, the Hands, and the Hardys, was a function of the Dorset peasant class from which they sprang, despite all Hardy's later attempts to represent his father as a professional builder and his family as the offshoot of an ancient stock which had come down in the world. It is surprising that these tales have not been more quarried by biographers, or inquirers into the Hardy enigma who might employ a Freudian approach, for they would reveal much of personal significance. Kristin Brady has written a workmanlike study of the stories and she has some good insights, particularly about *A Group of Noble Dames*, but neither she nor Hardy's latest and most authoritative biographer of all, Michael Millgate, draws attention to the starkness and simplicity with which the two sides of Hardy's nature come together in the tales.

In one of his poems, "The Convergence of the Twain", the liner *Titanic* and the iceberg that sank her are imagined as growing up together, though far distant from each other, until the moment of their fatal match and marriage. It is a homely but sinister conceit of the kind in which Hardy was fond of indulging. Other poems suggest that he saw the convergence of himself and Emma, from their two remote rural backgrounds, in the same light; and it may well be that he was also aware of a personal image of the cold, dominant will in him coming into its unique relation in his life and art with his warm, receptive, and wondering side.

There is no doubt that Michael Millgate has in his own way projected a more convincing "convergence" than any previous biographer, and has produced what will surely be the definitive life. It is easy to read, continuously interesting, and crammed with facts – some curious and new – mild, peaceable, and understanding in tone. Whatever Hardy himself might have thought of those who dug on his grave he would no doubt be fair-minded enough to view it, and the picture of himself which it gives, with a grudging lack of resentment.

Millgate effectively pulls together the mean and stark little Thomas with the great writer Hardy. One of the ways he does this is quietly to emphasize Hardy's remarkable sense of duty and fidelity, his unswerving loyalty to two incompatibles: his own close-knit family and the two wives who represented his own elected separation from it. His implacable and indomitable mother Jemima would have liked to decree that her four children would live celibate, in two pairs. She actually made this known to them: her younger son Henry, who followed his father in the building trade, and her two daughters, who became schoolteachers, in fact never married and lived more or less in each others' pockets all their lives.

The death of Hardy senior in 1892 offers a good illustration of the kind of thing that went on. His tranquilly reflective good nature had acted as a sort of buffer; wife and mother were now in direct confrontation, and Jemima expected her son to be in constant attendance. A first-class row broke out, with Hardy's sisters being virtually forbidden the entry at Max Gate – of course the mother had never come there – and this prohibition continued until Emma's death. Hardy stoically retained his relation with both sides and saw nothing incongruous in burying his first wife beside her old enemy and rival. They were all of the one family, and whatever had happened in life there was to be no division between them in death.

Millgate is very good at slipping through the walls of family silence, without actually summoning them to fall down as his predecessor Gittings had done. If Hardy's stories reveal in many cases a transmutation into art of the two sides of his nature, his novels use his sense of his own life in a different way. Millgate remarks of *The Return of the Native* that in it Hardy seems to try out another version of what might have gone wrong for him. A return to his native heath and a disastrous marriage leave Clym as the archetypal defeated and impotent intellectual, eventually reduced to a purely passive state and tolerated by society as a sort of quietistic and broken-down lay preacher.

There may be an element of wish fulfilment here, as in the background of so many great novels, for the real Hardy was constantly aggrieved and resentful at the attitude of publishers and public toward events and attitudes in his fiction. Emma particularly detested *The Hand of Ethelberta*, in which Hardy tries himself out as the daughter of a London butler who has succeeded in society as a kind of actress and poet-improvisatore and frequently finds herself at dinner tables where she is waited on by her own father. Like all really good plotting imaginations Hardy's was decidedly epicene: before the final, rather mechanical chapters he informs Ethelberta with a good deal of original and erotic life of his own; and in *Tess* the process is carried almost to its logical conclusion, Hardy being both the deer and the hunter, the persecuted girl and her pursuers.

The correspondence, which Millgate is editing in a meticulously produced series of seven volumes in collaboration with that other doyen of Hardy studies, Richard Purdy, tends in the third volume to bear out the general temperateness of his approach to the skeletons in the Hardy cupboard. Between 1902 and 1908 Emma's relations with her husband have usually been taken to be at their lowest ebb. She had detested *Jude the Obscure*; even more perhaps she had detested *The Well-Beloved*, whose pages bore ample evidence of Hardy's views on the impossibility of marriage and the hopeless pursuit of romance. She complained of Hardy to visitors, sometimes asserting that she was a writer too, almost in the same class as her husband: she had sacrificed her life to him and he had never given her thanks or encouragement. She wrote bitterly about this in her diary, which her husband read after her death. She retreated to two upper attics in Max Gate and led a hermitlike existence. It was even rumoured that she was certifiable, and Hardy wrote a poem with the epigraph: "I saw the form and shadow of madness seeking a home."

But this gloomy picture was not the whole truth or even in a sense the half of it. That old affections and intimacies continued unabated, and that they were by no means wholly perfunctory is shown by Hardy's letters to her during this period. They take for granted a life in common, passing on tidbits of news, giving a blow-by-blow account of visitors to Max Gate, if Emma was away, and of social life in London if she had remained in the country. Hardy remained a pertinacious attender of grand social occasions, but his letters show him doing this, as often as not, to give pleasure to relatives or dependants like his niece by marriage Lilian Gifford. He reports to Emma:

> I ate no dinner yesterday, & although I had to undergo the fatigue of taking Lilian to the Academy Crush, I felt no worse. It was such a novelty & a delight to her that I was so glad I took the trouble; she never saw anything at all like it before, poor child, & though I felt past it all, I enjoyed it in an indirect way through her eyes.

The important thing about that letter is that it is as true in feeling as is "After a Journey", the poem about revisiting the dead Emma. Hardy's observations are always in their way as "true" as those of the characters in Shakespeare, and his life has all the richly inter-mingled aspects of muted comedy and tragedy that one finds in the plays. Hence perhaps the kind of interest we take in it. Hardy, like an ageing Othello, is reporting to a Desdemona who had once lovingly urged him "to feed on nourishing dishes" and to keep warm. In the same spirit he had been, while his family was alive, in the position of a Hamlet obliged by deep and atavistic loyalties to keep in with his father's ghost as well as with his mother and his uncle Claudius.

A sharing of the commonplace and the pleasure of others is an elementary connubial satisfaction the Hardys never seem to have forgone, even in these years. More unexpectedly they shared their literary experiences.

> I have been reading H. James's "Wings of the Dove" – the first of his that I have looked into for years & years. I read it with a fair amount of care – as much as one would wish to expend on any novel, certainly, seeing what there is to read besides novels – & so did Em; but we have been argu-ing ever since about what happened to the people, & find we have wholly conflicting opinions thereon. At the same

time James is almost the only living novelist I can read, &
taken in small doses I like him exceedingly, being as he is
a real man of letters.

Much emerges from that, besides Hardy's views on the novel and
on "the man of letters". He thought the latter a superior concept
to the novelist *tout court*, and no doubt preferred to count himself
as one. On James he conferred the same dignity, for Hardy would
not have agreed with or even understood James's sense of the
novelist's high calling.

That letter is to Florence Henniker, daughter of that earlier "man
of letters", Monckton Milnes, and wife of a distinguished but
Philistine British officer. Hardy had met her in Dublin in 1893 and
been smitten at once, though she seems to have kindly but firmly
demarcated the lines and progress of their relationship, possibly to
his secret relief. The letters to her during this period have a slightly
resigned philosophical air, as if he were gently reproaching her for
her prudence while at the same time tacitly endorsing it. To "Em"
Hardy made no secret of this relation.

There are four short letters to Florence Dugdale, the quiet little
secretary with literary aspirations whom Hardy was to marry in
1914, two years after the death of his first wife. At this stage he
encouraged her attempts to write but gave up doing so after they
got married. He wrote after their first meeting: "I do not think
you stayed at all too long, & hope you will come again some other
time".

The strength of Millgate's biography lies not so much in its
scholarship, which the reader can take for granted, as in its balance
and its natural sympathy with the subject. Almost everything that
is likely to be known about Hardy is now known, but Millgate has
made nonetheless one important discovery which will be of considerable interest to devotees. Hardy met Eliza Nicholls, whose
father was a coastguard at Kimmeridge in Dorset, sometime in 1862
when he was working as an architect's assistant, and they seem to
have been more or less formally engaged from 1863 to 1867. (They
kept it quiet, but Millgate has turned up more or less conclusive

evidence.) A serious and deeply religious young woman, Eliza seems to have been of considerable support to the youthful Hardy, but her seriousness and her religion may eventually have caused them to drift apart. Though probably more deeply attached to him than he to her, she was no doubt shocked by his growing agnosticism and the free-thinking intellectuals whose tuition he sought, like his great friend and mentor Horace Moule, who was to commit suicide in 1873.

Eliza would no doubt have been no more successful as a wife for Hardy than her sister Jane Nicholls (with whom he seems to have flirted), or Tryphena Sparks, or Louisa Harding ("To Louisa in the Lane"), all of whose pretty features look out from the excellent photographs in Millgate's volume. Hardy was no Don Juan, and it is unlikely he had intimate relations with any of them, though Millgate rather surprisingly speculates that Emma may eventually have "caught" her evasive suitor by pretending to be pregnant, the same device that Arabella uses in *Jude*. Sexually Emma was probably more like Sue Bridehead than Arabella, though this in itself need not have seriously thrown the relationship off balance: Hardy was clearly more attracted to girls glimpsed twirling a sunshade than to girls in bed. Any that came there could not forever have nestled in his imagination and been commemorated in his poems. Yet that "I am just the same as when . . ." is never insincere, even on the occasion he told Edmund Gosse that the young Helen Paterson, his "best illustrator" who had done the pictures for *Far From the Madding Crowd*, was the woman he should have married "but for a stupid blunder of God Almighty". Wisely, no doubt, she married the fifty-year-old poet William Allingham in the same year in which Hardy began to take an interest in her.

> Had we mused a little space
> At that critical date in the May-time,
> One life had been ours, one place,
> Perhaps, till our long cold clay-time.

Perhaps. But one enduring fascination of Hardy's life to its readers, as to readers of the novels themselves, lies in the way his imagination fuses the literal and the humdrum with the might-have-been, with what his great admirer the poet Philip Larkin called

> the long perspectives
> Open at each instant of our lives.
> They link us to our losses. . . .

Life is never really suited to our imaginations of it, as Hardy continually found, and is continuously reminding us.

New York Review of Books, 1982

A Vanished Masterpiece

Leopoldo Alas, *La Regenta*, translated and
introduced by John Rutherford (London: Allen Lane)

What were the ten best novels of the 1840s to 1880s? The competi-
tion was formidable one hundred years ago, though it is possible
there would have been no more unanimity among the critics then
than there has been in the recent promotion schemes for the best of
our time. The Victorians, the great Russians, have only become
giants in retrospect, but it may be that our epoch will seem in
another hundred years to have produced no giants at all. Great
novelists, like Great Men, are out of fashion, and likely to remain
so.

This may be partly due to their change in tone, from open to
intimate, from public to private. Proust was the last novelist to
address his readers like a public meeting, as Dickens and Thackeray
and George Eliot had done. Formal and yet friendly, they spoke
openly to a wide circle of all the things that could be spoken openly
about. By contrast the tone of fiction today seems both too
compulsive and too relaxed, too indulgent of self and self's idio-
syncrasies. It is a voice that wants to be loved, and if we cannot love
it we turn elsewhere. This affects the status of the form and accounts
for the discrepancies among the judges. We do not sit at the feet of
novelists but have affairs with them, and love is notoriously blind.

Now a vanished masterpiece from the great period comes back
to us, speaking in form and at leisure (over 700 pages), addressing
all of us readers with politeness and good manners. Published in
1885, Leopoldo Alas's novel *La Regenta* had little success in its own
time and vanished from view, to be rediscovered not long ago in

Spain and hailed as one of the classics of Spanish letters. No doubt it is so, and I should say it had claims to be considered among the select band of "world novels".

This is partly because it has now been outstandingly well translated. John Rutherford, a specialist in Spanish literature at Oxford, has produced a version which is in the same class as Moncrieff and Kilmartin's versions of Proust, or Colquhoun's of *I Promessi Sposi*. The tone of Alas is both grave and witty, withdrawn and yet abandoned to the luxury of humour, and these Spanish manners have been wonderfully naturalized in translation. The jokes really are jokes, and the sadness and charity of Alas's stylistic temperament has a lack of pretension in English which seems just right, elegant – the note of a master. Proper, too – indeed essential – to retain the Spanish title, which could presumably mean female regent, regent's wife, judge's wife, wife of distinguished retired government official. Its importance is its important sound, its generalized implication.

The heroine is in fact the wife of a retired judge, a sweet old man, a landowner from Aragon whose passion when young was for theatricals, who never did very much official work. She is beautiful, the most beautiful girl in the sleepy old town of Vetusta, where the action takes place. This is in fact Oviedo, capital of the Asturias, a wooded and mountainous region of northern Spain where the climate (weather is very important in this novel) is unpredictable. March sometimes sweltering and May freezing. Alas was himself from Oviedo and has the novelist's love-hate for the place and its inhabitants. He was a professor of law at the university and a prolific critic and journalist, an isolated man, always in poor health, who died before fifty.

This was his one novel, built on a scale suited to the period, and Oviedo society hated it. One can see why. Many of the characters look like inspired reworkings of real people, and the author has put himself in the book as a particularly futile and grotesque minor participant. With a loving care that is like that of Balzac or the equally prolific Spanish master Galdós (a contemporary of Alas and much admired by him) the novel dwells on the rich, tedious frivolity of domestic and social existence in this supremely

bourgeois epoch, the intrigues, the rivalries, the envies and aspirations. Love, and leisure, though, are the words for this type of art.
"How Balzac loves his Valérie," wrote Taine of the repulsive little
Madame de Marneffe in *Les Parents Pauvres.* "What a strange taste if
he did," murmured an Anglo-Saxon critic, thereby earning, as
Henry James sharply remarked, "the highest prize ever bestowed
on critical stupidity undisguised".

It is just in this way that Alas loves his characters and achieves by
so doing that *saturation* in the milieu of his art which Henry James
so much valued. Like Galdós, whose novel *Fortunata y Jacinta* is a
lengthy and wonderful study of two women with different Madrid
backgrounds, Alas is a connoisseur of the whole world of Oviedo,
its cafés and priests, clericals and anti-clericals, the political attitudes
and the internal politics, the louche side and the respectable families.
Above all, he is a connoisseur of the sexual drive, its shamelessness
and pathos, its subtleties and disguises: he is totally frank and open,
amazingly so for the period, and this without any need for biological boastfulness or for arranging demonstrations in bed. It
strikes one, strangely, that Alas is infinitely more *grown-up* about
sex than emancipated modern novelists can afford to be. Still, it is
hardly surprising that his book was received with disgusted shudders
and swept under the carpet as soon as possible.

The three men in the life of Ana, La Regenta, are all marvellously
more than lifesize in their dreams and compulsions, their inner and
outer lives, and all with something about them of both Don
Quixote and Sancho Panza. Quintanar, the husband, devotes himself to shooting and do-it-yourself activities about the house, which
he proudly shows to his affectionate Ana. Mesia, the local Don
Juan, who is both a sexual spendthrift and a man carefully and
fussily rigorous in his sexual economies for specific ends, devotes
himself to her seduction. But the most remarkable character is the
local canon, a priest of Herculean physique, self-made, with a
powerful and loving mother who arranges pretty servant girls to
attend to his needs and then marries them off to their advantage.

All this sounds like that conscientious stirring up of muddy
depths which Zola, the "naturalistic" novelist well known to Alas,

was devoting himself to at the time. But in a Spanish context it is quite different. With an abundance of refinement, an agility of unselfconscious tenderness, Alas shows that nature in the raw is bound to be as comical as it is complex. More fundamentally democratic than our own – certainly than our own at that time – Spanish society as investigated by Galdós and Alas intermingles naturally at all levels of class and behaviour, like private theatres constantly rehearsing and playing to themselves and each other. Alas is adept at conveying the style of each consciousness in the words it uses, so that characters are described as if they themselves were speaking. He attributes the development of this *estilo latente* to the great novelists of the period, Flaubert, Galdós, Zola, who

> replace the observations which the author makes in his own voice about a character's situation by the character's own observations, using the latter's style – not however in the manner of a monologue, but as if the author were inside the character, and the novel were being created inside the character's brain.

Alas in fact uses the technique much more comprehensively and more subtly than the writers he mentions. Not until Joyce will the novel in English fully develop the same method, and in any language it can still remain a rare accomplishment in the novelist, a sign of complete and apparently effortless mastery of full material.

Accused in his own time of copying the plot of *Madame Bovary*, Alas did indeed very likely take the quadrilateral situation of wife, husband and two lovers, but there the resemblance ends. In contrast to Alas's treatment, Flaubert's looks solipsistic, his heroine (as he himself said) a projection of the total alienation he would himself have felt had he married and lived as a provincial bourgeois. Notorious as she became, Emma Bovary seems a shadow compared to Ana, whose physical and social reality for the reader is both relaxed and absolute. She is a virtuous girl, merry, volatile, naturally religious, looking forward to children. She and her elderly husband love each other, but sex somehow cannot get a foothold in their relation, for all Ana's attempts. Their relation is both comical and tender, nothing to be laughed at, and Ana herself a comic character, as in this sense we all are. It is striking that at the other end of Europe the German novelist Fontane was creating, in *Effi Briest*, another tenderly observed, frustrated and eventually adulterous wife, inspired by Emma Bovary but quite unlike her. Flaubert's personal predicament in relation to his art became, as it were, naturalized in the revealed experience of nineteenth-century European womanhood.

Ana is virtuous, but "to renounce temptation: that was too much. Temptation belonged to her – it was her only pleasure. What would she do if she had nothing to struggle against?" The irony of her situation is that she would have remained virtuous if the canon had not passionately fallen for her, his naive passion being the pander that lets in Don Alvaro Mesia, the professional seducer. Alas's account of how Ana and the priest struggle to sublimate their feelings, to act them out in a religious context, to mediate in society the kinds of fantasy fascination that each feels for the uniqueness of the other, is done with a frankness and an understanding that must have outraged the *bien pensants* of the Spanish church establishment. Yet it is done with the greatest charity – wry humour, too. Their mutual misunderstanding is total, and Ana is appalled when she finds that a priest, however physically handsome, feels for her in *that* way.

Sex, as Alas shows, can never escape from its conditioned stereotypes inside our feelings. It is an area he probes to particular effect. Ana recoils from the true and impassioned love of the priest into the arms of an unloving but satisfying seducer. The outcome is all too predictable, and Alas does not quite manage the problem, supremely difficult, even for a great novelist (Conrad has the same trouble), of winding up a story in the context of contrived event which has become almost too gripping in the other context of psychological and dramatic truth. His ending is not so bleakly adroit as that of *Madame Bovary* but is equally an anti-climax. But before he finished he had written a very fine novel.

The Listener, 1984

Pasternak, Rilke
and Cézanne

-⟨⟩-•-⟨⟩-

Boris Pasternak, Rainer Maria Rilke and Marina Tsvetaeva,
Letters: Summer 1926, edited by Yevgeny Pasternak,
Yelena Pasternak and Konstantin M. Azadovsky,
translated by Margaret Wettlin and Walter Arndt
(New York: Harcourt Brace Jovanovich/Helen and Kurt Wolff);
Rainer Maria Rilke, *Letters on Cézanne*, edited by Clara Rilke
and translated by Joel Agee (New York: Fromm International)

Nothing in literature is odder than the way in which the
"atmosphere" of poets changes between one generation and the
next. This extraordinary correspondence between Pasternak, Rilke,
and Marina Tsvetaeva, sensitively fashioned by editorial commentary into a kind of seriocomic drama, seems already fixed in the
distant past, light years away from any letters a poet might write
today, if indeed he bothered to write letters at all.

Pasternak was a schoolboy of ten when he met Rilke, who in
1900 was paying his second and last visit to Russia, accompanied
and looked after by his mother-mistress, Lou Andreas-Salomé.
Pasternak described the encounter, thirty years later, in his autobiographical work, *Safe Conduct*, which he dedicated to the
memory of Rilke, who had then been dead four years:

> On a hot summer day our express was about to leave
> Moscow's Kursk Station. Just then someone in a dark
> Tyrolese cape approached our train window from the out-
> side. A tall woman accompanied him. Father began talking
> to them about something that aroused the same warm

interest in all three, but from time to time the woman exchanged brief remarks with Mother in Russian; the man spoke only German, and though I knew the language well, I had never heard it spoken as he spoke it.

Rilke in fact was so seduced by the Russian language that he had made strenuous and successful efforts to learn it, and had already translated poems and stories into German. He had even written poems of his own in Russian, of which Lou Andreas-Salomé, a native speaker, observed: "Though the grammar is pretty awful, they still somehow are mysteriously poetic." Rilke's reverence for all things Russian was so great that he even determined to go and live there with his young wife, Clara Westhoff, but since he could find no prospect of a job the idea was abandoned. He went instead to Paris, where he acted for a time as Rodin's secretary, and developed the passion for Cézanne paintings which forms the subject of the letters written from Paris to his wife in 1907, letters that were probably intended to become a sort of extended critique and appreciation of the painter.

The artist Leonid Pasternak, the poet's father, introduced Rilke to Tolstoy, whose books he had been illustrating; and Rilke and Leonid corresponded in Russian. The high-minded cosmopolitanism of those days, at least among artists and writers and the intelligentsia, might make us weep for what seems a vanished golden age of European culture. We are cut off from that Eden, out of which they were expelled by revolution and war. Not unnaturally their letters, after they had been blown apart by the explosion, seem full of nostalgia for bygone days; the emotions expressed between each other by these three poets, extravagant as they may now seem, represent a kind of clinging together after the catastrophe, an attempt to keep alive an old civilization of the feelings, in their art and in themselves.

That civilization may have its affected side ("Rilke was a jerk," as the poet John Berryman crisply put it), but its leisure and interdependence nurtured art in a way that none has done since. Marina Tsvetaeva was not a poet to shrink from contemporary realities, but she insists with the greatest vehemence that the legendary status accorded to Rilke in those postwar years was owed to him because of the way his poetry had created a world of inner reality and inner values. Revolution had brought its own versions of togetherness, still invoked today, and the aspirations of socialism and fascism had been greeted by symbolists like Blok and Yeats with factitious fervour. Rilke stood alone, a baptist of solitude, and Tsvetaeva was no doubt right in claiming that European culture honoured him all the more for it.

She herself passionately believed that "writing poetry is in itself translating, from the mother tongue into another, whether French or German should make no difference".

> No language is the mother tongue. Writing poetry is re-writing it. . . . A poet may write in French; he cannot be a French poet. That's ludicrous. . . . The reason one becomes a poet . . . is to avoid being French, Russian, etc., in order to be everything. . . . Yet every language has something that belongs to it alone, that *is* it. . . . French: clock without resonance; German – more resonance than clock. . . . French is there. German *becomes*, French *is*.

These characteristically brilliant observations were addressed by Tsvetaeva to Rilke in a letter about the book of French poems he had written – *Vergers*. Tsvetaeva – herself German and Polish by origin as well as Russian – was writing to Rilke in German, on whose quality he congratulated her with a mixture of accuracy and delicacy, as he himself had once been congratulated on his letters in Russian by Leonid Pasternak. The idea of all poetry as not national, but always translation into a higher medium, is true for all three poets. Rilke had projected the abstraction of German into the height of his own sense of things, and in his last years wished to embody himself in the form of another language. Tsvetaeva writes that she is "not a Russian poet and am always astonished to be taken for one and looked upon in this light".

Psychologically the three poets and their relations present a strange picture, full of touching incongruities and misunderstandings; yet the way in which they communicate, in their loneliness and their longing to reach a fellow spirit, has something noble about it. Strongest of the three, Tsvetaeva is also the leading spirit of the correspondence and the most tempestuous; possessive, and yet also evasive, her love reaches out to both men, requiring its own sort of devotion in return. Physically she has suffered the most from the upheaval of war and revolution, living with her two small children as a penniless exile in France, unable to get her poems published even in émigré magazines because of her sympathy with Mayakovsky and the poets of the revolution. She had been separated for years from her husband, Sergei Efron, who had joined the Whites, but she remained doggedly loyal to him and they eventually came together in Prague. An ambivalent figure, he flitted to and fro in France, leaving her to cope with a family in a garret. ("No woman among your acquaintances and friends lives like that," she wrote to Rilke, "or would be capable of living so. Not to sweep any more – of that is my kingdom of heaven.")

There are sinister and tragic portents, too, behind her indomitable will to write poetry and keep in touch with her poets. Involved in the betrayal of émigrés, her husband was to become a finger man for the OGPU and be eventually liquidated by them. She herself would return to Russia, because her son and daughter so much wished to, and die miserably by her own hand, in desperate poverty and estranged from her son, who was killed in the army. Only her daughter Ariadna survived, after years in the camps, to edit her mother's work and write a memoir.

Rilke in 1926 had only a few months to live. Since the war he had been a recluse in the ancient diminutive chateau of Muzot in Switzerland, still supported by his faithful retinue of princesses, and with his reputation growing as the premier European poet. No doubt he was flattered by Tsvetaeva's ardent if ambiguous advances, which were cries for help and comfort as much as declarations of poetic love. ("Rainer, if I say to you that I am your Russia, I'm only saying (one more time) that I care for you. Love lives on exceptions, segregations, exclusiveness. Love lives on words and dies of deeds.") Intensely jealous, Tsvetaeva felt each of her poets as her own dream possession, and their sense of her must be exclusive to her. This could make her remarkably insensitive. Rilke was reticent about himself and his health, but she had no idea how ill he was, and continued to bombard him with love letters, which he eventually gave up answering. When he died of leukemia at the end of 1926 she was as puzzled and hurt as a child.

Pasternak revered Rilke, treasuring in his wallet till the end of his life two generous letters he received from him. About Tsvetaeva he was indifferent when they first met in Moscow during the chaos of the revolution, falling in love later first with her poetry and then with the poet by correspondence. Their letters afford a rich psychological contrast – his laborious, tortuously self-obsessed, yet with a kind of honest solidity like wood or stone; hers crackling with critical intelligence and wit, and with her own brand of egocentric love sparkle – a contrast which embodies at a domestic level the qualities of their poetry. Pasternak is constantly vowing to fly from his wife and child and join her in France. She wants him to belong to her but only at a distance. Jealous of his wife, she also looks down on her as a mere sleeping partner, incapable of what Pasternak calls their own "penchant for suffering". He is rather humourless but she can be very funny. ("Men shoot themselves for the lady of the house, not for a mere guest in the house.") They ardently discuss each other's poetry, though often giving the impression that the other doesn't understand it.

Translating and explaining tactfully, the editors are of particular help here. Pasternak is having trouble with his long poem *Lieutenant Schmidt*, a celebration of the pre-revolutionary hero who had attempted to take over the Black Sea fleet at the time of the Potemkin mutiny. Tsvetaeva has no patience with this, not because she doesn't approve of heroes and revolutions but because poetry is too lofty to take such matters with the kind of documentary seriousness Pasternak is attempting. She keeps telling him that it is he, the poet, who matters, not the martyred lieutenant. Nor does she grasp that Pasternak's aim was discreetly to go against the then conventional and accepted style of portraying the heroic revolutionary, and attempt to show Schmidt with sympathy, but as a very ordinary man in a confused and complicated situation.

Tsvetaeva was nonetheless right in seeing that this kind of thing went against the root of Pasternak's nature and talent. In a magnificently reverential letter to Rilke in German, beginning "Great, most beloved poet!" and introducing and pleading the cause of Tsvetaeva, Pasternak wrote: "I am indebted to you for the fundamental cast of my character, the nature of my intellectual being. They are your creations." If one makes allowances for what Dr Johnson called "the mutual civilities of authors", that is fundamentally true. Like Rilke and Cézanne, Pasternak embodied that rarest of qualities in an artist, the complete absence of the division – so marked in Pushkin or Byron, Keats or Rubens – between one side of himself and another, the total concentration on art as the world and self, and on the world and self as art.

It is this concentration that Rilke is exploring, in his own characteristic and peculiar fashion, in his letters about Cézanne. They are themselves extraordinarily peaceful and concentrated, seeping with the sense and recognition of Cézanne's colours, in nature as on canvas, colours which seem a part of Rilke himself, of the words and paper (he often wrote his poems on blue paper), and of his wife Clara to whom the letters are addressed.

Rilke remarks that in an art gallery he usually finds the paintings less real than the people looking at them, but that in the Cézanne room at the *Salon d'Automne*, "all of reality is on his side".

> ... in this dense quilted blue of his, in his red and his shadowless green and the reddish black of his wine bottles. And the humbleness of all his objects: the apples are all cooking apples and the wine bottles belong in the roundly bulging pockets of an old coat.

This is the same impression that he was afterwards to record in poetry.

> Doch als du gingst, da brach in diese Bühne
> ein Streifen Wirklichkeit durch jenen Spalt
> durch den du hingingst: Grün wirklicher Grüne,
> wirklicher Sonnenschein, wirklicher Wald.

(Thus, when you went, there sprang to this theatre a streak
of reality through the gap you went through: green of
real green, real sunshine, a real forest.)

Cézanne's aim of *réalisation* became Rilke's own, and Rilke revered
him too as a model for himself, a model of exemplary devotion to
the life of art. The Rilkean ego melts, as it were, into the colour of
Cézanne, so that it does not seem egocentric of him to state that
the "raptness" he must achieve in order to *be* in his poetry means
that he must never again be "delighted and awed" except by his
own work. As Cézanne said of his own life, he must remove himself from everything that could "hook him", in order to devote
himself entirely to that realization of things that his master had
achieved.

Reading between his lines must have been a sobering experience
for Clara, his wife, for the letters are an oblique statement by Rilke
of how he means to live, and must live, in the cell of his art. And
yet they are suffused with an affection and understanding that
seem to be supplied as much by her as by him; they seem to belong
to her in a very deep sense, as Rilke said (sometimes diplomatically,
no doubt) that all his works belonged to the person who had inspired them. They are also quite unaffected; they are suffused
instead with Cézanne's almost brutally humble instinct for the
nature of matter. His apples, as Rilke says, are neither ugly nor
attractive, his still lifes "refusing any kind of meddling in an alien
unity". He was struck by the expression used by a friend of his, the
painter Mathilde Vollmoeller, who remarked that Cézanne sat in
front of nature "like a dog, just looking, without any nervousness,
without any ulterior motive"; and he echoes it when he writes to
Clara about his desire sometimes to keep a quiet bookshop where
no business takes place, just with a dog sitting in front of the books,
"good-natured, or a cat that makes the stillness around them even
greater by brushing along the rows of books as if to wipe the names
off their backs".

New York Review of Books, 1985

Pasternak and the Russians

The Correspondence of Boris Pasternak and Olga Freidenburg 1910–1954, edited by Elliott Mossman and translated by Elliott Mossman and Margaret Wettlin (London: Secker & Warburg)

The flowering of European Jewry in the days before 1914 is a cultural phenomenon comparable to the "golden" periods of national art in Spain, France and England, even to the great years of the Italian Renaissance. Like other such peaks of civilization, it might have faded of its own accord had it not been brought to a tragic end by the xenophobia engendered by two world wars, by Nazism and Soviet fascism. It was, above all, cosmopolitan. Not for nothing (a favourite phrase of Russian critics) did Mandelstam observe that Acmeism, the literary movement which he helped to found in 1910 in St Petersburg, took as the inspiration for its poetry the whole European cultural tradition.

The particular ideas and ideals to which Mandelstam was referring, though naturally associated with pan-European Jewish culture, are just as much a part of the best German and Russian art at this time. Rilke and Musil, Joyce and Jules Romains, were all in a sense honorary Jews, the natural fellows of Proust or Svevo. It was a family atmosphere, in which German and Russian, Italian and French, were for members the natural media of intelligence and imagination. Pushkin's feeling for the family of art was as strong as Auden's, and Pushkin was a forerunner of this latterday renaissance of cosmopolitanism, however inevitably he is also Russia's great national poet. Even while the state xenophobia of Stalin was setting in, Pasternak made most of his living by translations of European poetry, from Shakespeare to Goethe and Petöfi.

And it is an insight into relations within such a family that comes to us from this correspondence of Pasternak with his cousin Olga Freidenberg, almost like the understanding we get from the art of a very good novel. Both Pasternak and his cousin belonged to predominantly Jewish families and clans from Odessa, the most cosmopolitan of Russian towns. Both families were Russianized: the Pasternaks, who lived in Moscow where the poet's father was an art curator and successful painter, especially so. Although this correspondence reveals how closely Pasternak was connected with family and cousinage, it does not indicate – or only by indirection – what decidedly equivocal feelings the poet had about his ancestry. As much as Blok had done, he identified in his life and work with Russianness and Russian history; and this Russianness, together with the tendency among admirers of his work – and even in the Party – to identify him with Ivan the Holy Fool of Russian folklore, was undoubtedly one of the factors that contributed to his remarkable immunity from the worst persecution. By background, temperament and culture he was as cosmopolitan a poet as Mandelstam, but Mandelstam was not only more obviously Jewish but belonged to those especially Europeanized circles of the Petersburg intelligentsia which came in for the most systematic persecution by Stalin and his henchmen. Pasternak, like his own Dr Zhivago, was emphatically a Moscow man, and in the course of the twenties and thirties the Party came to identify more and more with the old xenophobic Muscovite tradition.

Not that there was any rapport between them – just the opposite – but Pasternak, like Stalin himself, was in a sense claiming to represent the Great Russian people, their sufferings, their endurance, their loyalties, their "true way". So today is Solzhenitsyn. Thus while Pasternak belonged essentially to cosmopolis – like Rilke, whom he so much admired and with whom he corresponded – he also had local ideals and instincts of an atavistic, almost mystical kind. Nor were these in any Western sense liberal, no more than are Solzhenitsyn's ideals. In one of the excellent commentaries with which he has interspersed this very remarkable translation, Elliott Mossman points out how "élitist", in the current cant, was Pasternak's view of art and of the function and position of the artist. As it happens, the liberal and the communist or Soviet view of art's status more or less agree on the point that art is the possession of the people and the more of it the better – more and greater variety in the case of the West, more of the right sort in the case of Soviet communism. That was not Pasternak's view of the matter. Writing in 1958 to the young linguist V. V. Ivanov, he maintained that the "'majority' should not cross the threshold of poetry". He could never say, in Mayakovsky's words, "the more poets – good ones and varied – the better". He strongly objected to "a multiplicity of people working in art", because this inhibited "the emergence of someone . . . who will redeem their plurality with his singularity". Dr Zhivago is emphatically not Everyman, but a figure of mystic simplicity, or laborious and beautiful innocence, who will set up "Norms of a New Nobility of the Spirit".

Such ideals, which he himself sometimes recognized as naive, had been with Pasternak from an early age, in fact from well before the First World War, when he had associated them with the coming revolution. It seems likely that their mystic Russian primitivism struck no chord at all in Olga Freidenberg, whose background and tastes were both more sophisticated and more conventional – she aspired to be among the first women in Russia who would scale the heights of European Classical scholarship. In Pasternak's vision there was, by contrast, a kind of pastoral idyll, a redeemed Europe and Russia full of innocent and happy youths and maidens. "Boys and Girls" was in fact one of the earliest manuscript titles for the first part of the work that afterwards became *Dr Zhivago*; and more significantly still, another early title was "The Story of a Russian Faust". (Pushkin produced a *Faust* scene, an imaginary one to interpolate among the scenes of Goethe's *Faust*, Part II, which is among the liveliest of his poems.)

No doubt Pasternak in his early twenties was very much in love with his cousin, and she in her own way returned the sentiment. But apart from her own scholastic ambitions she was far too sensible and canny to think of marrying him. She was fascinated by him and he regarded her – or so it seems – as a quasi-maternal figure; after the first anguish and elation of love she remained to soothe and calm his emotions, to regularize the passion which she had aroused into a permanent exchange of thoughts, feelings and experiences. Though throughout the twenties and thirties he constantly urged her to visit him in Moscow, she never came, and one suspects that he too preferred it that way. Olga also kept a diary – sections of it are printed between the letters – in which she records the experiences of a bourgeois *intelligent* in the Petrograd of the First World War and during the siege of Leningrad in the Second. She was at her family's favourite watering-place in Sweden when the First World War broke out, and she served throughout the war in Russian military hospitals, falling in love with an officer much decorated for gallantry, who finally died of his wounds. Pasternak, exempted from military service by a childhood injury, spent much of the war working as a clerk in the Urals. After the Revolution, his family emigrated to Berlin, but he and his brother Alexander, who became an architect, remained in Moscow, sharing the once spacious family apartment with the horde of Soviet citizens for whom it had been requisitioned. He married his first wife Zhenya, and settled down with his usual industry to write poems, stories and translations. Olga became one of the first women, under the new Soviet emancipation, to join the Classics faculty at Petrograd University and in due course to defend her doctoral thesis. After the death of the officer she had loved in the war she seems to have had no further ideas of marriage, and looked after her mother – Pasternak's Aunt Asya – until the latter's death at the end of the Leningrad siege.

Pasternak seems to have depended for his art on a mode of life which was emotionally tumultuous – driven "at misery's full tilt", as he put it in a poem – in a manner which was at the same time warmhearted and naive, chaotic and selfish. It appears that Olga acted as confidante and family regulator, a kind of conscience of the tribe, one to which Pasternak could find solace in appealing without the need to defer to or obey. He lets her know his matrimonial troubles – he parted from Zhenya and then from his second wife Zina – but does not go into any greater detail about his emotional life. More important, they could exchange views on art and their theories about it. Taking her material from the field of the Greek classics, Olga became one of the exponents of the formalist theory in Russia, her work achieving the same importance as that of scholars like Viktor Shklovsky and Vladimir Propp. After successfully defending her thesis, she toiled with devotion for ten years on what she knew would be her masterwork, *The Poetics of Plot and Genre*, a study of form in relation to the themes and materials of ancient Greek literature. She worked in the few moments left free from having to help organize trade union committees among the university staff, who would select "shock workers" for various non-academic tasks, the nature of which is sufficiently indicated by the banner headline in the university newspaper for January 1935:

DISCOVER PEOPLE'S SECRET THOUGHTS

The book appeared, and sold well at all the bookstores, in accordance with that blessedly logical law in the Soviet Union that any reading matter unconnected with the regime and its ideals – no matter how esoteric it might seem for the common reader in normal times – was bought and devoured by the public. This in itself might have been enough reason for its withdrawal by the authorities after three weeks, but the immediate cause was an article in *Izvestia* entitled "Harmful Gibberish", in which the writer denounced it as a typical piece of "scholarship" from the Leningrad Institute of Philosophy, Literature, Linguistics and History. Granted that the Institute itself was under attack, it still seems extraordinary that a book on such an out-of-the-way and harmless topic as ancient Greek literary forms should arouse such suspicion and resentment. But Pasternak himself supplies the reason in a letter of passionate sympathy to his cousin. "Everyone knows Marx's opinion of Homer." The regime, in fact, as in so much else, was trying to have things both ways. We must have scholarship on obscure topics, but it must be researched and produced so that everyone can understand it in relation to existing ideological and party guidelines. Scholarship must both maintain its traditional loftiness and rigour and be accessible to every good Soviet citizen. No wonder Pasternak himself professed a wholly "non-liberal" view of art; and what is decidedly subtle – and significant from a Western point of view today – he saw, not only that more art means worse art, but that the irreproachably humanist ideal of art for all the people becomes, under a Soviet-style regime, a way of encouraging the kind of art that is good for all the people.

In fact, he takes too pessimistic a view: the perversity of human nature sees to that. What is fobidden is desired: hence cousin Olga's *Poetics of Plot and Genre* continued to circulate clandestinely and to reach many more readers than it would have done in a "free" society. This is the kind of paradox necessarily left out of account in such nightmarish visions of the modern state as those of Orwell and Zamyatin. And it works the other way too. Few among us would read the Russian dissidents if they were not so well touted by the Western propaganda machine. This delicate and intimate collection of letters, which reveals privacies and psychologies with the discreet indirection of a Henry James novel, has – like *Dr Zhivago* itself – been taken up by what the late Dr Leavis used to call the colour-supplement press, in the usual mechanical interests of anti-Soviet mythology.

And, of course, the martyrdom of Olga ("People avoided me so as not to have to speak to me – my friends ceased calling me up on the phone") does have all the usual gruesomeness associated with accounts of those years. Still conditioned by the high-minded revolutionary's assumption that behind all the mistakes and abuses the All-Wise and All-Good was working out their destiny, she wrote to Stalin, who did not reply. In the launching of the Yezhovshchina other matters preoccupied him. Pasternak did his best with the literary bureaucracy in Glavlit. "I was met first of all by sincere astonishment on the part of high-ups and officials," he reported to Olga. "They could not understand why I should come to the defence of colleagues when no one had harmed me or even thought of doing so." His own feelings about the regime were still equivocal, with a deep bias towards enthusiasm. With the big purge under way he was still writing to Olga: "The longer I live the more firmly I believe in what is being done, despite everything. Much of it strikes one as being savage, and then again one is astonished . . . even in the worst of times everything seems very subtle and astute."

Astute the great leader was certainly being, though hardly in the way Pasternak intended. Naiveté alone would not have saved him, but along with it he – and Olga too – had the instincts of survivors. Pasternak was not isolated like Mandelstam: he had loyal friends in high places; he had written such ideologically orthodox works as *Lieutenant Schmidt*, and, in spite of its verbal fantasy, the mystic joy of his most popular collection, *My Sister, Life*, made it natural even for the Party inquisitors to see him filling the role left vacant by Mayakovsky. The worst time for both Pasternak and his cousin came after the war, when hopes for some kind of liberalization were buoyant, even for Olga, utterly worn out though she was by her experiences in the Leningrad siege. In fact, the latent anti-Jewishness of the Stalin regime now became virulent. "Jews no longer receive an education, are no longer accepted at universities or for graduate study." Jewish academics were thrown out of work or forced to retire. "Professors who survived last year's pogroms are dying one after another from strokes and heart attacks." Olga's distinguished colleagues Eikenbaum and Propp fainted at their lectures, were taken to hospital, and after they died were granted magnificent funerals. "The Soviet authorities know how to honour their scholars."

For Pasternak, too, as his poem "Hamlet" says, everything was "sinking into pharisaism". Yet he remained hopeful, still identifying deeply, as Dr Zhivago does, not with his cosmopolitan past and background, but with a simple and visionary Russian future. "Perhaps everything will smooth over. There really was much foolish confusion in my early work. But my new-found clarity will prove to be much less acceptable." He was frenziedly translating Goethe's *Faust* in order to earn "the opportunity and the right" to complete the novel he knew could not be published in Russia. "I am not even writing it as a work of art, though it is literature in a deeper sense than anything I have ever done before." He continues, at the worst of times, to delight in his family and his children, and is intensely proud of Zhenya, his son by his wife of the same name, who had a successful military career in the postwar period and became an instructor at a tank school. His handsome features, like those of a Decembrist aristocrat, and his smart uniform with broad shoulder boards, confront us in one of the many marvellous family photographs in the book. Pasternak's own remarkable face shows its unchanging profile at all his ages; and there are many group portraits of parents, siblings and wives, Olga and her mother young and old, and together in the reproduction of a charming portrait painted by Leonid Pasternak. Everywhere in the text and pictures is the voice of "Eternal Memory". There is something magical in such survivals, as there was, for Pasternak and his cousin, in the continuity of such a relation as theirs. As he wrote to her mother, in 1941, "had anyone told us 25 years ago what would happen to each of us, we would have thought it a fairy-tale".

Charmed Life

Richard Freeborn, *The Russian Revolution:*
Turgenev to Pasternak (Cambridge: Cambridge University Press);
Guy de Mallac, *Boris Pasternak: His Life and Art*
(London: Souvenir Press); Ronald Hingley, *Pasternak: A Biography*
(London: Weidenfeld & Nicolson);
Boris Pasternak, *Selected Poems*, translated by Jon Stallworthy
and Peter France (London: Allen Lane);
Peter France, *Poets of Modern Russia*
(Cambridge: Cambridge University Press);
Edward Brown, *Russian Literature since the Revolution*
(Cambridge, Mass.: Harvard University Press)

The poet Blok once wrote about the "gloomy roll-call" in Russian history of tyrants and executioners, "and opposite them a single bright name – Pushkin". Quite true. But to put it like that is the equivalent of a single bright name outside the cinema – Omar Sharif as Dr Zhivago. The Russians have a word for the process – *poshlost*. This is not vulgarity, which is a good honest affair, but a factitious emphasis placed where none should exist, the facile forcing into expression and standardizations of what can only be true at the level of private, exploratory feeling. Television and advertising, politics and journalism, are the natural homes of *poshlost*, where it has its proper uses and its presence is so much taken for granted as to be relatively benign. Though bad art may embody *poshlost*, its pretensions are usually harmless and recognizable: worse things happen when good art is taken up by *poshlost*, and has the kind of qualities which it can take over.

When does this happen? Not with Mozart, with Shakespeare or with Pushkin, geniuses who can never be denatured, no matter what is done to them in the name of admiration or idolatry. Not even with Tolstoy, in spite of all the ballyhoo of Tolstoyism: his great achievements in art stand inevitably separate from the committed, parabolic aspects of his life. But the larger his talent the less easy it is for the twentieth-century writer to separate himself from the exploitation of his own personality, an exploitation which he initiates, with which he collaborates, and which continues after his death. This occurs in a very obvious sense in relation to an artist like D. H. Lawrence, but in a much more subtle and peculiar sense it is true of a great poet-artist like Pasternak. The tradition in English is different: the greatness in poetry of a Yeats or an Eliot, however complex a matter, does not depend directly on their "views", or upon their self-appointed role in society. Their legend is personal, not exemplary, and their achievement as poets is not a sort of holy collaboration with the national soul, a struggle requiring the poet to present himself as both prophet and sacrifice. And of course they had not participated, as Pasternak did, in the convulsions of a revolution and its aftermath. Pushkin did not consciously or voluntarily become the single bright name opposed to the record of Russia's rulers: he got on with the job of being an artist. But for Pasternak that job turned into becoming such a bright name, making a sacred identification of himself and his art with life, the life that had gone down into the grave and would rise again. The only thing of importance in the lives of the minor characters in *Dr Zhivago* is that they lived in the times of the great man; they could bear witness to the mystery and miracle of his existence.

In his excellent book on the Russian revolutionary novel Richard Freeborn discusses the many forerunners of *Dr Zhivago*, and implies, what is certainly the case, that the novels which had sought to come to terms with the new world of the Revolution – Fedin's *Cities and Years*, Veresaev's *The Deadlock*, Bulgakov's *The White Guard*, and perhaps most of all Olesha's *Envy* – all oppose to the new revolutionary phenomena a solitary *intelligent* who is unable to come to terms with them, and who tries to make something out of his life in terms of former mystical, national or artistic traditions, seeking unsuccessfully to reconcile the new with the old. Zhivago has plenty in common with such heroes, but he is not only incomparably more compelling, as a projection of his creator, in terms of art; he is also strong where they are weak and vacillating, filled with confidence and sureness where they are hollow and empty. Whatever his anguish in terms of his personal life and of the collective scene, Zhivago/Pasternak is a man who knows he is right. In terms of art he is as Lenin was in terms of politics. Unlike the traditional Russian *intelligent*, he opposes to the Bolshevik scene a conviction as convinced and as crafty, an ideology as sure of itself, as that with which Lenin and his entourage were able to seize power from the nerveless hands of the liberals and the *bien-pensant* Russian intelligentsia.

It is precisely this ideological confidence which lends itself to and collaborates with the kind of *poshlost* which in the Soviet Union is now in charge of the communist legend. Although Zhivago is dead before the great purges, he is in his own way a colleague in Stalin's cult of personality. Pasternak himself had a strange relation to Stalin, a relation involving a kind of mutual respect. "Don't touch the cloud-dweller," Stalin is supposed to have said about him, and the assumption is that the tyrant, who had a nose for such things, sensed that Pasternak was no threat to him but was admiring him in his peculiar way. The poet Gumilov, Akhmatova's husband, had actually taken part in an anti-Bolshevik conspiracy, for which he was executed, and if Pushkin had been present in Petersburg at the time of the Decembrist uprising, he would have been on the square with his friends. Milton and Petöfi are true revolutionary poets. Pasternak was no more capable of throwing himself into the struggle than Tennyson would have been, or Rilke. This is to speak frivolously of a terrible matter, but his role seems to have been ultimately understood by Pasternak rather than chosen by him – one can hardly speak of deliberate choice in such a context – because the figure of the sacrificial artist claimed the same kind of unique role and unique authority, at a given historical moment, as Stalin implicitly claimed. A saviour was needed, to lead the people back to life, as a new Tsar of steel had been needed, at least by the inherent logic of the Bolshevik ethos, to fuse the national sense of purpose, the will to drive towards the industrial future.

On several occasions Pasternak insisted that there could, as it were, be only one true artist at a given time. In addition to everything else about communist ideology, he utterly rejected the role of the artist as a kind of social engineer or welfare worker, playing his part beside his Party colleagues. This was the view that Mayakovsky promulgated, at least officially – that artists and poets must be turned out by the Soviet state in ever-increasing numbers, like tanks and lorries and doctors and TV sets. For Pasternak the saviour poet of the age must be a single figure, and the poems reveal his identity. In true art "the man is silent but the image speaks", as it does at the end of the last Zhivago poem.

> You see, the progress of the ages is like a fable, which on its way has the power to burst into flame. In the name of its awful majesty I will go down with willing torments into the grave.

> I will go down, and rise again on the third day, and as boats float on the river, the centuries like a caravan of barges shall float out of the darkness to me for judgement.

In representing Christ speaking in the Garden of Gethsemane, this extraordinary and deeply moving poem makes no claim on behalf of its author, but it exhibits a final realization of what his life and art have meant to himself and to his age. It is to become, as Solzhenitsyn described the purpose of literature in his Nobel speech, "the living memory of a nation". That echoes the opening words of *Dr Zhivago*: "On and on they went, singing eternal memory."

The relation between Zhivago and Pasternak is thus itself a unique one. We are familiar with a comparable kind of process, the relation of the poet's persona, the self that he makes in his poetry, to the actual self that gets through life like the rest of us. In the descendants of Yeats, Lowell and Berryman, the deliberate creation of such a self in poetry became itself art's function and justification. But paradoxically it is easier for a poet of this kind to avoid the *poshlost* process than it is for Pasternak. In the completion and creation of the self, art seals itself off from the powers of the media, as it does when a Pushkin or a Shakespeare writes. Pasternak's art was much more vulnerable, and it was a part of his sacrificial role to contribute to his own vulnerability. One contradiction is that though the artist accepted a sacrificial role, the man himself bore a charmed life. Mandelstam was martyred in the flesh. Pasternak lived on year after year in his comfortable dacha in Peredelkino, the writers' colony outside Moscow. Like Dr Zhivago, whose mysterious half-brother Yevgraf perennially reappears to assist from his high position in the Party hierarchy, Pasternak had a curious protector in Fadayev, a handsome Siberian author who lived near him in Peredelkino and was high up in the Writers' Union. Fadayev was also liked and trusted by Stalin, and could be relied on to interpret zealously the Party line and take the correct view of those who transgressed it. But he was also human and retained human weaknesses. De Mallac has a story of his calling on the Pasternaks because he was very fond of Mrs Pasternak's baked potatoes, with which he would consume very large quantities of vodka and talk with monumental indiscretion. Next day Pasternak would ring him up and say: "Don't worry, Sasha, you told me nothing." Sometimes denouncing Pasternak in public but supporting him in private, Fadayev continued in his powerful position as secretary of the Writers' Union until the Khrushchev thaw, when he was demoted for his Stalinist loyalties and committed suicide. The Byzantine nature of Soviet literary intrigue is shown by the fact that Tvardovsky, the comparatively enlightened editor of *Novy Mir*, another human being and hard drinker, lost his post at the same time. Paying his last respects in Russian style to Fadayev in his coffin, Pasternak is reported to have said: "He has rehabilitated himself."

Both of these biographies tell the story of Pasternak's life and art with the authority of a complete and up-to-date scholarship. De Mallac's is the more hagiographical, but that in a sense is to be expected, and may even be fitting: a modern saint's life bears witness against the forces of evil, and it was against just such forces in Soviet Russia that Pasternak's art and his personality bore witness.

For this reason they have a historical importance that is not comparable with the personalities and gossip of our own literary scene; the recorder has a responsibility towards them, whether as scholar and critic like the present biographers, or, in the case of writers like Solzhenitsyn, as a creative presence comparable with Pasternak's own. Solzhenitsyn bore the same sort of witness when in *The Oak and the Calf* he told the tale of himself and the Soviet literary establishment.

Nonetheless, Hingley's book, tauter, more economical, more balanced, and containing some good translations and commentary on the poetry, must on balance be considered the better biography. The two books also complement each other, one being essentially sceptical, the other by a devotee, and on occasion they agree to differ. Pasternak's cousin Olga commented on his "maidenly purity retained until comparatively late years". How late is "comparative"? asks Hingley, querying de Mallac's rather coy observation that his hero, like the young Tolstoy, "was not above calling on ladies of easy virtue", and that this "will be documented by some later, less bashful biographer". But can it be? asks Hingley. There is no evidence one way or another. De Mallac's suggestion is illustrative of his tendency to try to get as close as possible to his subject and to exhibit him as like one of ourselves in all his lovable frailties. In fact, as Hingley recognizes, there is something especially impenetrable in Pasternak's personality: he is not at all an easy man to get to know, and the famous monologues to which he treated his friends as well as interviewers seem designed to hold them off while giving the impression of a deep and delphic intercourse.

But of course Pasternak's celebration of life means that everything is transfigured in his eyes, and for his poetry, by the act of living. Meanness, anti-climax, ironic reversal – they seem not to exist in the vision of his art and of his being. His idealism offers a kind of parallel to early Soviet idealism, ignoring it, certainly not celebrating it, but not so far from it in the spirit. Mayakovsky, the official poet of the Revolution, passionately admired Pasternak's poetry, and the older poet Bryusov, a shrewd critic who had also joined the Communist Party, wrote that it was "without its author's knowledge saturated with modernity, and could only have crystallized in our conditions". Pasternak himself remarked in a discussion of his first collection, *My Sister, Life*: "I saw on earth a summer that seemed not to recognize itself . . . as in a revelation. I left a book about it. In it I expressed all that can possibly be learnt of the most unprecedented, the most elusive aspects of the Revolution . . . the feeling of eternity having come down to earth and popping up all over the place; that fairy-tale mood I sought to convey."

This process of "making it strange", as the formalists would say, is conveyed in the selection of poems translated by Jon Stallworthy and Peter France, and in France's excellent study *Poets of Modern Russia*, which besides that on Pasternak contains informative essays on Blok, Akhmatova, Mandelstam, Tsvetaeva, Mayakovsky, and the poets of today. A particularly admirable feature of this Cambridge series is that the Russian text is given before the translations. It's a pity that this sound convention isn't more generally followed in the now numerous books of translation from the Russian poetry of this time.

A pictorial analogy, perhaps the paintings of Van Gogh, seems apposite for the early poems of Pasternak, whose father was a well-known artist, and Hingley refers to Christopher Barnes's suggestion that the painting of the Expressionist school – Munch, Kandinsky, possibly Chagall – seeped sideways, as it were, into the young poet's vision,

> Where the air is as blue as a bundle of clothing
> In the arms of a patient discharged from a clinic.

The poems had a breathtaking freshness which, as Hingley says, is of the kind which shows that the Russian language possessed resources which might have remained untapped if this poet had not taken up his pen. It is also in some degree leprechaun verse, lacking the quietness of feeling. That came later, as a result of persecution, but it is arguable that Pasternak the artist could only have strong feelings about himself. One looks in vain for anything like the infinitely touching little poem ("We'll sit together in the kitchen,/ The white paraffin smells sweet") which Mandelstam addressed to his wife at the time when his time was running out. Pasternak's art is as lacking in intimacy as in humour – two qualities usually found together.

His inability, in the context of art, to examine himself or to take a close interest in others, is an all but fatal handicap to Pasternak as a novelist, but as an idealized autobiography *Dr Zhivago* has the same amazing freshness as the early poems – the awe and joy in both the verbal equivalent of the red figures dancing on Matisse's great canvas in the Hermitage. There is a painful contrast between the Lara of *Dr Zhivago* (the freshness of the book sliding with fatal ease into the *poshlost* of the film) and the actual personality of Pasternak's mistress, Olga Ivinskaya, on whom the dream projection is based. A shrewd, accurate and by no means uncharitable observer, Lidia Chukovskaya, who had been a colleague of Pasternak's mistress on the staff of *Novy Mir*, recalled how "slovenly, pathologically mendacious, boorish" she had seemed, and much given to vulgar boasting about her love affairs. A more serious accusation is that she had stolen the food parcels and money entrusted to her by a mutual friend for dispatch to a woman who remained in the Gulag, and whom Ivinskaya had known there before her own release. The poetess Akhmatova wished that those who knew or suspected this should tell Pasternak, but they refused, wishing to spare the poet's feelings. It seems likely, in any case, that he would have paid little attention, for he was one of those geniuses for whom other people have no existence outside the one he has imagined for them. Other artists and their art had no real existence for him, not even Akhmatova herself, for whose work he professed great admiration, but without apparently having bothered to read it properly. Akhmatova saw this and forgave it, not however without remarking, in her quizzical way, that Pasternak's behaviour could be "intolerable".

All this, as Hingley says, is part of Russian literary folklore; and it is the kind of folklore which, given the peculiar conditions of Soviet literature, means a great deal to those who have taken part in it. It accreted around Pasternak precisely because his psychology did not mesh with it, because of what Edward Brown in *Russian Literature since the Revolution* calls "his long exile inside himself". Brown's beautifully informative study, now republished in a revised and considerably enlarged version, is incidentally a store-house of such folklore, which becomes the more essential the more it keeps alive memory and memorial in such an age as these Russian writers lived through.

Pasternak's personality, like Pushkin's, does have that mysterious brightness which transcends the conditions in which they worked and the people they consorted with. Both poets were a mixture of shrewdness, compromise and "holy fool": Pasternak's relation to Stalin was not so very different from Pushkin's with Nicholas I. But Pasternak had to do consciously and with painful craft what for Pushkin seems to have been instinctive: adapting himself to the regime while retaining wholeness of being. For Mandelstam and Akhmatova such a process was impossible. They either did their own thing, or else wrote, under compulsion, pieces in praise of Stalinism of such grotesque badness that no one was deceived. Pasternak was not like that. His attempts at work that would immortalize revolutionary annals (always the emphasis on history as a seamless garment), *The Year 1905* and *Lieutenant Schmidt*, had been popular, and they were serious attempts to reconcile a personal vision with a communal revolutionary one. As de Mallac points out, the attempt is more impressive though even more self-conscious in the 1932 collection of poems, *Second Birth*, in which "the poet states his intention of including 'everything' – his past experiences, his present ideals and aspirations, his place as a poet in Soviet Russia". Where Pasternak is concerned, such an attitude is quite compatible with what the great Polish poet Milosz, himself a deep admirer of Pasternak's poetry, called "a programmatic helplessness in the face of the world", and "a carefully cultivated irrational attitude".

Pasternak's later sense of isolation, of abandonment in the Garden of Gethsemane, together with the messianic sense of being a chosen witness that went with it, arose as much as anything from the fact that in seeking to be all-inclusive he displeased both camps: both the Marxists, who found that his "civic poetry" laid too much stress on "intimism", and atavistic opponents like Akhmatova, who knew that true art can never be produced by enforced idealism and enforced communality. Pasternak in his own way soon came to know it too, and during the purge years adopted what Babel called "the genre of silence", producing no original work but only translations. Nonetheless, his curiously ambivalent attitude to the regime, and especially to Stalin, persisted. Undoubtedly he was fascinated by Stalin, whom Mandelstam saw as a murderous and barbaric thug, and by the power he wielded, in the same way that Pushkin's imagination had responded to power embodied in the statue of Tsar Peter. When Stalin's wife died, by suicide or possibly by murder, thirty-three prominent writers published a letter of condolence in the *Literary Gazette*. Pasternak declined to add his name to this fulsome document but produced his own personal statement, added as a postscript. "I share the feelings of my comrades . . . I was shaken exactly as though I had been present, as though I had lived through it and seen everything." This odd form of backing into the limelight may have gratified Stalin, establishing Pasternak as his personal poet-seer. When Pasternak received the famous phone call from the Kremlin, asking for his views on Mandelstam, he expressed a wish to have a long talk with Stalin, "about love, about life, about death", upon which the dictator rather naturally hung up.

Pasternak's evasiveness about Mandelstam himself may have helped the other poet or not: opinions vary, and Mandelstam's destruction was in any case imminent. What is certain is that news of the phone call made all the hard-line functionaries of the Writer's Union forget their hostility and fawn upon Pasternak. On the other hand, it is said that he refused to translate some youthful poems by Stalin, who had expressed the wish that he should do so. Apart from other considerations, he must have lost a lot of money from not doing this, for most of his income came from his translations and he had done many versions of Georgian poets, two of whom – friends of Pasternak's – were killed in the purges.

His second wife, Zinaida Nikolaevna, remarked on Pasternak's "tortuous meekness" – a striking phrase from one whose lack of intellectual sympathy appears to have been deplored by his friends. What woman would have been worthy of the man who aroused in and expected from his friends the sort of worship that he did? As Hingley comments, Pasternak's meekness, though perfectly genuine, is indistinguishable from "profound immodesty". His self-disparagement, as his brilliant cousin Olga Freidenberg remarked, was a way of disguising vanity. The women in the life of a genius of this type both "see through and revere". And yet Pasternak was genuinely humble, confused, even masochistic, essentially like Goethe's good man who in all his difficulties knows the truth. And this in a very evil time. "Should one suffer without falling prey to any illusions," he wrote to an émigré, "or thrive while deceiving oneself and deceiving others?" There is a special force of simplicity in his use of a Russian proverb in the last line of a famous poem. "Living your life is not like crossing a field." Certainly he had no appetite for disaster, and no need for it; he was no Baudelaire or Berryman, nor had he any conventionally artistic bohemian tastes. Where marital complications were concerned he was exceptionally good at staying on the sidelines and leaving the women to fight it out. In his work habits he resembled his father, Leonid, who, though the most sociable and affectionate of friends and fathers, hated "having a good time" in the sense understood by his fellow artists. Like his father and brother, Pasternak was in an important sense a professional man, needing quiet and space for his twelve-hour day as poet and translator, and he went to great lengths to hold on to the family flat in Moscow and to the dacha in Peredelkino that the Writers' Union had awarded him. Mandelstam, a true bohemian in his way, was amused by its air of bourgeois comfort and stability.

The tormented poetess Tsvetaeva, who herself probably loved him, was probably thinking of herself when she said that Pasternak could never be happy in love. Certainly he reproached himself bitterly when she hanged herself in despair in 1941, evacuated to the godforsaken Tatar settlement of Elabuga, neglected by the Writers'

Union and, as he felt, by Pasternak himself. In those times one's own life had somehow to be lived. Pasternak in fact fell in love with a good deal of prudence, preferring like a Turgenev hero the sort of strong women who either refused him outright or took him on in a businesslike spirit and without illusions. Olga Ivinskaya seems to have had a good deal in common with his second wife Zinaida Nikolaevna, who looked after him devotedly in the critical time before the war, and from whom he never became totally estranged. He needed women who possessed, in de Mallac's quaintly expressed phrase, "a certain Telluric stability". There are drawbacks to such women, as D. H. Lawrence found, and Pasternak needed much more than he the long hours of quiet concentration and craftsmanship. De Mallac, who in spite of his hagiographic approach has a knack for telling in a wide-eyed way the revealing story, describes a typical nocturnal scene at Peredelkino, with Pasternak shut up in his study, his wife playing cards and the gramophone and fortune-telling with Nina Tabidze, widow of the Georgian poet martyred in the purges, and Yury Krotkov, protégé of his fellow Georgian Lavrenty Beria, whose speciality in the KGB was blackmailing foreign diplomats by means of beautiful Soviet agents, called "swallows" in secret police jargon. Krotkov was also an author who wrote several anti-American plays including one called *John, Soldier of Peace*, based on the life of Paul Robeson. While Pasternak worked, this strangely-assorted group would sit up smoking and playing till dawn.

Hingley is detached, dry, basically unforthcoming: de Mallac enters into the legend with warmth and abandonment. With a story like Pasternak's there is something to be said for this approach: in its loving recapitulation with all the trimmings, all the recollections, all the *dévoué* gossip, *poshlost* is inevitable, and one might as well meet it head-on. This de Mallac certainly does, understanding perhaps that in Russia as in California the thing can be done on an heroic scale and not just as in the *Reader's Digest*. If you are writing about a modern saint it is not unfitting to do it in a traditionally hagiographical manner. Thus we are told: "During his walks he stopped to talk to those he met, gazing at them with his large radiant dark-hazel eyes with an air of trustfulness. To the children who sometimes followed him he gave candy from the supply stuffed in his pockets." This, in a sense, is the price the poet pays for the wholeness of his being, for the fact that biography and auto-biography, gossip and reminiscence, are all involved in the vision of life that he saw, that he wished to give and *be*. A far from sympathetic Soviet critic, Zelinsky, grudgingly admitted that no writer of the age had given such intense realization in his art to the Russian ideal of *zhivaya zhizn* – "living life" – although this quality of "inner wholeness" had to be "bought at the price of biography".

This is a profound judgement, as is Zelinsky's other, sharper comment that the poems in Pasternak's *Second Birth* are "full of the hieroglyphs of his biography". And the critic wrote that long before the ballyhoo began. In such a poem as "The Garden of Geth-semane" Pasternak seems to give himself to biographical *poshlost* with the impassive fervour of Christ surrendering himself to the servants of the high priest. In a bargain of such totality good taste cannot be included, any more than with Tolstoy or St Francis, and their life and work do not include their biography in the deter-mined sense that Pasternak's seem to. Thus there is a certain right-ness and inevitability in Milosz's prediction that there will one day be a statue of Pasternak in Moscow, and even in the way in which de Mallac takes leave of his hero in the churchyard, where "the grave has been kept meticulously clean by one of Pasternak's devoted admirers – an ordinary workman in baggy trousers and muddy shoes". As John Strachey enthusiastically wrote in a 1963 *Observer* piece, "Pasternak's Children", annual pilgrimage is made from Moscow to the Peredelkino cemetery, and sometimes young girls sing the poem "Winter Night", accompanying themselves on the guitar.

All poets, as Auden wrote in his poem on Yeats, "become their admirers", but Pasternak has done so in a specially complete and sacrificial way. Even his remarkable face, like that of a soulful horse, seems ours now and not his, reproduced as it is in its sombrely conscientious grandeur on almost every page of de Mallac's narra-tive. His father, also a remarkably handsome man, but in a more conventional style, recounts in his memoirs how he was asked in his youth by a famous artist to sit for a picture of Pushkin's Don Juan. That could not have happened to his son, who resembled no one but his own photographs, and his identification with them becomes oppressive after we have been exposed to so many. This lends a certain pathos to one of the most interesting comments that Pasternak ever made on his art, in a letter in English to Stephen Spender: "Nineteenth-century art, either in painting or poetry but above all in the great novels of the period, is fixed in narratives which are irrevocable, like verdicts or sentences, beyond recall." The fixedness is that of the individual, the Flaubert, the Dickens, the Tolstoy. In *Dr Zhivago* life itself is the hero, and may at any time go in any direction, determined by the living play of coincidence. Nothing in a sense "happened" to Zhivago, or it does not matter what happened; events do not determine his individuality.

The architects of the Revolution wished to construct such fixed nineteenth-century-style narratives, and in their theories and actions there is, as Zhivago reflects, "everything that is rejected by life itself". Pasternak's aesthetic has a certain logic about it, but in practice both the art and the artist (as the photographs show) remained intensely self-conscious – more so if possible than those narratives and individuals of the nineteenth century. In any case, when we say of a work of art that there is "life" in it (still a good and ready criterion), we do not mean that it has been deliberately constructed to embody life. Pasternak takes to the limit of self-consciousness the idea that is implicit in all realistic narrative, although his art, his novel, and particularly his poetry, are not oppressed by the theory in them. Yet his life itself now is, because the biography on which his art depends can never become "life" as he understood it. Our Pasternak is bound to be an imitation.

Poems with a Heroine

⋖⋗●⋖⋗

Anna Akhmatova, *Poems*, selected and translated by
Lyn Coffin, introduction by Joseph Brodsky (New York: W. W. Norton);
Sharon Leiter, *Akhmatova's Petersburg*
(Philadelphia: University of Pennsylvania Press)

Anna Akhmatova had been in her youth one of the "Acmeist" poets, along with her husband Gumilev and Mandelstam. Acmeism was essentially a reaction against the symbolist movement in Russian poetry, a movement that tended, as such things do in Russia, to extremes, in this case extremes of uplift, mysticism, apocalypse. Acmeism by contrast was concerned with poetry as architecture, and poems as objects of weight and mass-produced as if in a workshop (the poets' guild or workshop was one of the group's other names for itself). The most important early influence on Akhmatova was her discovery of the poems of Innokenti Annensky, an expert translator and scholar of ancient Greek, who had written – they were published posthumously – a volume of verses called *The Cypress Box*. Her early poems are precise evocations of places, moments, loves, deceptive intensities of being, carved out with reticence and a kind of inner dignity.

It is significant that the Russian symbolist poets, notably Blok and Bryusov, hailed the revolution of 1917 in their whole consciousness. They were fascinated by the *idea* of such a thing. Their attitude was not unlike that of Yeats in "The Second Coming" and "Lapis Lazuli", joyfully greeting the end of order and the coming of the "rough beast" in a spirit of "gaiety transfiguring all that dread". Terror was merely an exciting and poetical idea to them, as the rough beast slouching towards Bethelehem was for Yeats. The Acmeists' reaction was very different: they recognized facts and truths when they saw them. Pasternak in *Dr Zhivago* refers to Blok's line, "we children of Russia's terrible years", and he remarks dryly that those years really had been terrible for those who had been killed, bereaved, or imprisoned. The symbolic status of revolution was not the same thing as what actually occurred, and the Acmeists were only interested in what actually occurred.

Because of this common sense, as one has to call it, Akhmatova, like Mandelstam, can write about virtually anything. It is hard to think of any poetry in English, and certainly of none written in the last century, that has the range of hers, and the amazing power to rise to an occasion. Mandelstam said that great poetry was often a response to total disaster, and it is true that we may think of Milton, blind and at the mercy of his political enemies, setting out to write *Paradise Lost.* True in some heroic ages perhaps, but not much in our own, when poets in their sufferings have been more apt to lose themselves, like Pound muttering in his *Cantos,* or to say with Yeats: "I think it better that in times like these / A poet's mouth be silent." With her husband shot and her son imprisoned, Akhmatova wrote her poem *Requiem* between 1935 and 1940, telling of her experiences in the Yezhov terror. They were common experiences, as she emphasizes in the simple sentences of prose that preface the poem, describing how one day a woman in the great queue that stood permanently outside the prison recognized her and said in a whisper, " 'Can you describe this?' And I said: 'I can.' "

She could. Rare indeed for a poet to rise like that to such a challenge. But the whole poem has about it the dignity of utter simplicity, without false modesty or any attempt at the common touch. She describes her experiences as if they happened to her only, like words in a gospel, the equivalent in art of what she called the severe and shapely spirit of Russian Orthodoxy. In this spirit she concludes by saying that if her countrymen ever want to make a monument to her she would consent if they put it outside the prison gates where she had stood, and where the news she longed for never came through the door.

> And may the melting snow drop like tears
> From my motionless bronze eyelids,

And the prison pigeons coo above me
And the ships sail slowly down the Neva.

That is D. M. Thomas's translation, from a rendering of *Requiem* and *Poem Without a Hero* published in 1976. In her new version from a selection of Akhmatova's poems, Lyn Coffin attempts, and not without success, the flowing meter of the original.

Let from the lids of bronze, unmoving eyes
Snow melt and stream like the tears each human cries,
And let in the distance the prison pigeons coo,
While along the Neva, ships pass quietly through.

That has the movement but not the weight, or the calm simplicity. Thomas is better at giving an idea of that. As usual the problem is insoluble, but never mind: Coffin's is a good try that deserves as much credit as the cautious versions, or more. In her long poem sequences Akhmatova uses metres of great robustness and subtlety in the Russian which when transposed into English can often sound all too like Shelley or Poe at their most ebullient. The strong accents and stresses of Russian have a variety and flexibility that iron out a regular beat that would otherwise dominate the more docile English syllables. The metre of *Poem Without a Hero*, for example, has an extraordinarily commanding and stately rhythm, reminiscent of the *Dies Irae*, which could be Englished with its rhyme scheme as follows (the section refers to the ponderous march of the twentieth century, "the real not the calendar one", advancing on Petersburg like the stone effigy of the commander in *Don Juan*):

Thus up every street there came drumming,
So past every porch it was coming,
The shape finding its way in the gloom.
Gusts tore the placards off the palings,
Smoke spun a dance over the railings,
And the lilac flowers smelt of the tomb.

It was the metrical movement, percussive and minatory, that first started itself in Akhmatova's head, so she tells us, before any words came. In the Russian it sounds measured and relaxed, as calm as the stride of a great cat. The experts would say that the Akhmatovan line here consists of two anapests with an amphibrach, or two with an iamb, a combination so rare as to be virtually extinct, and certainly never found before on this scale. Annensky would no doubt have appreciated it, but it seems unlikely that Akhmatova herself would or could have worked it out theoretically.

The most complex and enigmatic of her works, *Poem Without a Hero* (*Poema bez geroia*), combines the personal and the historical somewhat in the manner of *The Waste Land*, but a great deal more dramatically. It is a poem of expiation, both for the personal sins she felt she and her contemporaries in St Petersburg were guilty of, and for the national sorrows and horrors in part expunged by the great struggle for liberation against the Germans. It is certainly an arcane poem – Akhmatova called it "a Chinese box with a triple base", but its personal and literary allusions do not disturb its majestic liturgical flow. Even more than *The Waste Land* it is a poem that seems to call for explanations and yet does not really need them. It is essentially a voice poem, in the tradition that Pushkin stylized in the figure of the "Improvisatore" in "Egyptian Nights", who denies any idea of how complex verse can suddenly come into his head, rhymed and in regular feet, so that it can be instantly declaimed. Like many Russian masterpieces, especially by Pushkin, of whom Akhmatova was a profound student and critic, her *Poema* has the form of an open secret, at once spontaneous and enigmatic.

"I hear certain absurd interpretations of *Poem Without a Hero*," she writes in the foreword. "And I have been advised to make it clearer. This I decline to do. It contains no third, seventh or twenty-ninth thoughts. I shall neither explain nor change anything. What is written is written." And not in her voice alone, or that of her muse. She wrote the poem at intervals over twenty years, committing it entirely to memory because she feared to write it down, and it ends with a dedication to "its first audience", the fellow citizens who died in Leningrad during the siege. "Their voices I hear, and I remember them when I read my poem aloud, and for me this secret chorus has become a permanent justification of the work."

This combination of unashamed individuality with a public voice is characteristic of the best Russian poetry since Pushkin, who drew a sharp distinction between himself as an ordinary, idle, and fashionable man about town, gambling with friends and running after women, and himself as the vehicle for an unknown and inexplicable inspiration, a voice that might speak with the accents of private friendship or of public authority. Akhmatova had something of the same dual persona: the dandy of Petersburg society, the arrogant beauty involved in bohemian intrigues at poets' cafés like the Stray Dog, and at the same time the grave poetic voice of conscience and religious awe, the voice of Russia's severe and disciplined spirit, silenced for a while by the anarchic envy and clamour of revolution, but speaking out in the fine series of poems dedicated to London at war (unprinted and unheard of, of course, while Soviet Russia was the ally of Nazi Germany), and in the sonorous poem "Courage", a summons not to the Soviets but to her fellow Russians, which actually appeared in *Pravda* a few months after the German invasion.

She was a Russian Orthodox believer and a Russian patriot. Her poetry flowed from both kinds of faith, and as the opening lines of *Requiem* pronounce, she was deeply proud, too, of having remained in Russia while so many others of her class and kind had fled into emigration. The four lines are very simple, but their tone sets a notorious problem for the translator:

> No foreign sky protected me,
> no stranger's wing shielded my face.
> I stand as witness to the common lot,
> survivor of that time, that place.

This attempt by Stanley Kunitz Americanizes the translation, and makes one realize how deep and subtle is the difference between "great simple verses" in the American tradition and in the Russian. The difference was even more marked when Robert Lowell reconstituted the lines in his own fashion.

> I wasn't under a new sky,
> its birds were the old familiar birds.
> They still spoke Russian. Misery
> spoke familiar Russian words.

Those are wholly American words, and an American tone. Lyn Coffin is the best at getting some equivalent of the original's weight and *gravitas*.

> No, it wasn't under a foreign heaven,
> It wasn't under the wing of a foreign power, –
> I was there among my countrymen,
> I was where my people, unfortunately, were.

"Unfortunately" could have been an unfortunate word, but its complex English connotations in fact just provide the right note, stopping just this side of the ironic. "Unhappily" would have verged on the portentous.

With the war over, the Soviet state returned to "normal". In 1946 Akhmatova was denounced by the cultural commissar Andrei Zhdanov and expelled from the Union of Soviet Writers.

> Akhmatova's subject matter is . . . miserably limited: it is
> the poetry of an overwrought upper-class lady who fran-
> tically races back and forth between boudoir and chapel. . . .
> A nun or a whore – or rather both a nun and a whore who
> combines harlotry with prayer . . . Akhmatova's poetry is
> utterly remote from the people. . . . What can there be in
> common between this poetry and the interests of our
> people and state?

By using words like "overwrought" and "frantic" Zhdanov showed he had not the faintest conception of what her poetry – or any other, probably – was about. Remote from the people in a sense it certainly is, but the people did not seem aware of the fact. Her poems were immensely popular in *samizdat*, and the few official printings were instantly sold out. Perhaps the nun and the whore was the popular touch, as a symbolist like Yeats – oh so self-consciously – might have claimed. Yet the people who admired Akhmatova would not be likely to be interested in symbolist personas. Yeats or Blok might adopt the mask of libertine or sage, but Akhmatova, like Pushkin, was herself through and through, whether as woman or as poet.

Though she admired Blok, and perhaps briefly loved him, she regarded him as some sort of unstable demon, an actor in a seductive but dangerously wicked farce. She declared: "One does not ultimately behave like that," and she says the same thing in the same tone to state tyranny, to the horrors of the *Yezhovschina*, to all the destructive manifestations of inhuman conceit. She knows that offence comes, but woe unto them by whom it cometh, whether from the frivolity of the individual or the wickedness of the state. *Poem Without a Hero* (the ironic reference is of course to the new "Soviet-style" heroes of official Soviet poetry) irritated some of Akhmatova's own friends and well-wishers, as well as the Soviet officials, by resurrecting for guilt and expiation some of the old private St Petersburg sins as if they were one with the new torments of Leningrad.

Lyn Coffin is probably wise not to attempt this poem, for her rhymed versions could not come near it, though they are frequently and rather unexpectedly effective when she renders in this way the shorter and earlier poems. Early Akhmatova often has a crisply matter-of-fact quality, which transposes well into an American idiom. Here is Coffin's version of one of Akhmatova's earliest poems, "While Reading Hamlet".

> A dust-covered patch to the right of the cemetery.
> Beyond that, a river of unfolding blue.
> "Get thee to a nunnery," you said, "Or marry
> An idiot – It's up to you."
>
> That's the sort of thing princes always say,
> But I won't forget it as I grow older.
> May your words keep flowing as centuries wear away,
> Like an ermine mantle tossed over someone's shoulder.

"But I won't forget it as I grow older" hits just the right note, more so than Kunitz's more sober and impersonal "but these are words that one remembers". (Kunitz's version, though, had the Russian on the other side of the page – an excellent arrangement – and the added advantage of an essay by Max Hayward, by far the best and most concise introduction to Akhmatova yet written for readers in English.)*

Lyn Coffin succeeds again in the short, tart poem in which Akhmatova glances at her unhappy relations with her husband, the poet Gumilev. She married him in 1910, after many proposals by him, one of them accompanied by a suicide attempt. Although an original poet, an explorer, and a gallant soldier (after the war he was shot by the Bolsheviks for alleged conspiracy), Gumilev was clearly not an easy man to live with, and Akhmatova herself seems to have been quite innocent of all the ordinary domestic virtues.

They had one son who because of his name was arrested in the purges, and for whom his mother spent the hours of anguish outside the Leningrad jail which are commemorated in *Requiem*. Released to fight in the war, he was rearrested after it. Sadly, after his final release he became estranged from his mother. The son of the poet Tsvetaeva, who hanged herself in 1941, had done the same. Even in a situation of apocalypse the gap between life and art can often have the same dreadful old commonplaceness about it. Had it not been for revolution, tyranny, and violent death, Gumilev and Akhmatova would no doubt have quarrelled, been jealous of each other's loves and poems, and finally separated like any other writers anywhere. As it is the little poem written only months after her marriage has a terse clarity about it which includes, even if it does not foretell, the future. There is humour in it too, as well as sympathy and a kind of wry fellow-feeling.

> The three things he loved most in life
> Were white peacocks, music at mass,
> And tattered maps of America.
> He didn't like kids who cried and he
> Didn't like raspberry jam with tea
> Or womanish hysteria.
> . . . And I was, like it or not, his wife.

* Hayward's essay is reprinted in the collection *Writers in Russia:1917–1978*, edited and with an introduction by Patricia Blake (New York: Harcourt Brace Jovanovich/Helen and Kurt Wolff).

Kunitz's version has rival virtues, but ends, "And he was tied to me" – which leaves the relationship ambiguous. Lyn Coffin cleverly gets her rhyme on the first and last line even though she has to pad out the latter. The Russian states merely: "And I was his wife."

There are some excellent versions too of the poems written during the First World War and in the early days of the Revolution, when Akhmatova was beginning, as it were, to rise to the occasion: "I Hear the Oriole's Voice", "The Tale of the Black Ring", "The Muse", and the magnificent "Lot's Wife", which celebrates the woman who looked back at her old home in "red-towered Sodom", and deliberately paid the price. "Dante", a poem on the same theme, was memorably rendered by Kunitz. The poet sends Florence "a curse from hell / and in heaven could not forget her": he refused to bow the knee to the town that was "perfidious, base, and irremediably home". Lyn Coffin's version weakens this somewhat, but her version of the almost equally memorable "Cleopatra" concludes well.

> Tomorrow they will chain her children. And yet
> She has something left in the world to do – one more jest.
> And the little black snake, as if a parting regret,
> With an equable hand, she puts on her swarthy breast.

In these poems Akhmatova invokes historical precedents for her fate without any scrap of pretension. The metre, unfortunately, is a mere jingle compared to the Russian, but nothing can be done about that. What comes faintly through is the quality that Joseph Brodsky isolates in his introduction to this translation – the true classic. "Nothing reveals a poet's weaknesses like classic verse," he says, "and that's why it's so universally dodged." As a poet in the same tradition, he is the best possible perceiver of what gives Akhmatova's verse its inner strength.

Continually we hear echoes of the true classic in her verse, but they are neither assumed nor something she is trying to conceal; they are deliberate. As Brodsky says, "She came fully equipped, and she never resembled anyone." She did not have to make herself like Yeats: she knew what she was. She was Anna Akhmatova, not Anna Gorenko. Her father, a naval architect of aristocratic birth, told her to write poetry by all means, but not to "sully a good name" by publishing under it, so she adopted a name from the distant past of her mother's family, a name which, as Brodsky points out, has a distinctly Tatar flavour. It went with her appearance – "five feet eleven, dark-haired, fair-skinned, with pale grey-green eyes like those of snow leopards, slim and incredibly lithe, she was for half a century sketched, painted, cast, carved and photographed by a multitude of artists starting with Amadeo Modigliani". Bizarre, after this, that Brodsky compares her to Jane Austen (". . . her syntax resembles English. From the very threshold of her career to its very end she was always perfectly clear and coherent"), but the point is an exceptionally shrewd one. Neither cared in the least about originality, or even about being an "artist": they just were so. Akhmatova, according to Brodsky, disliked the very word "poet".

She was as much identified with Petersburg as her source of inspiration as Jane Austen with her "three or four families" in an English village. *Akhmatova's Petersburg* is a scholarly and imaginative study of her themes, her friends, and her poetry, in relation to the city that since its foundation by Peter the Great has exercised such a fascination over Russian poets and writers. Sharon Leiter quotes as one of her epigraphs a conversation with Akhmatova recorded by Lidia Chukovskaya in 1939, in which they agreed on the particular suitability of Petersburg as a setting for catastrophe. "This cold river, with heavy clouds always above it, these threatening sunsets, this operatic, frightful moon. . . . Black water with yellow gleams of light. . . . I can't imagine how catastrophes look in Moscow; there they haven't got all that. . . ." Blok and Bely would have agreed with her, while the stories of Gogol and Dostoevsky, and his *Crime and Punishment*, had already sounded the same theme.

And yet the town, like Dante's Florence, was "irremediably home". For her, as for her contemporary Mandelstam, it was the home of the "blessed word". There is a significant contrast here between the attitude of the two Acmeist poets to Petersburg (in my view Mandelstam's prose memoir *The Noise of Time* is the best evocation of it) and that of Blok. For Blok it was a symbolist hell, a *huis clos* whose only exit is bloody apocalypse. A famous two-stanza poem of his describes the immobile night scene, "a street, a street-lamp, a drugstore", with "no way out" in past or future. Akhmatova and Mandelstam let in all the light and air of story and legend (Acmeism for Mandelstam was "a nostalgia for world culture") and about the town they are, in their curious way, both more affectionate and more homely. In her "To Osip Mandelstam" she writes a poem of marvellous classic serenity, whose lilt – unheard before – nonetheless echoes both Pushkin's most famous lyrics and the nineteenth-century German lyrists who loved the Greeks.

> There, where Eurydices circle,
> Where the bull carries Europa over the waves;
> There, where our shades rush past,
> Above the Neva, above the Neva, above the Neva;
> There, where the Neva splashes against the step, –
> Is your pass to immortality.

The triumphant line – *"Nad Nevoi, nad Nevoi, nad Nevoi"* – with the accent on the last syllable of each phrase, conveys the dithyrambic movement, and Sharon Leiter's text is greatly enriched by making all quotations bilingual.

As she points out, the word "pass", *propusk*, is used by Mandelstam in his wonderful poem that begins, "We will meet again in Petersburg / As if we had buried the sun there. . . ."

> I don't need a night pass,
> I'm not afraid of sentries:
> For the blessed meaningless word
> We will pray in the Soviet night.

Though it was published in *Pravda*, as part of the official drive to mobilize the Soviet people's morale, Akhmatova's poem "Courage" also subtly undermined Soviet values by proclaiming that the struggle was to "keep you alive, great Russian word", the same word that Mandelstam invokes and prays for in the night of

Leningrad. As Sinyavsky saw, the poet's word in Russia has an unambiguous authority that is the secular state's mysterious rival. The poet in Russia is the custodian of the word, and leaves the last word to God.

New York Review of Books, 1984

Women Are Nicer

Simon Karlinsky, *Marina Tsvetaeva: The Woman,
her World and her Poetry* (Cambridge: Cambridge University Press);
Julia Voznesenskaya, *The Women's Decameron*,
translated by W. B. Linton (London: Quartet Books)

Trotsky, who had a certain wit, even in literary matters, thought that women wrote poetry for only two reasons: because they desired a man and because they needed God, "as a combination of errand boy and gynaecologist . . . How this individual, no longer young and burdened by the personal bothersome errands of Akhmatova, Tsvetaeva and others, manages in his spare time to direct the destinies of the universe is simply incredible." Trotsky's view of God was as conventional as his view of women. All tyrannies with a new spiritual pretension, from Zealots and Anabaptists to the Ayatollah, want to keep women in their old place, and the Bolsheviks were no exception. After the first heady days, with Madame Kollontai preaching free love, and poetry and drama doing what they pleased, the Soviet government discovered that it needed censorship as much as, or more than, any other repressive system. "Dictatorship, where is thy whip?" enquired *Pravda*. A charmingly candid demand, which shows, among other things, that the Soviet system was not so hypocritical then as it has since become.

The proletariat's dictators were not going to put up with nuns and whores masquerading as poetesses. From adolescence Tsvetaeva had the urge to defend anything that was getting the worst of it, whether it was the Tsar or Kerensky, the Communards or Napoleon. An admirable urge in a poet, and – surprisingly – it kept her for many years out of the worst sorts of trouble. She quarrelled with the Russian émigrés over her defence of Mayakovsky and the Soviet poets, and she recited to a Moscow audience, full of Party members and Red Army men, her poem-cycle *The Demesne of the Swans*, a passionate elegy for the White Guards. Faced with such irresponsible independence, the kinds of cultural commissar who turned their heavy guns on Akhmatova, and denounced her as a nun and whore, could only shrug their shoulders. What could they have made of Tsvetaeva's ironic but also frenetically sincere manifesto to fellow writers: "The TRUTH is a TURNCOAT!" Her daughter, and her husband, became in time convinced and faithful servants of the Party, and as a result her husband was shot and her daughter sent for seventeen years to a labour camp. The poet herself the regime didn't bother to touch. After managing, during the German invasion, to get evacuated with her son to Soviet Asia, she came to the end of her own tether, and hanged herself in a mood of private hopelessness, humiliation and despair. She wanted, as she wrote before the end, not to die, but not to be.

Both Akhmatova and Tsvetaeva were extremely personal poets, for both of whom it was nonetheless natural – as Russian poets – to seem seers and public figures, through whom was expressed the whole of the country's suffering, its true being and awareness. No pretension is involved in this, any more than it is when Akhmatova writes in *Requiem* that the statue her country will erect to her should stand outside the prison where she used to wait, with the melting snow weeping from its bronze eyes, and the ships sailing past it up and down the Neva. Or when Tsvetaeva, whose actual grave was unrecorded, imagines her funeral procession, through the streets of Moscow, followed by writers, ministers, the populace. So Pushkin was buried, with universal mourning. But Akhmatova and Tsvetaeva are nonetheless very different kinds of poet. It would be possible, even desirable, to read and reread Akhmatova's complex masterpiece, *Poem Without a Hero*, in a state of complete ignorance about the poet herself, although the poem is full of cryptic intimacies and references to friends and events, both public and private. But Tsvetaeva's poetic dramas and poem-cycles to friends, or in memory of them, really do require a background of detailed knowledge about her life and personality. It is impossible to imagine the job being done better than by Professor Karlinsky. His knowledge of and research into the period are encyclopaedic, and he has the same understanding of his subject that he showed in his brilliant study of Gogol.

She wrote a great deal. One feels it came as naturally to her as could be, and from 1922 to 1940, when she and her family were émigrés in Czechoslovakia and France, she wrote to earn money in the émigré journals produced in Berlin, Prague and Paris. The general effect, however invidious comparisons may be, is of a mixture of Browning, Hugo Von Hofmannsthal and Robert Lowell, with something of Whitman's breezy effect of easing himself in poetry's words. If that sounds bizarre – well, she is in many ways a bizarre writer. Her ways with rhythm and sound effects seem too spontaneous to be experimental, though they can have, like Mayakovsky's, an aggressive quality which has not worn particularly well. A Russian ear is clearly needed to detect and enjoy her best effects. Her sounds can be more subtle than what she says, and there is an absence of an "inside" to much of her verse that can make it disappointing to reread. For most readers she is at her best when most immediate, as in the extraordinarily moving cycle, *The Demesne of the Swans*, written when she was still very young, though already a wife and mother. It has been well translated by Robin Kemball.

Tsvetaeva's background was as much European as Russian. Her father was a distinguished and absent-minded professor ("my attentively uncomprehending father") who came from a family of Orthodox priests: but her mother, his second wife, was from the Baltic, and had Polish and German forebears. All her life Tsvetaeva retained a passionate admiration for things German. In one of her explosively brilliant love letters to Rainer Maria Rilke she was to proclaim that, like all true poets, she wrote her own language, which was not French, German or Russian. Be that as it may, in her 1919 essay "O Germanii" ("On Germany") she wrote that her passion for German literature and culture revealed two sides of her inmost being which could only be expressed in that language –

übermass, a state of excess or extravagance, and the gushing ecstasy of *schwärmerei*. She adored the German sentiment of Nessler's opera, *Der Trompeter von Säkkingen*, which her mother, who had always longed to be a concert pianist, used to sing to her:

> Behut' dich Gott! Es war zu schon gewesen,
> Behut' dich Gott, es hat nicht sollen sein!

In the same way the victory of the White Armies was to seem to her something too beautiful ever to be, something belonging to the world of yearning and romance. A friend called her an incorrigible 'mythomaniac', creating and half-believing myths about her own life and everything else, and this is true insofar as twentieth-century myth-making poets, like Yeats and Blok, are direct inheritors of European Romanticism, giving it a personal and individual life. Tsvetaeva was in a sense a more thoroughgoing, a more absolute romantic, but, like Yeats, she had a tough, practical, earthy side, and a pungent natural style that was never derivative or dreamy.

Yet even the most striking of her longer poems – "On a Red Steed", "The Pied Piper", "Poem of the Air", "Poem of the Staircase", "Poem of the Tsar's Family" (most of this unpublished) – suffer from a discrepancy between the vitality of the style and the oddly old-fashioned laboriousness of the "meaning". The two things seem distinct in a way that would be impossible for Eliot, Rilke or Akhmatova, and the feeling again is of a throwback to German Romanticism and to the long poem which allegorizes the spirit of man, the ever-womanly, the victory of enlightenment, or whatever. "Poem of the Staircase" takes the image of a sordid back-staircase to excoriate the poverty and materialism of modern life; "Poem of the Air", inspired by Lindberg's Atlantic flight, celebrates a passionate dislike of, and escape from, physical limitation; the protagonist of "On a Red Steed" is exposed to three temptations, from each of which she is rescued in the nick of time by a knight on a red steed who is, as the poem makes all too clear, her poetic genius. Notwithstanding the Germanic weight of the main significances, the texture of the poems can be highly obscure, dense with private reference and the talismanic meaning for the poet of events, places, heroes, like Napoleon's son "l'Aiglon", romanticized in the lush verse drama of Rostand, which Tsvetaeva fervently admired. All this is very engaging in its way, and symptomatic of a spirit totally uncrafty and uncalculating, in her art as in her life. She did what the spirit impelled her to do with none of that canny instinct for the *zeitgeist*, and what they could make of it, which is so marked in great poets like Yeats and Eliot. This almost childlike indifference to fashion is the most attractive thing about Tsvetaeva as a poet, and it goes with her sense that "Truth is a Turncoat", that fashion goes with fanaticism and all the hardness of ideology.

But that said, it must also be admitted that her frenetic personality has something non-individual about it. It conforms too much to a type, the type of one of her most ardent childhood infatuations, Mary Bashkirtsev, the legendary young diarist who died of tuberculosis in 1884, and the publication of whose journals caused a European sensation. Simone de Beauvoir was to cite them in *The Second Sex* as the archetypal example of "self-centred female narcissism", but also as the discovery by the female of her independent personal existence. The young Katherine Mansfield worshipped them too, and modelled herself on them, and there is a striking similarity, in the appearance of face and hair, between Mansfield and Tsvetaeva. Although a much greater talent than Katherine Mansfield, the latter, too, never escaped from being the period type, and representing its intensest form.

This is shown in the contradictions of her married life. While still a girl, staying at the poet Maximilian Voloshin's house at Koktebel in the Crimea, she fell in love with another young literary aspirant called Sergei Efron, half-Jewish, tall and handsome, with Byzantine features and enormous dark eyes. They married and remained married through all subsequent vicissitudes. There is a remarkable photograph taken around 1912, of their two solemn and childish young faces gazing at the camera, his lean and hollow, hers chubby and round. Efron, the perpetual student, had no sooner escaped from Russia with the White Army than he enrolled on an art course at the University of Prague: the generosity and cultural concern of the young Czechoslovak republic was one of its brightest features and Tsvetaeva and her husband continued to receive an allowance from the Czechs for many years afterwards. When they were separated by the war Tsvetaeva had sworn that she would be her husband's dog for ever if she ever found him again, and she kept her vow, in her own fashion. Before the war she had had a tremendous affair with the notorious Sophie Parnok, sometimes making love with her in a monastery cell in Rostov, and she was to continue all her life having tempestuous affairs with women, with Sonechka Holliday, even with the famous Natalie Barney, the wealthy and elegant Amazon of the Parisian thirties, for whose soirées the privileged bought themselves special frocks from the grand couturiers. Tsvetaeva turned up looking as if she was wearing an old sack.

In addition to the women in her life she fell frequently for young men, but her passions here were usually brief, highly maternal and probably sexless. As Karlinsky observes, she loved "frail and vulnerable Jews", like the young publisher Abram Vishniak in Berlin, but she often put them in a difficult position and soon became disillusioned herself. With Rilke she conducted a love affair by correspondence, in a series of letters coruscating with wit and telegraphic insights about poetry. The German poet was cautious, clearly enjoying her unbounded admiration but reluctant to go so far as a meeting; with her usual impetuosity Tsvetaeva ignored the fact that he was gravely ill, and was deeply hurt when he gave up writing back. She was fiercely protective of her own family, however, and looked after them with devotion, through all the ups and downs of poverty and emigration. But in this context, too, things went bad. Her younger daughter died of starvation in an orphanage during the famine of the Civil War. The elder girl, Ariadne, was very close when young to her mother, who confided to her all her griefs and loves, but became estranged at the age of ten, absorbed only in an ideal vision of the Russian communist paradise. Her son, whom she doted on (Pasternak called him her "Napoleonid"), grew up into a spoilt, oafish boy, endlessly complaining and mistreating his mother. When, entirely for his sake, she returned to

Russia in 1940, he hated it and accused her of ruining his life. He showed no remorse at her suicide, and there is evidence that his death in the Red Army two years later was not in action but the result of insubordination and cheeking his sergeant.

Tsvetaeva, in short, was one of those unfortunates who pay for their genius, and their generosities too, by a dire failure in human relations. Her swans, whose demesne she had once so movingly celebrated, all turned out to be geese. She was unswervingly loyal to her husband but seems to have had no idea what he was like. He had become, in fact, a fanatic for the communist cause, and was employed by the OGPU as an undercover agent, planning as the head of a front organization in France at least two political murders and abductions. A friend described him as unintelligent and kind, "an enthusiast, an idealist, utterly sincere and extremely naive. That, it seems to me, exhausts the subject." Only when they were briefly re-united again in 1940, at an OGPU safe house outside Moscow, did Tsvetaeva grasp what had long been known to the émigré community in France: that her husband was a spy and a murderer. Nor did it do him any good. The legend is that after his arrest he was interrogated by Beria himself, with whom he became violently angry, presumably out of incredulity that one who had become so devoted a servant of the Soviet state should be disposed of out of hand when his job was done.

Naive as he may have been, Efron could be perceptive about his wife. In a letter to Voloshin he wrote that "to plunge into a self-created hurricane has become a necessity for her, the air of her life. Who the instigator of this hurricane is doesn't matter . . . everything is built on self-deception. . . . Today it's despair, tomorrow it's ecstasy, love, total surrender of self, and tomorrow it's despair again." That sounds a familiar diagnosis, but ignores not only the fact that her talent as a poet was a necessary part of this psychology, but also that she possessed a hard, penetrating, Voltairian intelligence – humour too – which gave the equally necessary stress and balance to her art. Whatever her fellow émigrés thought, and however much they despised her gullibility and what Karlinsky calls her status as a "Dostoevskian infernal woman junior grade", I would suspect that in a part of her divided spirit she was quite well aware of what her husband was up to, but chose to turn the blind eye of loyalty. It was part of her "absolute maternal care", and it expressed a temperament that – significantly – was apt to repel the more masculine of her fellow artists. Alexei Remizov, author of that remarkable novel *The Clock*, noted that "I strongly dislike Tsvetaeva for her posturings, her ignoble character and her *female irresponsibility*. And for her extraordinary vanity." The Nobel Prize-winner, Bunin, wrote that he "couldn't stand that psychopath with her leaden eyes, gifted, but lacking in shame, taste".

Great writers not infrequently do lack shame and taste. And to understand Tsvetaeva's greatness we have to understand how she lived, and sympathize with what she was like. Karlinsky's study enables us to achieve this. It is a landmark in the scholarship of one of the most talented as well as tumultuous periods of Russian poetry. The paradox is that for all her "Europeanness", her insistence that she wrote no language but her own, Tsvetaeva is for a foreigner actually the hardest of all of her poetic generation to approach and understand as a poet's voice in the Russian language. Akhmatova, Pasternak, Mandelstam are all far more accessible, more comprehensible in terms of the poetic art that was going on in their time in Europe.

It is not easy to say what Tsvetaeva would have thought of Women's Lib. She herself combined, in extreme form, maternal impulses and passions with the wish to lead a wholly independent existence, like a Peter Pan or a Pied Piper. Such a division is normal enough, indeed the mark of sanity in one sense, and she would have thought nothing of it, just as she made no distinction, in her own life, between men and women. As Karlinsky says, she made a bit of a myth out of her "kitchen martyrdom", though it was real enough; she never expected her son or husband to do a hand's turn to help her – that was not "man's work" – and she doted on them so much that they were privileged beings in the household. Yet she could write to her friend Teskova that "marriage and love are destructive of one's personality. . . . I've lived my life in captivity, and, strange to say, a freely chosen captivity." She wryly remarks that no one asked her to take everything so seriously, but that it was "in my blood, its German component". "If I get to live another time, I'll know what to do."

Living one's life in captivity is a state taken for granted by the narrators in *The Women's Decameron*, a remarkable book by a writer born in Leningrad and educated in a Siberian labour camp, before being forced to emigrate to West Germany, where she now lives. She was the founder of "Maria", the first Russian Independent Women's Group, and is the subject of the American feature film, *Julia's Diary*. There is a certain comedy, which would have appealed to Tsvetaeva, and perhaps to Boccaccio too, in the idea of Russian Women's Lib, with all the harsh and elemental experience it is based on, encountering its Western counterpart. Traditionally wives have been more physically abused in Russia even than in other countries – seventeenth-century Russian books of domestic management actually give wife-beating an official status – and yet in the great flowering of Russian literature from Pushkin to the Revolution women are invariably portrayed as stronger, more enterprising and more dominant than the uncertain and often superfluous heroes. Women's Lib would probably justly comment that one way of keeping women in captivity is to make out that they are stronger than you are. Certainly the strong Russian woman is a male literary invention, and by the time there are women writers, like Akhmatova and Tsvetaeva, the myth becomes irrelevant, though it is true to say that both poets were very dependent on men, and on being the centre of authority in their family.

Ten young women in the maternity ward of a Leningrad hospital learn that they have been put in a ten-day quarantine, and decide to borrow the Florentine writer's idea and pass the time telling each other stories. By the book's end one hundred have been told. The device works well, because the Soviet background seems curiously and compellingly similar to that of the actual *Decameron* – basically medieval, in fact – and though the stories illustrate the trials, sufferings and ingenuities of women, their greater effectiveness is to show what real life in Russia is like. It has virtues which we have lost or are losing, and this comes out all the more clearly because the women tell their tales without shame or sentiment. One tale, told by an air hostess, concerns a foreign diplomat who falls in love with a Russian girl when he sees how well she looks after her old grandmother, who lives in the same tiny flat – virtually the same room – as the rest of the family. He is engaged to a Western girl who has put her parents in a nice home, and it occurs to him that she would treat him the same way if the need arose: and so he decides to marry Katenka, "a wife with whom I could calmly face sickness and old age". Another story describes an *Othello* situation (itself from an Italian novella) in which a tough lesbian *zek* in a Gulag, who has a timid and wholly faithful lesbian "wife", is betrayed by another female *zek* whom she has ignored. This *zek* steals and wears the blue scarf the butch Othello has given to her Desdemona, and the girl is too frightened to admit she has lost it. She is stabbed by her jealous lover but survives, and the twist is that when she comes out of the camp hospital her Othello has got another girl and will have no more to do with her. The Desdemona can never prove she is innocent.

These stories are not masterpieces, but they exploit and develop a convention very successfully. They suggest an all too likely world, not necessarily a Russian one, in which human nature does not change, nor the position of women, nor their need to outwit men and protect themselves against them. The Russian background makes these facts stand out more starkly and in stronger moral relief. It may be, too, that the author is deliberately doing what Russian male writers used to do more unconsciously: showing that women are tougher and more resourceful than men, as well as nicer.

London Review of Books, 1986

Chalk Between
His Fingers

Michael Scammell, *Solzhenitsyn* (London: Hutchinson)

Query: what categories do Russian writers most neatly divide into? Answer: shamans and schoolmasters. Pushkin, Gogol, Dostoevsky enchant their audience like magicians, work upon them like wizards. Belinsky, Tolstoy, Solzhenitsyn sit their readers down in the classroom, take up a piece of chalk, and proceed to draw great sweeping diagrams upon the blackboard. On his estate Tolstoy taught for years by his own principles in his own school; and when he was released from the Gulag, Solzhenitsyn's greatest joy was in being able to teach once more, to feel the chalk, as he says, between his fingers.

At first it was only mathematics he was teaching, his star subject, the mastery of which had made him an artillery captain in a special spotting battalion during the war. But a rage to instruct had always been at the bottom of his passionate desire to be an author. To fulfil it he would sacrifice everything – himself included. One sometimes has the feeling that his rejection of Lenin and Stalin, and all they stood for, was a deep resentment of rival pedagogues, who had tyrannized the Russian kindergarten, filled the pupils with false doctrine, and beaten them black and blue into the bargain.

This enormous biography is worthy of the most industrious traditions of the classroom. Mr Scammell has certainly done his homework, not only drawing on Solzhenitsyn's own monumental account, in *The Oak and the Calf*, of his struggles with the Soviet bureaucracy after he had become a famous novelist, but filling in,

165

in detail, every aspect of his life – childhood, boyhood, years in the Gulag, and his present existence as an industrious hermit on a guarded estate in the woods of Vermont.

It may be that readers are becoming just a little bored with Solzhenitsyn and his legend, for the same reason that the fickle Athenians banished Aristides because they were so tired of hearing him called "the Just". If so, this biography should certainly revive the interest. Quite apart from its technical fascination to the Cold War trade, it can itself be read as a kind of spacious Russian novel – particularly absorbing, like many family novels, on the background into which the hero was born and the conditions in which he grew up.

These were chaotic enough. Solzhenitsyn was born in 1918, not the best of years anywhere, in his uncle's villa in Kislovodsk, a spa town in the Caucasus. His paternal relatives were small farmers, but his father had married into a more prosperous family, and his maternal uncle, though far from being a capitalist, was actually one of the nine people in Russia to possess a Rolls-Royce, of which Scammell has managed to find a splendid photo. Much was made of this allegedly bourgeois background by Solzhenitsyn's persecutors during the attacks on him that led to his expulsion from Russia.

His father, in fact, was a not untypical product of late Tsarist enterprise and social mobility. He had got himself a good education, joined up at the outbreak of the First World War and was posted to the artillery, in which he served with distinction, marrying while on leave after a whirlwind and romantic courtship. When revolution came he made his way home, and died shortly afterwards from a wound received in a hunting accident. His son was born six months later, and his widow found herself engulfed in the savage civil war between the Whites and the Reds which raged for the next two years over south Russia.

Solzhenitsyn's mother Taissia had a hard time over the ensuing years and developed TB, but the sacrifices she made for her son meant that he had a fairly normal Soviet childhood, filled with the new idealism and hopes for the future; he was determined both to work for the cause and to fulfil his own educational ambitions for himself. He was good at everything at school, always keen to be a writer. A school essay, of the "what I did in the holidays" type, was sent by his headmaster to Maxim Gorky, and the great man returned it with encouraging words. Solzhenitsyn idealized the memory of his father, and as early as 1930 had written sections of a long novel about the First War and the beginnings of Bolshevism which he was later to recast and incorporate in *August 1914*, though with a very different message. His father was the hero of these early unpublished works, and appears in *August 1914* as the officer Isaaki Lazhenitsyn.

The bosom friend of Solzhenitsyn's student days was Nikolai Vitkevich, with whom he once hitchhiked on the railway as far as Kazan, where they acquired an ancient dugout canoe and made the descent of the Volga as far as Kuibyshev. This was in the year of the purges and the height of the Great Terror, of which the two innocents were no more conscious than probably was the mass of the Soviet population. They did once encounter guards apparently looking for escaped prisoners, but thought nothing of it, resuming their intoxicating dialogue about man, nature, freedom and the wonders of Marxism.

Having scoooped up all available educational honours Solzhenitsyn was approached at this time, as many of the cleverest students were, for a job with the NKVD, which might have led to the highest Party honours. He declined the opening, not from principle but because it seemed to him dull and respectable.

In the later part of the war he and Vitkevich, now both captains at the front, continued to write to each other, and it was their innocence, once again, that betrayed them. It was *because* they were such believers that they talked so freely to each other, as young Russians always have done, exchanging views about life like Pierre and Andrew in *War and Peace*, which Solzhenitsyn had first read at the age of nine, and many times thereafter. The censorship took a different view, however. Solzhenitsyn, whose young wife had been living with him at the front – a remarkable testimony to the happy-go-lucky nature of at least some aspects of the Red Army –

was now racing with his battery through East Prussia, full of the joyful excitement of the final conquest of Nazi Germany. Summoned one morning to his Brigadier's office he was arrested by Smersh and stripped of his insignia, the Brigadier, with great courage, shaking his hand and wishing him happiness as he was led away, a gesture Solzhenitsyn never forgot. Shells were falling all round, and the Smersh limousine drove off accidentally towards the front, a detail the new prisoner had to draw to his captors' attention.

His friend Vitkevich had also been arrested, and the two were to meet again during and after their Gulag experiences; but their friendship was never resumed. Vitkevich, who subsequently became a respectable Party member and a chemistry professor, had no wish to identify with his old friend's rise to fame as an author and his stand against the regime; he kept his head down and his nose clean – a very natural reaction after the ardours and illusions of youth. Solzhenitsyn's wife, though she loyally sent him food parcels during his imprisonment which must have helped to keep him alive, finally lost heart after a series of quarrels and reconciliations, and set up with someone else.

Solzhenitsyn's Gulag time was in fact much mitigated by the long spells he spent in a *sharashka*. These were special camps, filled with scientists and experts of all kinds, which were run more or less like factory estates, with the inmates receiving comparatively good treatment. Solzhenitsyn describes them in *The First Circle* and they were very different from the kind of camp which figures in *One Day in the Life of Ivan Denisovich*. After he developed a cancerous tumour, probably from a neglected childhood condition, he was invalided to Tashkent, and afterwards exiled in Ryazan, where he resumed work as a teacher and began to write.

One of Scammell's two well-chosen epigraphs is a comment by the Frenchman Jacques Vache: "Nothing kills a man like being obliged to represent his country." The other is a noble tribute by Octavio Paz, for whom Solzhenitsyn's real achievement is not a political or even a moral one, but rather that of the ancient religious concept – bearing witness. It could equally be said, of course, and not disparagingly, that Solzhenitsyn was a writer in search of his true subject, and that what he has achieved is the result of his fanatic determination to succeed as a writer. Equally inevitable that much of his campaign has been conducted with what Scammell once acknowledged to be "cold egocentricity". Though his biographer defends him stoutly, Solzhenitsyn's personality does not come over as a particularly attractive one. His story gets murkier as it goes on, fuller of accusation and recrimination, particularly bitter ones from his wife, who refused for years to give him a divorce. Naturally the authorities tried to discredit him on these domestic grounds. His own lengthy account of the struggle with them is given in *The Oak and the Calf*, in which the most important figure is not Solzhenitsyn himself but Tvardovsky, the editor of *Novy Mir* who "discovered" him, a touching, tormented Frankenstein who in the end was virtually destroyed by the inflexible monster he had created. Solzhenitsyn's appearance at his funeral – even making the sign of the cross over the coffin, to the scandal of Soviet believers – became a triumph of international publicity.

But all that is in the past. The disquieting thing is that Solzhenitsyn, and all he stands for, may now seem old hat, even among Russian dissidents. His successors have different attitudes, reflected in their style and approach. Sinyavsky, Aksyonov and their younger contemporaries have taken to writing in the Western manner, with a fantasy and frivolity which does not so much oppose the Soviet system as find it boring and irrelevant. The young may soon regard Solzhenitsyn as just another species of the old guard against whom he bore witness.

The Listener, 1985

Making It Strange

-{}-•-{}-

Vladimir Voinovich, *Pretender to the Throne*
(New York: Farrar, Straus & Giroux)

Any nation's best and most pungent humour usually doesn't travel
well. Like poetry, it gets lost in translation, both in the literal sense
and in terms of acoustic nuance – those numerous verbal gestures
and tropisms that encrust a culture. The subtlest humour is, as the
structuralists would say, metonymic: it presupposes a linkage of
anticipated connections with one abruptly left out, or with a link
to some quite different set of expectations. We must have an
unconscious and atavistic awareness of this mechanism, an awareness dictated by class and culture, for the element of surprise to have
its full effect.

Vladimir Voinovich's lighthearted, picaresque new novel
prompts such reflections. *Pretender to the Throne*, the successor to
The Life and Extraordinary Adventures of Private Ivan Chonkin (1977),
is a further instalment of Chonkinian fantasy by this celebrated and
controversial writer, whose skirmishes with official Soviet policy
culminated in his departure from the country last December.

In its comparatively brief span, Russian literature has produced
many satiric masterpieces: Pushkin's *Tales of Belkin*, Gogol's *Dead
Souls*, Saltykov-Shchedrin's *Provincial Sketches* – to name only a
few. Dostoevsky was a virtuoso of grotesque comedy. Tolstoy, a
much cooler genius, imported from Europe the device described
by the Russian formalist critic Viktor Shklovsky as "making it
strange". When, for example, Natasha, in *War and Peace*, attends
the theatre for the first time, Tolstoy evokes only the actors'
mechanical motions – "the singer waved his legs about a good deal
and sang something in a high voice" – thus literalizing into

ludicrous travesty a complex ritual that depends for its success upon a collective suspension of disbelief. In this way, we are made to view a familiar transaction in a new light and as if for the first time. Tolstoy borrowed this technique from Voltaire, who makes the innocent eye of Candide unable to adjust to the collective hallucination required by such human activities as warfare, patriotism, and religion. Instead of being inspired by the sight of soldiers playing a martial air on a drum, he can see only "murderers six foot high clad in scarlet and beating on a distended ass's skin".

Voinovich inherits and uses the same technique. His Chonkin owes something to the old Russian tradition of Ivan the Fool, the holy simpleton of folk tales, but he is still quite a familiar figure. Indeed, there is something distinctly *déjà vu* about him, which may make the Western reader somewhat less than enthusiastic about his adventures.

When a novel ridicules the Soviet system by conjuring up an ordinary citizen oppressed by bureaucracy, we tend to be sympathetic; but that doesn't mean the novel is a masterpiece. There is something a little patronizing in our enthusiasm for Chonkin; it is as if the Russians finally caught on to a type that we have long since recognized as universal.

Such condescension, however well-meaning, hardly does justice to the peculiar nature of Voinovich's talents. Like Gogol, he is both a humorist and a poet – traits difficult to put across in translation, though Richard Lourie had done a valiant job. Besides, Chonkin is only a convenience, and in this sequel he figures a good deal less than in the original novel, disappearing for pages at a time while his creator gives the full satiric treatment to the fantastic world of wartime Russia, where there is not only no heroism but no fighting. The Catch-22 element runs riot, just as it did in Alexander Zinoviev's monumental ragbag of a novel, *The Yawning Heights*.

There is an idyll in the background of most satires. Bureaucratic and ideological nightmares may seem inescapable, but the garden of Eden still exists somewhere. Private Chonkin's idyll began, readers of the first instalment will recall, when he was sent by his sergeant to guard an aircraft that had crash-landed near some remote village. There he was befriended by a buxom local lass and settled down to a life of pristine simplicity. This primitive Eden would always have been enough for him; he would never have had an urge to bite the apple and confront the challenge of Soviet civilization.

The sharp division between modern Soviet man and an unchanging rural background obsesses Voinovich. But where the adventures of Chonkin are concerned he treats it in terms of farce. When the army comes to investigate what is going on in the village, Chonkin, true to his orders to guard the crashed plane, mistakes the investigating soldiers for bandits and fends them off. At the opening of *Pretender to the Throne*, we find him under arrest while his mistress goes from one office to another in the hope of obtaining his release.

The Chonkin case soon prompts a spate of bureaucratic fantasies. It seems that a Prince Golitsyn once owned the village Chonkin came from, and perhaps Chonkin is really a changeling, a prince in disguise (hence the book's title), dedicated to the overthrow of Soviet society. Or perhaps he has been leading the notorious Chonkin detachment of White Guards? Such notions thrill the bureaucrats, intent as they are on the virtually incompatible goals of winning prestige from the case and passing the buck further on up. Meanwhile the Germans invade, and in the ensuing war fever news of the Chonkin affair travels swiftly to the Kremlin and engages the attention of Lavrenty Beria, the OGPU chief, and then of Stalin himself. Even Hitler hears of it, and gives orders for a tank column to change direction in order to rescue the gallant prince, who as an anti-Bolshevik may be a potential recruit for the Nazi cause. Eventually, however, the higher-ups tacitly agree that Chonkin is best forgotten about, and at the end of the novel the hero heads home to the village and his mistress, only to find it occupied by the Germans, who are making the same threats and promises to the local inhabitants that the Soviet commissars used to make.

Pretender to the Throne recalls the late Alexander Tvardovsky's *Vasily Tyorkin*, an immensely popular verse narrative about the adventures of a simple Soviet soldier during the Second World War. Tvardovsky, the editor of *Novy Mir*, was the darling of a regime to which he owed everything; yet in Solzhenitsyn's *The Oak and the Calf* he appears as a pathetic martyr, torn between his loyalty to the system that had made him what he was and his passionate commitment to good writing – the very kind of writing that the system prevented him from publishing in his magazine.

This sort of anguished contradiction isn't usually found in émigré authors, who can solace their homesickness by attacking with the most wholehearted contempt and ridicule the regime that has expelled them. Yet Tvardovsky's Tyorkin and Voinovich's Chonkin would get on: they are essentially birds of a feather, even though Tyorkin is a war hero – one of the few convincing ones in Soviet hagiography – and Chonkin the instrument of an anti-Soviet propagandist. Having been created by artists, both are true in themselves despite the polemical purposes for which they were made – truer, oddly enough, than the simple soldier of *War and Peace*, Platon Karataev.

In their own ways, both Tyorkin and Chonkin reveal the virtues of the Russian character, virtues that in the one case are brought out and glorified by the communist system and in the other continue to exist in spite of it. But for Voinovich, this effect is accidental; like any satirist, he would be lost if he tried to transform a negative attitude into a positive one. His dilemma echoes that of Gogol, whose portrait in *Dead Souls* of human evasiveness and inertia – everything that Russian syntax comprises in the phrase *ne to* – reveals by negation our natural preference for living in a world of unreality, a world in which the notional and the non-existent absorb all aspiration and vitality. Yet his attempt, in a sequel, to reform his hero, direct him to useful activities, and encourage him in positive thinking was a disaster, and Gogol burned the manuscript in despair.

More than a hundred years later, the exponents of socialist realism are still finding out how difficult it is to encourage and portray the civic virtues. Traditionally, Russian literature has polarized a situation endemic in Russian society: in one novel after another, the longing for order, for *pravda*, is balanced by an equally profound nostalgia for unregenerate secrecy and chaos. Today, however, the nature of that polarity has changed. "Order" has assumed an ideological form; and its opposite has no choice but to appear in the guise of a negative or counter-ideology. The worst disservice that Soviet doctrine has done to literature is not so much to have incubated a whole class of dreary conformist authors but to have compelled the truly talented to spend their whole talent on being against that doctrine.

The result is a peculiar form of parochialism, which even Solzhenitsyn shows signs of: a parochialism of protest. Again, the precedent is there; the literature of protest is a tradition in Russia. Turgenev's *Sportsman's Sketches* played as important a role in the emancipation of the serfs as *Uncle Tom's Cabin* did in the freeing of the slaves. Dostoevsky's *Notes From Underground* began as a polemic against Benthamism and the Utilitarian quest for the greatest good of the greatest number. Even the majestic canvas of *War and Peace* started out as Tolstoy's answer both to the intelligentsia who execrated the patriarchal way of life of the old nobility and to the standard patriotic version of the events of 1812. But as these works acquired the immortality of great art, the local and polemical element ceased to matter.

In our own day, that element is frozen into a perpetual predominance. Voinovich, Zinoviev, and Andrei Platonov, to name only three of the most talented (and most "counter-revolutionary") of recent Russian prose authors, are dedicated to a species of protest that eventually takes over the whole work – its content, its form, even its language. Joseph Brodsky, the most distinguished Russian poet writing today and the most perceptive critic of Russia's literary scene, maintains in the introduction to an American edition of Platonov's work that Soviet "Newspeak" required a counter-language to neutralize and undo it, a counter-fantasy to the fantasy that serves as the official Soviet version of life in Russia. But there is something fatal in this logic, because it implies a kind of imitation: if you can't beat them, copy them. Soviet society, as Brodsky put it, "turns out to be capable of generating a fictive world and then falling into grammatical dependency on it". The same phenomenon befalls the protesting writer.

To be fair to Voinovich, it must be said that his world has a clarity and candour about it, an effect of getting back to fresh and simple things; it is closer to Gogol than to Platonov. But what all three of them demonstrate is the way in which society not only corrupts the natural man but liberates the primitive, predatory, unregenerate aspects of his nature. The hero of *Dead Souls* exploits the bureaucracy of serfdom, which its apologists would have said was intended to look after and protect the serfs. The socialists in Platonov's fantasy *Chevengur* have grown so accustomed to the doctrines of their strange world that they cannot conceive how anyone could actually love or feel concern for his neighbours and relatives; and they even go so far as to wonder whether a true communist system shouldn't endeavour to organize demonstrations of "artificial sorrow", supposing that the flavour of communism might be improved by a little salt.

One of Voinovich's characters relates how he used to denounce fellow Bolshevik workers, finding that the more talented they were the more unsuspicious: "To destroy talented people is the pleasantest and safest of tasks." Normal human envy found its happiest expression in this activity. And the most unsuspicious of all were the officials themselves: "There is no government more trusting in the world. No matter what nonsense I wrote they believed it." The informer had a bad moment when he protested to a superior that he was acting out of pure love of the cause. This created instant suspicion, until he hastily added that he had nothing against taking money for his services. The official nodded happily: "Of course it isn't the money any of us work for, but we are materialists and we don't hide the fact."

Snobbery plays an important part in the style of intrigue:

> After Chonkin was discovered to be of high birth his case was removed from among the ordinary cases, and it was directed "up top". . . . Before receiving those instructions the lower officials displayed a certain indecision which was reflected in the documents and other materials of the investigation, where Chonkin was called simply Chonkin, and the "so-called Chonkin", and in certain

cases even "Chonkin the White". However, now there were occasional glimpses of the dual surnames Chonkin-Golitsyn and Golitsyn-Chonkin.

Chonkin's virtues are wholly negative: that is one of the most effective points Voinovich makes. Not only is he not against anything but he is in no sense warm or generous. Having no taste for revenge simply reflects his selfishness, his desire to be left alone with his mistress in the little village.

By not seeking to set up Chonkin as a symbol of "humanity", an honest Russian intended to serve as a rebuke to Soviet corruption, Voinovich has largely neutralized the novel's polemical force. But what would Tolstoy and Dostoevsky have thought of it? It is an ironic comment on the ethical system promulgated by communism that the moral fervour so vivid in Russian literature should have dwindled – in its own service, so to speak – to a point where a serious author can recommend only the minimum of decent self-interest.

Kundera and Kitsch

-{}--{}-

Milan Kundera, *The Unbearable Lightness of Being*,
translated by Henry Heim (London: Faber and Faber)

There is always comedy in the ways in which we are impressed by
a novel. It can either impress us (if, that is, it is one of the very good
ones) with the sort of truths that Nietzsche, Kafka and Dostoevsky
tell us, or with the truths that Tolstoy and Trollope tell us. To the
first kind we respond with amazement and delight, awe even. "Of
course that's it! Of *course* that's it!" The second kind of truths are
more sober, more laboriously constructed, more ultimately re-
assuring. They are the truths necessary for fiction, and therefore
necessary for life. The first kind contribute brilliantly not to life
itself but to what seems an understanding of it. And that too is
necessary for us, or at least desirable, and enjoyable.

Milan Kundera's latest novel is certainly one of the very good
ones. It is in fact so amazingly better than anything he has written
before that the reader can hardly believe it, is continually being lost
in astonishment. In manner and technique it is not much different
from his previous books, but the story here at last really compels
us, and so do the hero and heroine. Kundera's great strength has
always been his wit and intelligence, and his particular way with
these assets. He was a Nietzschean truth-teller rather than a Tolstoyan one. But this new novel dissolves my distinction while at
the same time drawing attention to it. Its impact is considerable.
Whether it will last, whether one will want to read it again, are
more difficult questions to answer.

Salman Rushdie described *The Book of Laughter and Forgetting*,
which appeared in English in 1980, as "a whirling dance of a book",

and went on to bury it under all the chic epithets, sad, obscene, tender, wickedly funny, wonderfully wise, "a masterpiece full of angels, terror, ostriches and love". It was not as bad as that.* But Kundera was like a man let loose among all the literary fashions of the West, grabbing this and that, intoxicated by the display of patterns of freedom. On the publication of the book the Czech government revoked his citizenship. Both this decision and the book itself followed logically from Kundera's early novels and stories, like *The Joke*, published in Prague during the Prague Spring. *The Book of Laughter and Forgetting* (the title is shorter in Czech and sounds better) used every device of French and American "fictiveness", and its pornography, though cheerful, was so insistent in repudiating any shadow of Iron Curtain puritanism that it now seems as didactic and determined as the evolutions of Komsomol girls in red gymslips.

Unfair maybe, but circumstances made the book weightless, cosmopolitan. Despite its title, there is nothing weightless about *The Unbearable Lightness of Being*. In one sense, indeed, it satirizes its predecessor. Nor could it possibly have been written by a Frenchman or an American. It is deeply, centrally European, both German and Slav, as Nietzsche himself was both Pole and German. Prague is the centre of Europe, and with this book we are right back in Kafka's city, where neither Kafka nor Kundera can be published. Nonetheless, Kundera's intelligence has quietly forsaken contemporary Western fashion and gone back to its deep roots, in Europe's old repressions and nightmares, to a time and an art long before the cinema and the modern happening.

Both in Poland and in Czechoslovakia the cinema represented

---

* To the Editor of the *London Review of Books*:
SIR: In spite of the absence of inverted commas, I owe Mr Rushdie (*LRB*, Vol. 6, No. 12) an apology for quoting, or seeming to quote, his review of Milan Kundera's *The Book of Laughter and Forgetting* (Vol. 6, No. 10). The extract from his review printed on the cover of Kundera's new novel suggested the ghostly presence of all the praise words favoured by current critics of the novel, from "wickedly funny" to "wonderfully wise" to "tenderly obscene". But his complete review probably did not give this impression at all, and I am sorry I was not able to refer back to it.

JOHN BAYLEY

a method of escape into the modernity which the communist system rejected and forbade. Kundera was a professor of film technology and his pupils produced the new wave in the Czech cinema. His work, even the present novel, has been influenced by film techniques, but they have here been thoroughly absorbed into the forms of traditional literature, and Kundera now seems positively old-fashioned in the way in which he combines the authorial presence with the "story". The author is the purveyor of Nietzschean truth, but the story is of the Tolstoyan kind. Lightness of being is associated with the author's voice, with the cinema and sex, with irresponsibility and definition, with politics. Weight or heaviness of being, on the other hand, is associated with the love and fidelity, suffering, chance, fiction, form and content ("The sadness was form, the happiness content. Happiness filled the space of sadness"), death.

The story has weight, though it is lightly told. A Prague surgeon, an insatiable womanizer, visits a hospital in a small provincial town. He gives a kind smile to a waitress at the hotel, who falls in love with him. She follows him to Prague. She has weight (her whole background is described). They make love in order to sleep together afterwards (he has never been able to sleep with a woman before, only to make love to her). They are necessary to each other, but he cannot give up other girls. At night his hair smells of them, though he always remembers carefully to wash the rest of himself, and Tereza in her unbearable jealousy has nightmares, dreams that are part of the lightness of being. He marries her to make up for it.

He gets a good job in Zurich, but his habits continue, and Tereza leaves him, goes back to Prague. Realizing he cannot live without her, he goes back too, just in time for the Russian invasion. He loses his job, becomes a window-washer, then a driver on a collective farm. With their dog Karenin he and Tereza remain together. Fate is a story; fate is Beethoven's *Es muss sein*. Karenin dies of cancer, a moving episode – for animals, being powerless, have all the weight lacking in human consciousness. We learn that Tomas and Tereza die in a car accident, but the novel goes on, leaving them at a moment of settled happiness not unlike the tranquil ending of a traditional novel, on what is presumably their last night on earth. Tomas might have been a successful surgeon in Zurich; he might have emigrated to America, as one of his weightless mistresses, Sabina, has done, and lived in the permanent limbo of non-fiction. But his destiny is the Tolstoyan story and Tereza, who could never "learn lightness".

In one sense, then, Kundera's novel neatly turns the tables on today's theorists about the novel. It is, after all, ironical that we are now told all the time how totally fictive fiction is, while the writers who hold this view do not in practice make much effort to render their novels thoroughly fictive – that is, convincingly *real*. When the novel begins to insist that it is all made up, it tends to strike the reader as not made up at all. Kundera's aim is to emphasize that the novel is, or was, true to one aspect of human life, while the free play of thought and consciousness is true to another.

> What then shall we choose? Weight or lightness?
> Parmenides posed this very question in the sixth century before Christ. He saw the world divided into pairs of opposites. . . . Which one is positive, weight or lightness?
> Parmenides responded: lightness is positive, weight negative.
> Was he correct or not? That is the question. The only certainty is: the lightness/weight opposition is the most mysterious, most ambiguous of all.

Kundera thus ingeniously suggests that the aspects of life that constitute a novel about it, a determined story, are as authentic as the sense of consciousness, the lightness of being. To understand either we require both. Tomas stands for lightness, Tereza for weight. This sounds as if they were not "real" characters: but they are, because of the opposition between them.

> It would be senseless for author to try to convince reader that his characters had actually lived. They were not born of a mother's womb; they were born of a stimulating phrase or two or from a basic situation. Tomas was born

of the saying *"Einmal ist keinmal."* Tereza was born of the rumbling of a stomach.

Tereza was overcome with shame because her stomach rumbled when Tomas first kissed and possessed her. It was empty from the strain of travelling and she could do nothing about it. Not being able to do anything about it is the sense in which we live as if we were being controlled by the plot of a novel. Tomas is a personified symbol of the German saying, of the idea that nothing ever happens to us because it can only happen once. Because nothing ever happens we can control it – it becomes as light as feathers, like history. "Because they deal with something that will not return, the bloody years of the French Revolution have turned into mere words, theories and discussions, frightening no one." We also read this:

> Not long ago I caught myself experiencing a most incred-
> ible sensation. Leafing through a book on Hitler, I was
> touched by some of his portraits: they reminded me of my
> childhood. I grew up during the war; several members of
> my family perished in Hitler's concentration camps; but
> what were their deaths compared with the memories of a
> lost period of my life, a period that would never return?
>   This reconciliation with Hitler reveals the profound
> moral perversity of a world that rests essentially on the
> nonexistence of return, for in this world everything is
> pardoned in advance and therefore everything cynically
> permitted.

Well, it doesn't follow. Nietzschean discoveries, however sensational, in practice leave common sense and common morality much as they were. One such reconciliation with Hitler does not alter the general sense of things, or even that of the man who has made this discovery. Much more important from the point of view of the novel is Kundera's manipulation of two sorts of awareness of things: the light and the heavy, the perpetual and the fictional. It is as if he had decided to write a novel – and perhaps he did – which would acquire its reality by contrasting two theoretical views of how the novel presents it: Virginia Woolf's idea of the perpetual transparent envelope of consciousness, helplessly receiving impressions, and the "row of giglamps", the sequential and determined tale told by a novelist like Arnold Bennett.

The transparent envelope of promiscuous Tomas is dragged down to earth by the determined – in all senses – weight of the faithful Tereza. He is compelled against his nature to become a character in a novel, the character that she by nature is. Their relation is both funny and moving, dominating the book and giving it the dignity of fiction and its weight. (Kundera reminds us that the rise of the novel is both the expression of ever-increasing self-consciousness, and its antidote. By representing ourselves in fictions we escape from the unbearable insubstantiality of awareness. In Cartesian formula: we create the Archers, therefore we exist.)

Kundera has always been a flashy writer, his chief interest in sexual discussion and gossip. This is of course so common now as to be standard practice, at least for writers in the West, and it always involves a degree of self-indulgence. His flashiness here becomes an asset, however, blending nicely with his fictive strategy, which is to separate the splendid and various experience of sex – the area of lightness and the will, conquest, curiosity and enterprise – from the heavy, fated and involuntary area of love. Love shapes the novel, sex provides the commentary: a facile arrangement, perhaps, but effective. Like Stendhal, Kundera categorizes with engaging relish the different sorts of womanizer, notably those whose obsession is *lyrical*, founded on a romantic ideal which is continually disappointed and continually reborn, and the *epic* womanizer, "whose inability to be disappointed has something scandalous about it. The obsession of the epic womanizer strikes people as lacking in redemption (redemption by disappointment)."

Tomas belongs to the second category. Being a surgeon he could not, with his mistresses, "ever quite put down the imaginary scalpel. Since he longed to take possession of something deep inside them, he needed to slit them open." Sabina, Tomas's female counterpart, is similarly questing and capricious. For her love is a kind of kitsch, a breaking of faith and truth, spoiling an honest relationship. As an epic-style female Don Juan she is the ruin of her lover Franz, whose obsession with her is of the lyric variety.

All this schematization is fairly glib: in his miniature play *The Stone Guest* Pushkin handles the theme of the light-hearted mistress, and the seducer endlessly fascinated by feminine diversity, with a true depth of art, and it seems likely that Kundera has recalled what Pushkin termed a "dramatic investigation", and made it diagrammatic and explicit. More compellingly original is the political aspect of lightness, and the fact that, as Kundera perceives, it forms the normal social atmosphere of a communist state. No one believes any more in the false weightiness of the ideology of such a state, and since that ideology has replaced old-fashioned and instinctive morality the citizens' personal lives are left in a condition of weightlessness.

Sabina associates the kitsch of love with the overwhelming kitsch of the communist regime, seeing any long-term personal fidelity or integrity as if it were an analogy of that apotheosis of kitsch, the "Grand March" towards the gleaming heights of socialism. This Kundera suggests is the vilest outcome of the totalitarian kitsch of our time: that it negates any natural and individual pattern of responsibility and weight in private life. Indeed, in a communist regime there is no private life, but only bottomless cynicism on the one side and measureless kitsch on the other. Sabina had been trained as a painter in the socialist realist manner and she soon learned to practice a subterfuge which in the end became her own highly original and personal style, and makes her rich and successful when she gets away to the West and then to America. She paints a nicely intelligible socialist reality, but with the aid of a few random drops of red paint, or something of the kind, she conjures up an unintelligible reality beneath it, an evocation of meaningless, and therefore to her saving and liberating, lightness of being. She is filled with repulsion when her admirers in the West mount an exhibition, after she has got out, showing her name and a blurb against a tasteful background of barbed wire and other symbols of oppression conquered by the human spirit. This is the same old kitsch by other means, and Sabina, who has a fastidious taste in such things, protests it is not communism she is rejecting and getting away from, but kitsch itself. "Kitsch," observes Kundera, "is the aesthetic ideal of all politicians and all political parties and movements . . . . The brotherhood of man on earth will only be possible on a basis of kitsch."

It is unfortunately typical of Kundera to run a good idea into the ground, to become increasingly entranced in the development of a lively perception until it spreads too easily. It is thus with kitsch, the concept he opposes to lightness of being, and which he deals with in a lyrical analysis in the penultimate section of the novel. The point of this is that though kitsch opposes itself to lightness of being, the true antithesis to kitsch is the weight of love and death in Tereza, the weight with which she envelops Tomas. Kitsch has no answer to death ("kitsch is a folding screen set up to curtain off death"), just as it has no relation to the true necessities of power and love. Sabina is wholly accurate in her perception of the relation between kitsch and communism: what she loathes and fears is not communist "reality" – persecution, meat queues, overcrowding, everlasting suspicion and shabbiness, all of which is quite honest and tolerable – but Soviet idealism. "In the world of communist ideal made real", the world of communist films and "grinning idiots", "she would have nothing to say, she would die of horror within a week".

The term "kitsch", as used by Kundera, oversimplifies the whole question of the mechanism by which we accept life and open our arms to its basic situations. All good writers, from Homer to Hemingway, have their own versions of it. If we accept his definition, all art would be as full of kitsch – the stereotyped formula of gracious living – as any Hollywood or Soviet film. What matters, surely, he also recognizes, is the purpose behind kitsch today, the ways in which commercial and political interests have taken over and control a basic human need. Kitsch – the word and its meaning – arrived in the nineteenth century as a substitute for the other kinds of human illusion, religious and chiliastic, which were withering away. "What makes a leftist is the kitsch of the Grand March." Yes, but what makes living endurable is the kitsch of life itself. Here Kundera, it must be said, makes a nice distinction.

> Kitsch causes two tears to flow in quick succession. The
> first tear says: How nice to see children running on the
> grass!
> The second tear says: How nice to be moved, together
> with all mankind, by children running on the grass!
> It is the second tear that makes kitsch kitsch.

Even Sabina comforts herself sometimes with the image of herself
as part of "a happy family living behind two shining windows",
but "as soon as the kitsch is recognized for the lie it is, it moves into
the context of non-kitsch, thus losing its authoritarian power and
becoming as touching as any other human weakness". By always
recognizing kitsch, Sabina shows herself incapable of those deep
involuntary movements of the soul experienced by Tereza, and
by Tomas-with-Tereza. Sabina can only know the unbearable
lightness of being.

These are old platitudes dressed up in new styles? Inevitably so,
to some extent, and like all Nietzschean demonstrators, Kundera
cannot afford to admit the relative aspect of things. Kitsch does
not define an absolute concept; it only suggests tendency and style.
Kundera has a Continental passion for getting things defined, as
when he gives us Tereza's dream vision of her death and Tomas's:

> Horror is a shock, a time of utter blindness. Horror lacks
> every hint of beauty ... Sadness, on the other hand,
> assumes we are in the know. Tomas and Tereza knew
> what was awaiting them. The light of horror thus lost its
> harshness, and the world was bathed in a gentle bluish
> light that actually beautified it.

In spite of this, his ending is imaginative and very moving, as
moving as the end of Kafka's *The Trial*. Indeed Kundera could be
said to have written a kind of *explication* of Kafka's novel, shedding
light on its basic allegory and at the same time making use of it
for the structure of a new work. Kafka's title is a deep pun. The
German word for trial – *Prozess* – could also refer to the process of

living, and it is living which is impossible for Kafka's hero, because all life has been sentenced to death. The strangest moment in *The Trial* is when the hero, about to suffer execution, sees a light go on in a nearby house and someone lean out of the window. That someone is unaware of his fate, or indifferent to it, as the process of living is unaware of death. Kundera the novelist is exceptionally aware, as Kafka was, of the difference between that process and the state of consciousness, of what he calls the unbearable lightness of being. But whereas living for Kafka was not a feasible process, for Kundera it is extremely so. And for him the real enemies of life are not Death and the Law but kitsch and the politician.

Off the Record

Vasily Grossman, *Life and Fate*, translated by
Robert Chandler (London: Collins Harvill)

Robert Chandler writes: "*Life and Fate* is the true *War and Peace* of
this century, the most complete portrait of Stalinist Russia that we
have or are ever likely to have." Chandler, who has had the Herculean task of making a good translation of this long, moving and
very remarkable novel, puts forward that claim in his introduction.
When a long honest novel comes out of Russia today comparisons
with Tolstoy are routine – I have made them myself – but in this
case it seems worth asking rather more rigorously than usual what
they really mean.

In the first place, no novel that merely resembled *War and Peace*
could be anything like it, or indeed any good. Tolstoy himself
said that *War and Peace* was not a novel, nor a piece of history, but
something unique which he felt he could make, and which the
situation called for. But apart from that, all long socialist realist
novels coming from Russia since the Revolution, including those
of Alexei Tolstoy, have in fact taken *War and Peace*, consciously or
unconsciously, as a native model. That is one reason why most of
them are so bad. What works for a genius will not do so for those
who try to avail themselves of what seems his formula. *War and
Peace* depends as heavily on the social and fictional conventions of
its time, and on the way of life of the Russian nobility, as it does on
Tolstoy's genius. You cannot transpose its method into a wholly
different social ethos and scene.

Technically speaking, the panoramic method of *War and Peace*,
which made Henry James refer to it as a "loose baggy monster",
is far more cunningly ordered than it looks. No one is dropped or

forgotten; scene dovetails neatly into scene; above all, the central event – the attempted seduction of Natasha by Anatoly Kuragin – works by placing a girl, whose "reality" has been totally established, in a totally conventional fictional situation. Tolstoy's timeless truths depend on their liaison with stock events in the novels of his time, just as his characters get their living three-dimensional selves from a participation in such events.

The instinctive confidence his characters feel in themselves comes from the fact that Tolstoy always starts on the inside of life, always with what it feels like to be oneself. From this extreme natural awareness, which first sprang into words in *Childhood, Boyhood and Youth*, comes the whole spacious breadth of the external world in *War and Peace*. And this personal inwardness is of course something altogether alien to the spirit of Soviet Russia which its literature wishes to present, and which is indeed presented in big-scale socialist realist novels, good and bad, from Sholokhov's *Quiet Don* to Grossman's *Life and Fate*.

Grossman's method is indeed socialist realism, used with a wholly Tolstoyan truth and honesty. This itself makes a disturbing, an explosive mixture. But where creating individuals is concerned, Grossman uses Tolstoy's art just as ineffectively as the merest party hack. It is not his fault. Though individuals remain basically the same, their true innerness has no chance to be revealed in a work devoted to the miseries and splendours of Russian wartime society. External pressures are too great. Grossman simply cannot afford the sense of leisure and repose which is the ground of Tolstoy's art, even though Tolstoy's *deux cent familles* offer some kind of correspondence with the Soviet *Nomenklatura*, the list of in-people suitable for high office which is kept by the Party. These persons have neither the time nor the inclination to be conscious of themselves, and they offer decidedly meagre fare to the novelist who wishes to establish his characters in a solid perspective of familiarity. So a gap yawns in the centre of *Life and Fate*. The Shaposhnikov family not only do not have the great unifying function exercised by the Rostovs in *War and Peace*, but are the only characters in Grossman's novel who are positively null, even boring.

War and Peace is much more a large-scale domestic novel than in any sense an "epic" (how much Jane Austen would have enjoyed Vera Rostova, and the incomprehensible, but absolutely authentic difference between herself and the rest of the family), and it may be that art can no longer handle that basic material of the individual and the family. It is no longer thought of as "serious" and "important". (And yet was it ever seen as being so? Probably not.) Grossman replaces it with a pattern of arbitrary fates – who was killed where, who starved, drowned, was shot, gassed, or relapsed into anonymous existence. We follow to Auschwitz Sophia Levinton, a Jewish doctor, a major in the Medical Corps, captured at Stalingrad, because she happens to be a friend of Yevgenia Shaposhnikova. The latter's brother-in-law Viktor, an atomic physicist, the most important but least realized character in the novel, is there to make the painful points about the scientist's role and responsibility under Soviet communism.

By the same paradox that operates in *Dr Zhivago*, the author, in the process of operating the random arbitrariness of coincidence and destiny, puts himself too much to the fore and becomes an all-powerful instrument of fate rather than an artist. Tolstoy is all-powerful too, but, as he himself emphasized, the novelist must by some mysterious divination of art know what is, as it were, the true fate of each character, instead of merely allotting them a part. No doubt that is simply not possible these days, and the artist who aspires to paint on the widest canvas the travails of a revolutionary society in war and peace can only imitate the honest eye-witness who is doing it "for the record". Grossman in fact bows to this technique, using it in a way that is quite exceptionally powerful and moving. His novel is a series of scenes and records, which Tolstoy's is not, although it may seem to be. In some ways Grossman is much more like Isaac Babel, on a huge scale.

So much for the stock claim in terms of construction, technique, effect. But what about the message of *War and Peace*, its celebration of Russian life, the drive of its propaganda? This is a different and more complex matter, and it must be said at once that Grossman really has managed to breathe into his novel something of the inner spirit of Tolstoy's. Tolstoy never pretended that he was writing about the whole people of Russia. What interested him was his own class, and the part it had played during the French invasion and the glorious year of 1812. Yet with his massive and almost invisible diplomacy Tolstoy manages to associate all that was best and simplest in Russia with that class – which was under strong attack at the time he was writing *War and Peace* – and with its achievement. He suggests that "good" Russia is, and always has been, classless. Such a claim is never uncommon among those at the top of the tree in any country, but Tolstoy makes it with great certainty and subtlety. So although the literary method is quite different, inevitably different, there is an almost exact subterranean correspondence between what Grossman wishes to say and what Tolstoy wished to say.

Both see with penetrating clarity that everything bad comes from the state "machine", from the people who create it and devote themselves to it, and the mass of people who submit themselves – often willingly – to its disciplines. With the French occupation of Moscow in 1812 this "machine" (his own term) is seen by Tolstoy as working with its own particular sort of mad efficiency. The "human" French soldiers consent and defer to it utterly when they are required to shoot civilians or march out the prisoners. And by one of his characteristic sleights Tolstoy suggests that the "machine" is a peculiarly French organization, pitted now against good-hearted Russia and the simple human instincts of Russians. So compelling is the machine that it not only dehumanizes the naturally good and makes them do evil acts, but paralyzes those who have created it and are a part of it. Under its influence Napoleon has no choice but to march on Russia, and further into Russia.

This business about the machine, and the human goodness it corrupts and nullifies, is of course sufficiently old hat, and it takes a creative writer of the first power, like Tolstoy, to bring home to us what it means, and to move us deeply with the spectacle. It says much for Grossman that he can do this too, using the same basic ideas, and conveying them with the same transforming passion of art. But though his position is essentially Tolstoyan, it is more complex than that of Tolstoy in *War and Peace*. Without straining the probabilities too far Tolstoy was able to oppose Russian "humanity" to French "machine". For Grossman, naturally enough, the picture has to be different: his "machine" achieves a virtually identical perfection in two places, Stalinist Russia and Hitlerite Germany. Germans have the same *entrée* to *Life and Fate* as the French had in Tolstoy's novel, and their language is frequently used in a Russian context. This tacit but significant interchangeability – of the one country and the other – would itself be abhorrent to the orthodox Soviet line, even if there were no other offences in the novel. Its time sequence is that of the siege and relief of Stalingrad, though there are frequent references back and forth, particularly to 1937, the year of the purges. A number of scenes take place on the German side, in German camps, on the trains to Auschwitz and Dachau, and in the dug-outs and headquarters of the German Sixth Army at Stalingrad: and there is no great difference in tone between the reflections and conversations on both sides. Real persons are introduced in speaking parts, as in *War and Peace* and in Solzhenitsyn's *August 1914*; there are identical attitudes, ambitions and ideologies among Soviet and German *fonctionnaires*.

The genius of both novelists appears in the compelling and spontaneous way they juxtapose the human and the non-human in scenes of swift unspoken analysis. Towards the end of *War and Peace* Colonel Denisov, now a partisan commander, discusses the fate of the French prisoners with the sinister roué Dolokhov. He is furious with Dolokhov for expressing total cynicism on the point, even though he admits the prisoners will probably die anyway, of cold and hunger. An almost exactly similar scene occurs after Stalingrad between two Russian officers, one of whom has just casually kicked a wounded German by the roadside. The fury of the other, and their quarrel, illustrates with silent irony the difference between spontaneous human goodness and the equally spontaneous need to maintain appearances. The two things depend on each other, and validate the conviction that Russians, or Germans, or English, just don't behave like that. "Are we Germans or something?" cries Natasha, when it is a question of the wounded using the carts in which the Rostovs are evacuating their belongings. How *we* behave fuses nationality with humanity in a way essentially absurd, but also saving. The machine, whether Soviet, German or English, has no time for such incongruities.

In the face of the machine, even certain kinds of smallness and selfishness become allies of human dignity. When Field-Marshal Paulus surrenders at Stalingrad his captors wait curiously for him to utter some appropriate sentiment – appropriate, that is, to one machine that has been put out of action by another. What went wrong? Where was the decisive error? Instead he says shyly: *Sagen sie mir, bitte, was ist Makhorka?* A heavy smoker, he is enquiring about Russian tobacco. All he can think of is will he be able to get something to smoke and eat, be given some warm place to sleep. He has been reduced to just the same small preoccupations and anxieties as the ordinary soldier.

Grossman was a war correspondent who worked for the army newspaper *Red Star* and witnessed the disasters of '41, the defence of Stalingrad and the eventual fall of Berlin. As a popular wartime newsman, he was second only to Ehrenburg. In a way, he was in the position of Pierre at Borodino, whom Tolstoy uses as an inno-cent observer, whose eye makes the routine horrors of battle strange, and thus even more terrible. Tolstoy himself had been in the same kind of dangerous and yet privileged position at Sevasto-pol. But for Grossman as a writer his firsthand knowledge and penetrating sense of the truth ("My hero is truth," wrote Tolstoy in *Sevastopol Sketches*) is touchingly undermined by years of con-ditioning in socialist realist propaganda. Many of the scenes of the Stalingrad fighting in *Life and Fate* are as heroically stylized as those in any of the innumerable Russian novels about the war years. It looks as if Grossman had decided to include much of the same standard material that he had already used in *For a Just Cause*, the epic about Stalingrad which he had begun in 1943, and which had been published in *Novy Mir* after the war. Favourably reviewed, and frequently reprinted, it eventually earned the author in 1955 the coveted decoration of "the Banner of Labour". But in the previous years, before Stalin's death, Grossman's position, as a

Russo-Jewish writer, had become decidedly insecure. Fadayev, watchdog and lackey of the Writers' Union, had attacked him. With the thaw, and Khrushchev's denunciation of Stalin's crimes, his fortunes revived, and Fadayev switched over to praising his work.

It seems likely that Grossman hoped that the change of climate would make *Life and Fate* acceptable, which is why he made much of the Stalingrad material as conventional as *For a Just Cause*. He may thus have hoped to smuggle into print a wholly new attitude to the Patriotic War, at a time when, in spite of Stalin's death, Russian chauvinism was increasingly a feature of the Soviet machine. If so, he was soon undeceived. The Cultural Section of the Central Committee pronounced the novel anti-Soviet (they were right), and the KGB stepped in, confiscating every piece of MS they could get hold of. Suslov, the leading Party ideologue, himself wrote to Grossman that the novel could not possibly be published for the next two hundred years, a pronouncement which, among other things, carries echoes of the Fifty Year Rule and the Thousand Year Reich. State machines have an *Alice in Wonderland* attitude about their own longevity. The Soviet émigré writer Vladimir Voinovich, who managed twenty years after its completion to get a copy to the West, observed that Suslov's remark was at least a tribute to the novel's lasting importance.

Grossman was isolated, not arrested. He continued to write, and the short novel, *Forever Flowing*, which he began in 1955, a meditation on the camps, the kulaks, and the fate of Russia generally, was published in the West in 1972. By then, Grossman had been dead for nearly ten years, living at the end alone and in poverty, and uncertain whether his great book had survived and would ever come out. As Robert Chandler observes, the strength of Grossman is that of an insider, who had participated closely in Soviet society and was as familiar with its old-boy network as Tolstoy had been with the Tsarist establishment. Like many Russian Jews, he had been particularly loyal to the regime throughout the war and the purges, and unlike Pasternak and the Mandelstams, he had spoken its language and known it from within. He strikes one, ironically, as a native member of the *Nomenklatura*, just as Tolstoy was a native of the aristocracy: both have the common touch, in the particular sense of enjoying and celebrating what the Russians call a *byt*, a way of life natural and dear to them; and both combine this sense of belonging with a penetrating and wholly independent intelligence which, in the end, will not let them belong. It is an interesting question whether Grossman's growing realization of the way things were, and his need to record them, derived wholly or in part from the persecution of the Russo-Jewish intelligentsia at the time of the doctor's plot.

Pushkin's scribe Pimen, in *Boris Godunov*, is a recorder of all that goes on in the Russian state, in "war and peace", a phrase that may well have given Tolstoy his title. Grossman's aim, too, was such a record, sober and accurate, the more so, in a sense, from using the conventional literary form of the time – socialist realism – as Pimen had used the monkish chronicle. In formalistic terms, the falsities, which are also the received conventions, stand to the truths of his narrative as the conventions of an epic or thriller do to the real world it reveals. Thus extended scenes or dialogues, like those between fighter pilots, tank men and other heroic figures, sound all wrong, although in a manner the reader is quite used to. This may reflect the Russian admiration for Kipling's version of the way professionals talk at their work, although it is obvious that both Kipling's and Grossman's characters are talking, not for each other's benefit, but for the reader. In both cases, this is the falsity produced by the realistic reportage of a good war correspondent.

But in between the surfaces of this conventional stuff are small, understated perceptions and awarenesses which gradually transform the whole and give it a secret and a truthful life. Many of these are ironic or funny, building up a deliberate contrast between the war correspondent's official version of things and how it actually was. The hero of the main Stalingrad defence, General Chuikov, is so angry with a chief of staff who disagrees with him on the exact position of the front line that he knocks his front teeth out. He also abandons his command post to attend a dinner on the safe bank of the Volga to celebrate the founding of the Cheka. The soldiers watch the grandees arriving for this as if they were colourful fish in a warm glass tank. Such details are not for the official record, and neither is the real story of what happened in a strong-point cut off by the Germans and defended by a brilliant "housekeeper" in a manner quite at variance with proper Soviet practice. The political instructor who gets through to it reports back in a shocked way that they are behaving "like some kind of Paris commune rather than a military unit". Grossman's account of "House 6/I" blends a sentimental romance between a young soldier and a girl radio operator with a sardonic picture of what happens to heroism which can't be fitted into the proper mould. As Tolstoy says, intrigue on one's own side is always worse than the malice of the enemy. The real threat to "House 6/I" is not the Germans (though they eventually wipe it off the map) but the politicals at the rear who are trying to take it over for their own purposes. An unexpected touch of surrealism is added by an old soldier who refuses to believe that *War and Peace* is not about this war, in which Tolstoy himself must be fighting, because his reports are so much truer than those of the correspondents.

Faithful to the spirit of his model, Grossman celebrates the defence of the homeland against the Germans, as Tolstoy did against the French: but both deprecate the un-Russian spirit of mean efficiency, and ruthless indifference to the human cost, which seeks to carry the war into the enemy country and liquidate him like the kulaks or the party dissidents. When her sons have saved Russia the Party steps in and takes the credit, giving the cold shoulder to uncommitted loyalty and decency. Stalin in the Kremlin reflects that success has now condemned his victims to limbo: "Nobody quarrels with a victor." The commander of the tank corps which successfully completed the encirclement of Stalingrad is reported on unfavourably by the corps commissar for holding up his attack for a few minutes in order to ensure his men won't be decimated for lack of artillery support; and at the end of the novel he seems headed for demotion and possible disgrace. As at the end of *War and Peace*, victory seems only to have confirmed tyranny and made it both more confident and more suspicious.

Of course everybody knows this now. Grossman's fervour is years out of date, and even at the time must have seemed a voice crying in the wilderness. The old paradox obtains. What for Suslov must not be published for two hundred years, lest it amaze and confound the faithful, is in the West merely a repetition of what we have been told many times, or what we can work out for ourselves. We can also raise our own objections, for Grossman's propaganda is no more absolutely true than Tolstoy's. Patriotism and decency are all very well, but what won the war was the sheer brutal discipline and drive of the Red Army and the Party – their ability, by whatever means, to keep up the ammunition supply, to get the guns and the conscripts into action. No one who reads John Erickson's account of the four-year Russian campaign, lifeless and over-documented as it is, can fail to be struck by the extraordinary achievements of that vigorous and dynamic totalitarianism, achievements in the tradition of Genghis Khan himself. And all this was, so to speak, a family affair, giving intense pride even to the most non-political of Russians, for Grossman's parallels between the Nazi and communist systems ignore the continuous political tradition on the Russian side. Stalin was no mystic Fuehrer but Khosain, the owner, the boss, just like Peter the Great, and he himself was fully aware of the relation. It is ironic that the Party never referred to the Nazis but always to the Fascists, for "National Socialism" was altogether too near home. But though the two systems functioned in an identical way, the national difference between them was nonetheless very great.

Assent on both sides was equally overwhelming, and in a sense still is. Rather engagingly, Grossman has a weakness for the old thriller technique in which villains love to make long speeches to helpless heroes in defence of their policies, speeches of great elegance and philosophical subtlety. O'Brien does it in *1984*, and the interrogator Gletkin in *Darkness at Noon*. In *Life and Fate* a cultured SS officer of high rank, a friend of Eichmann, enjoys long discussions with his old Bolshevik prisoner from Stalingrad, remarking that it doesn't really matter which side wins, since both stand for the same thing, and thus victory for their joint policy is assured.

Towards the end of the novel the same kind of talk takes place in a cell in the Lubianka, where Krymov, one of the Party faithful arrested at Stalingrad for not taking a more vigorous line about House 6/I, finds himself incarcerated with another unexpected victim, a veteran Chekist whose aesthetic love for the whole system is so great that he imagines a time when there will be no difference between being in a camp and outside one.

Naturally, the old Bolsheviks are appalled and agonized by the cynicism of the SS man and the old Chekist, who treat them as no different from themselves. To the reader, however, the tableau is both commonplace and unconvincing. Russians love to talk, and the way they talk (lying under an idea as if under a stone, as Chadayev said) is more intense and dramatic than anything that usually takes place in a free society. But conversations designed solely to emphasize a point to the reader are unconvincing in any fictional context. SS and KGB men are far cruder and more naive types than this, and their conversation would most likely be meaninglessly depressing, or as banal as the chat of businessmen in a bar. Equally unconvincing are the sentiments of the heroic "housekeeper", Grekov, to the lads in House 6/I.

> No one has the right to lead other people like sheep. That's something even Lenin failed to understand. The purpose of a revolution is to free people. But Lenin just said: "In the past you were led badly, I'm going to lead you well."

Unexceptionable sentiments, but they are fatally compromised by being set in the socialist realist mould. They might fascinate and appal the Russian reader (though would they really today?), but us they excite as little as would their mirror image in the same style of a young soldier proclaiming Lenin's beneficent divinity. The medium, in a sense, nullifies the message. We can also understand why, in a piece entitled "Le Cas Grossman" in a French periodical (*L'Age d'Homme*, 1983), Simon Markish quoted a Russian friend's comment on *Life and Fate*: "Yes, all this is noble, elevated, morally irreproachable, but I don't need a follower of Leo Tolstoy's."

That reaction is natural, almost unavoidable, and yet the novel survives it triumphantly. I strongly agree with Chandler, who in his excellent introduction is aware of all such criticisms ("the novel is indeed a remarkably old-fashioned one") and yet remains convinced of its inherent freshness and importance. The defects and drawbacks are obvious: ideology, propaganda, "the clash between freedom and totalitarianism" – all these things take on an academic quality from the fact that they are painted as the old academicians used to paint. And yet the novel can still present a disturbing, an explosive mixture.

Structurally, it is dead: spiritually, it could not be more alive. There is even a certain justice about the fact that Grossman, who detests all forms of political and moral organizations, should himself be unable as a writer to organize his book on such lines. Although the scale is so impressive, the detail so varied and compelling, the true life of the book seems obstinately to exist independently, between and among all these forces that have been marshalled to make it. This is its truest, most secret relation to *War and Peace*. It also contrasts very sharply with the method and outlook of Solzhenitsyn in his big novels, particularly the current *roman fleuve* of which the first instalment was *August 1914*.

Solzhenitsyn has a passion for dogmas and explanations which represent, it could be said, the other side of Tolstoy, his overbearingly dogmatic side. Grossman clearly regards Solzhenitsyn's attitudes with deep dislike. One of his conversation tableaux, in a gulag, sets the "mystical obscurantist" types against those who merely want "the path of freedom and democracy" for Russia. (The young opponent of the "obscurantists" is proud of the fact that unlike the others he is there for a real reason: he has written an article entitled "The State of Lenin and Stalin", and distributed it to his students.)

What fill the mind at the end of *Life and Fate* are the innumerable glimpses the book contains of "senseless kindness". This is the phrase used by a dotty old creature who has ended up in Dachau, and who has managed to preserve a kind of essay, a very Tolstoyan document, on what men really live by. This gets into the hands of the SS officer Liss, who maliciously conveys it to the old Bolshevik

prisoner Mostovskoy, whom he loves to talk with and ideologically torment. Both regard the document, whose insertion has
a parallel in the Grand Inquisitor passage in *The Brothers Karamazov*,
as a piece of crazy nonsense, beneath contempt: and yet the old
Bolshevik, who will soon be liquidated anyway, is secretly tormented by it as much as he is by the SS man's affable intimacies.

Senseless, unwitnessed, such kindness is "outside any system of
social or religious good". It is "as simple as life itself", and yet
"even the teachings of Jesus deprived it of its strength". Christianity
in its time killed it as effectively as modern totalitarianism. The
sentiments of the holy fool are not particularly original – indeed it
could be said that acts of "senseless kindness" are usually no more
than gestures of human self-satisfaction, the universal sentiment
Tolstoy understood so well – and yet in some extraordinary way
Grossman's entire novel endorses the old mad man's point with all
the secret force of which the language of art is capable. "Art" is the
operative word, for Grossman's old-fashioned simplicities, and his
extensive use of secondhand techniques, might lead the reader to
suppose that he is not an original artist. The proof that he is is
shown more than anything by the fact that we are not "moved"
or "horrified", in the obvious sense, by the most memorable scenes
and sequences in the novel – like the one in which a trainload from
Eastern Europe arrives at Auschwitz, to be followed through the
"bath-house" into the gas chamber. Art here shows itself to be
deeply, and as it were naturally, in league with "senseless kindness",
as at the moment when a woman in the queue for the gas chamber
painstakingly brushes the mud off the back of another's dress, or
when a small boy sees the movement as a fan starts in the ceiling to
suck in the cyanide, and thinks that some bird or animal has been
trapped up there. One of the most memorable scenes in the novel,
quite near the beginning, simply describes how a mother goes to
the cemetery of a military hospital to visit the grave of her son, a
lieutenant who has just died of wounds. She hugs his grave, as if
she could still warm him and comfort him inside it.

Art in the novel is no good without a personality to go with it.
Not only is Grossman's extremely appealing, but it is part of the

nature of the appeal that it escapes from "the machine" – the full gruesomeness of whose impact upon the lives of Soviet citizens it continually but almost incidentally reveals – without rejecting it. It sets up no counter-philosophy, like Solzhenitsyn's, to fight the system: and partly for this reason, Grossman's personality and awareness of things are much more congenial than Solzhenitsyn's. Only a man indifferent to the real voice of art, a man who insists that the novel must above all things be *novel* – aligned with whatever kind of Modernism is currently valid – could dismiss *Life and Fate* as merely "noble, elevated, morally irreproachable". It is a work whose greatest recommendation is that it has no need to be in tune with the times. And yet, as Suslov inadvertently pointed out, in his act of refusal and denial to its author, the times are all too likely never to be out of tune with what Grossman has written, and how he has written it.

Waiting for Real Water

Andrei Voznesensky, *Nostalgia for the Present:
Selected Poems* (Oxford: Oxford University Press)

One tradition the Soviet Union has failed to carry on from nine-teenth-century Russia – indeed one among many – is that good art is more deeply political than bad art. There is a sense, of course, in which this is true with us too, but we need not take much notice of it. Yet good poetry, to paraphrase Péguy, does begin in the indivi-dual and end up in the political. Larkin say, or Lowell, would not be the poets they are if this were not the case: their attitudes are not a question of liberal beliefs or party allegiances, yet they are in-tensely if obscurely important to our sense of the whole of a society.

The same is true of one of the best Russian poets writing today, Voznesensky. If any truly individual voice in art sharply modifies our sense of the political, how much more must this be the case in Russia? There have always been elements of cipher and subterfuge in Voznesensky's work, just as there were at times in Pushkin's, but this is a question for the reader's intuition, as it would be in such a poem of Larkin's as "Homage to a Government". The seasoned Russian reader could detect something going on in the title poem of this collection, "Nostalgia for the Present", and he would no doubt refer its indefinable political point, as one should, not to society but to other poetry. In the timeless continuum of the Soviet state it would be easy for the past to seem attractive, and banal to be looking forward to the future, the gleaming heights of socialism, or the yawning heights, as Zinoviev punned on them.

> Whatever is past is past. So much the better.
> But I bite at it as at a mystery,
>   nostalgia for the impending present.
>   And I'll never catch hold of it.

There is a probable echo of a poem by Tvardovsky.

> In history's golden book of fame
> No doubtful comma, not a crooked line
> Shall cast a shadow on our name.
> What's done is done.

Tvardovsky was an excellent poet, and this poem, in part fulsome praise of Stalin for his war leadership, is by no means bad. But Solzhenitsyn bitterly attacked the "what's done is done": it seems likely that Voznesensky noticed it too. So things crawl under the surface of his "Nostalgia for the Present" poem, just as they should do, but they are more involuntary, more dangerous and vulnerable, than they would be in a poem written in England or America. Like other religions, communism has no time for the present: revelation was in the past and salvation in the future. Auden's "Spain", in its curious half-false, half-true way makes the same point. Voznesensky's poem has also its underground contraditions.

> And when the Mafia laughs in my face
> idiotically I say:
> "Idiots are all in the past. The present
> calls for fuller understanding".

But then follows a metaphor of water beginning to run clear.

> Black water spurts from the faucet
> Brackish water, stale water,
> rusty water flows from the faucet – I'll wait
> for the real water to come.

The poem muddles itself deliberately, but does not muddle its subterranean attack on dogma and stagnant idealism.

Voznesensky loves America, is mad about blue jeans and campuses and the fads that go with them. And the mostly American poets who have adapted into a kind of American poetry the literal translations provided for them have done an excellent job, as have Vera Dunham and the late Max Hayward, whose services to Russian literature will be sadly missed. Like most of the younger Russian poets Voznesensky's poetry is written to be spoken, indeed declaimed theatrically, and he has a very special kind of virtuosity with sounds and syllables which of course vanishes, but an equivalent kind of American idiom is an acceptable alternative. Robert Bly, Lawrence Ferlinghetti, Stanley Kunitz, Louis Simpson and William Jay Smith are poets whose idiom, given language differences, is wholly congenial to that of the Russian, and the results are as felicitous as might be expected from that.

Nevertheless one sees why Akhmatova had such a contempt for Voznesensky's work – it was not just the jealousy of the old master for the expertise of the young and wholly Soviet product. There is something altogether too *winning* about his poems, though this can be itself the key to a deeper kind of success:

> O Suzdal Mother of God
> shining on the white wall,
>   like that lady cashier
>   in her oval ticket window
> provide me with a ticket
> to that movie
>   that can only be seen
>   by those under sixteen

That is winning but very moving too, and applies as much to our odiously secularized pornographic society as it would to the equivalent in officially aetheist Russia. William Jay Smith and Vera Dunham make a most moving translation too of "Prayer" ("Lord I grow for Thee, for Thee alone") which contrasts oddly with their offbeat rendering of "Picture Gallery".

> "Mama, who's that funny man up there
> Flying with his arms out off that cross?"
> "That must be some instructor of calisthenics, dear,
> Whose act may be tough to follow, of course."

The completely different tone is typical of Voznesensky, who can command a great variety. His simplest religious imagery does not exactly fit into the poetry of American cosmopolitanism, but that is part of the charm. Where so much else in the poetry mingles with it effortlessly – the uncannily good translation of "Requiem" might be rendered with banjos at any student gathering – there is a private intensity and loneliness at the heart of the Orthodox imagery which keeps even in the depersonalized idiom of cosmopolitanism its national character.

Otherwise this is a highly social poetry and very conscious of reaching hands across the sea. The poem to Robert Lowell, and another in memory of him, make that almost too clear. The latter recalls his visit as a tourist to places of historic and poetic interest in Moscow, and Voznesensky's return visit to Lowell's grave in Massachusetts, bringing berries that in Russia are a symbol of the Resurrection:

> . . . And bring these berries from Pasternak's rowan tree
> For all the good that rowanberries do.

The most interesting poem in the collection, though not the best, is "Story Under Full Sail", a narration in parts based on the remarkable story of Nikolai Rezanov, who rose to be captain of Catherine the Great's guards and then went exploring in the Bering Sea and terrorized the coast of Japan before he sailed over to Vancouver Island and San Francisco. Here he fell in love with the daughter of the Spanish governor. His feelings were returned, and the pair persuaded their parents to let them be betrothed, but before the marriage took place Rezanov had to return to Russia to report his spectacular achievements, and died half way across Siberia. When she learned of his death, the governor's daughter took the veil and became the first nun in California. This romantic piece of history has, as one might imagine, a strong appeal for Voznesensky, who gives it allegorical overtones. The link between Russia and Californian civilization goes with his feeling for cosmopolitan possibilities, and indeed it might have been more than a link: if Rezanov's schemes had matured and been implemented the entire western littoral of what is now the USA might have been solidly settled by the Russians when the American pioneers arrived there.

Brodsky and Auden

It would be tempting to say that Brodsky and Auden are the only really civilized great poets of their respective generations, and of the past few decades. Tempting, and in spite of the difficulty of saying what one means exactly, far from untrue. Civilization, in their context, is an affair of basic humour, a humour which is naturally present in every aspect of their being and their works, like salt in sea water. With most poets, and writers generally, there is a point at which humour stops, if it has ever started. Many poets, like other writers, can be skittish, or funny, or deeply and wisely comical; and they cultivate these qualities – as Robert Frost did, say, or as Robert Lowell did – in league with their personalities and poetic will. But humour only really exists as the spirit of civilization if it is everywhere inside it, and inside the poetry that can be its expression.

Humour is also an involuntary aspect of personality, the motor nerve of its unconscious linkage to art. Wallace Stevens is at least as great a poet as Auden or Brodsky, but his poetry is extruded on a quite different principle, one sign of which is that one knows exactly where in it the humour begins and ends. Stevens could never have written in a poem "We must love one another or die", and then changed it to "We must love one another and die". But possibly Goethe could: in fact on the evidence of the Roman Elegies and some of the poems in the *Ost-Westlicher Divan* he certainly could. For Goethe, surprisingly enough, was a poet of total humour, as of total civilization, despite all evidence to the contrary. And Brodsky reminds us that twenty years after he wrote "September 1, 1939" Auden expressed a desire to "become, if possible, a minor Atlantic Goethe". Brodsky calls this an extremely significant admission, and indeed there is all Auden's humour (and Brodsky's own in the recognition of it) in the juxtaposition of "Goethe" with "Atlantic". It is the comic apotheosis of civilization's possibilities, and yet – like all the best humour – expressing itself with no deliberate consciousness of itself.

Brodsky's discussion of "September 1, 1939" is based on a class given at Columbia University, taped and transcribed by two of his students. It is detailed and quite long, and may well, one feels, have started up a lifelong love of Auden's poetry in many students. It is not a bit theoretical, and it contains a great deal of information – some of it controversial – about love, poetry, politics and sex. In tone and inspiration it is not unlike Nabokov's lectures on the Russian writers and on Kafka (in the course of which he had a good deal to say about exactly what sort of beetle Gregor Samsa had been turned into in *The Metamorphosis*, and why he made no attempt to unfurl his wings from their wing-cases and fly away). It is, that is to say, a free monologue by one poet on another's poem, which reveals to what extent both poets possess the humour and the civilization I speak of.

> I sit in one of the dives
> On Fifty-second Street
> Uncertain and afraid
> As the clever hopes expire
> Of a low dishonest decade:

Brodsky points out that the first three lines contain a large variety of suggestions and gambits. The opening line is both factual and metrically inert, but the second firmly establishes the trimeter rhythm, a rhythm which identifies itself from then on with any and every shift of sense and expression. The first two lines announce a kind of toughness – the seasoned observer or journalist looking out for copy – but the third line unexpectedly contradicts this image. The locality given, and the word "dive", shows a poet both confident in the idiom and geography of a new country, and drawing attention to his confidence. At the same time he is "uncertain and afraid". The poem is, among other things, a charm to overcome those feelings, as well as to naturalize the poet's idiom in a new country, and among the hospitalities of its own ways of speech.

For Brodsky, who has also become a multilingual poet and writer, this extension of language as the vessel and vehicle of civilization is of great significance. It is the resourcefulness, and above all the adaptibility, of language as poets and writers can manifest it that saves cultures and societies from the night, and from the "unmentionable odour of death". "September 1, 1939" owes its remarkable memorability and power to the fact that although civilization looks like collapsing, language is not: neither is language being subjected to the dreadful humourlessness of tyranny, to those ogres who – as Auden was later to put it in an epigram on the Russian invasion of Czechoslovakia – "cannot master speech". To master speech, as Auden and Brodsky have done it, matters far more than any amount of earnest protests or right-thinking exhortations. Brodsky refers to Hellenic Greece, and by implication to demotic Cavafy, as an example of how language can triumph when empire fails; and emphasizes that the vitality of English, extending "from Fresno to Kuala Lumpur, so to speak", is embodied by Auden's poem, written at a time when the English polity was in a parlous state. No matter what their local and parochial affiliations, his audience can be inspired, partly by the poem's aid, "to become citizens of the Great English Language".

There is no pretension in this, and the process, like the genius of the language itself, is essentially a humorous one. But for Brodsky there is nothing funny about what has happened to his own native tongue. He sees the effect on the Russian language of the Revolution as "an unprecedented anthropological tragedy, a genetic backslide whose net result is a drastic reduction of human potential". Poetry may have survived, in inner or outer exile, but Russian prose could not escape in that way, or survive the embrace of the state. Because the new state could not master speech it forced Russian prose to talk its own gobbledygook. Significantly, Brodsky thinks that Platonov, the author of the fantastic novels *Chevengur* and *The Foundation Pit*, is the truest and most imaginative master of Russian prose since the Soviet state began, because he successfully recreated Russian syntax and exposition to show – by his own kinds of exaggeration and distortions – what the Soviet mentality was doing to them.

> What's interesting about Platonov's style is that he appears to have deliberately and completely subordinated himself to the vocabulary of his Utopia – with all its cumbersome neologisms, abbreviations, acronyms, bureaucratese, sloganeering, militarised imperatives, and the like. In a sense one can see this writer as an embodiment of language temporarily occupying a piece of time and reporting from within. The essence of his message is LANGUAGE IS A MILLENARIAN DEVICE, HISTORY ISN'T, and coming from him that would be appropriate. Of course, to get into excavating the genealogy of Platonov's style one has inevitably to mention the "plaiting of words" of centuries of Russian hagiography, Nikolai Leskov with his tendency to highly individualised narrative (so-called "skaz" – sort of "yarn-ing"), Gogol's satirical epic sway, Dostoevsky with his snowballing, feverishly choking conglomeration of dictions. But with Platonov the issue is not lines of succession or tradition in Russian literature but the writer's dependence on the synthesising (or, more precisely, supra-analytical) essence of the Russian language itself, conditioning – at times by means of purely phonetic allusions – the emergence of concepts totally devoid of any real content.

Soviet Russian linguistic usage became like a sort of Potemkin village, and Platonov was doing what Orwell could not have done: inventing his own sort of newspeak and subverting the whole concept from inside. But, as Brodsky points out, it is by no means clear that subversion was Platonov's aim: the language and style he invented, with their own massive volume of inchoate humour, does it for him. The hero of *Chevengur* gets it into his head that socialism may have emerged somewhere in a natural, elemental way; so he gets on his horse, which he has named Rosa Luxemburg, and sets off to discover whether or not that is the case. It is language, not socialism, that emerges in a natural, elemental way, and the Soviet establishment has tried to create one as it has created the other. It viewed Platonov with the gravest suspicion, and would probably have proceeded against him if he had not already been terminally ill with tuberculosis, contracted while looking after his son, who had been in a labour camp. *Chevengur* and *The Foundation Pit* have never been published in the Soviet Union.

In "Catastrophies in the Air", his essay on the trend of the recent Russian novel, Brodsky suggests that the anti-Soviet novel has been insensibly compelled to adopt the language strategies of its opponent. Solzhenitsyn's *Cancer Ward*, for all its power and its sympathy, is socialist realism in reverse; and Brodsky comments on the moment when he felt the writing in the novel was about to take off, so to speak, while describing the daily grind of a Soviet woman doctor, but this never happened. To show the idiocy of the system Solzhenitsyn was conscientiously pursuing a technique designed to show the heroic virtues of the system. Except for immediate purposes of propaganda the message was fatally trapped in the medium, at least as regards what Brodsky feels to be the true traditions of Russian art. That art – Gogol's or Platonov's art – does nothing so banal as merely to guy the system, or even make serious criticisms of it. "The power of devastation they inflict upon their subject matter exceeds by far any demands of social criticism. Platonov had a tendency to see his words to their logical, that is absurd, that is totally paralysing, end. In other words, like no other Russian writer before or after him, he was able to reveal a self-destructive, eschatological element within the language itself, and that, in turn, was of extremely revealing consequences to the revolutionary eschatology with which history supplied him as subject matter".

For Brodsky, Platonov is a touchstone indicating what is wrong with other recent Russian prose, whether inside the Soviet system or in revolt against it. Even such a moving book as Vassily Grossman's *Life and Fate*, a "family" novel which takes place in Russia at the time of Stalingrad, does suffer from being locked into the system, stylistically speaking, so that its powerful scorn for the Nazi and communist ideologies, which it regards as virtually equivalent, cannot escape from the stylistic atmosphere which they have perpetuated. Brodsky clearly has great respect also for Sinyavsky and for Voinovich, but it might be felt that fate and history have placed them too outside the vanished world of civilization and humour to which he and Auden in some way belong. So too do their younger successors like Aksyonov, Dovlatov and Limonov, all writers to whom it is second nature to use fantasy and the grotesque as protest. Brodsky is probably right to suggest that as a result of the "genetic backslide" nothing in recent Russian prose has equalled what it achieved and promised in the twenties and thirties.

But to return for a moment to Auden's poem, and to Brodsky's relations with it. He perceives the way in which the art of the poem – its humorous civilization – in fact tolerates and accepts the didacticism and unease to which it gives expression. Auden's style had always specialized in exhortation within a framework of family comedy, the threatened civilization of ourselves. Now there is a note of kidding in the level, with the charmed circle really under threat, and yet still possessing the confidence and the spell of art. Auden was wrong in thinking that the famous poem showed "the preacher's loose immodest tone", and banishing it from his collected corpus. As Brodsky says, "We must love one another and die", the modification which Auden made before deciding to scrap the whole thing, is "a platitude with a misleading air of profundity". "We must love one another or die", the original, is far from being a simple directive: it parodies itself in the act of utterance, confirming the "understanding" of the civilized family, and its real loss of nerve, in the gesture of imitating a more impersonal and evangelical authority. The whole poem asserts the personal "in a rapture of distress", and while asserting that the personal is done for, and that sterner, more comprehensive measures are needed to combat the march of false ideology.

Brodsky's own poetry shows why this poem is so congenial to him, and so worthy of extended commentary. Many of his poems,

"Cape Cod" for instance ("A codfish stands at the door"), are saturated with an Audenian fullness of humour. More important, a poem like the one on Marshal Zhukov's funeral – one of Brodsky's very best, to my mind – in the collection *A Part of Speech*, shows how naturally he joins in with the annals of civilization, and their celebration, which includes the writing of fine tributes to generals, princes, fellow poets, assorted grandees. When such poems are at their best, and alive, they are always funny, never obsequious. There is a good deal of irony in the fact that Brodsky and Auden are so good at writing these public and commemorative poems which most other good poets – poets in the West especially – would fight distinctly shy of. It is partly because "the public", for these two poets, is an extension of their own large world of civilized privacy. They experience none of that anxiety and guilt which most poets today feel at the idea of privilege and grandeur – "culture is 'elitist' by definition" remarks Brodsky in the course of his essay on Nadezhda Mandelstam – the guilt which has an inhibiting effect on poetry's becoming a part of the grace and decoration of high life. There is a good deal of irony in the fact that dozens of Soviet hack poets would have been willing and able to produce tributes on the death of Marshal Zhukov – if it had been a good thing politically which in his case it probably wasn't – as they had produced flocks of odes to Lenin, Stalin, Kirov, Khrushchev, etc. The ease with which Brodsky and Auden move among the great in their poems is of course the opposite of the expedient sycophancy which constrained even Akhmatova to produce a poetic greeting to Stalin (she hammed it up deliberately so that friends could read between the lines). But the touch-me-not fastidiousness of Western poetry is in some ways as regrettable as the vulgar sycophancy of Soviet poets. Certainly Auden would have loved Brodsky's poem on Zhukov, and appreciated to the full its adroitly Marvellian mixture of admiration and criticism, together with the way in which metre, sound, and sentiment echo the eighteenth-century Russian poet Derzhavin's "Bullfinch" (the soldiers' fife), a poem celebrating the death of the great Marshal Suvorov.

Brodsky's title piece, "Less than One", takes us back to his

Petersburg childhood, and "A Guide to a Renamed City" is a wonderful evocation of the former capital, a city in which a man "spends as much time on foot as a good Bedouin". Although "Less than One" is vitriolic on the subject of Russian politics, the general effect of these essays is of an intelligence as lyrical and benign as Auden's own. The two pieces on him are outstanding, and there are equally brilliant essays on other poets, on Akhmatova, Tsvetaeva and Mandelstam, Dante, Montale, and Derek Walcott – the last the most illuminating and understanding appraisal that has been written about the West Indian poet. There is a remarkable meditation on Byzantium, another on the background of Cavafy; and finally a section on childhood, parents, and early days in Leningrad (universally known by its population as "Peter") titled "In a Room and a Half", the unit of accommodation in which the young Brodsky lived with his father and mother.

I found these recollections even more entrancing, if possible, than Nabokov's *Speak, Memory*, or Mandelstam's memoir *The Noise of Time*. Born in 1940, not a propitious year, Brodsky was the only child, and very close to both his parents. His mother was from Latvia, originally a German speaker; his father, also Jewish, came from a Petersburg family who kept a print shop. By profession a journalist and photographer, he became an officer in the Soviet navy during the war and was stationed in the far east. After the war he was appointed a curator of the Naval Museum, situated on Basil Island in the centre of the town and one of its most beautiful buildings, with wide views up and down the Neva. (When I was there on a brief stay as a tourist it was unfortunately always closed, or said to be closed, as if the authorities viewed with suspicion the idea of a Westerner taking an undue interest in Russian naval history.)

Brodsky used to meet his father there after work and the pair of them would walk home together.

> There is something in the granular texture of the granite pavement next to the constantly flowing, departing water that instils in one's soles an almost sensual desire for walking. The seaweed-smelling headwind from the sea has

cured here many hearts saturated with lies, despair, and powerlessness.

Although now so much a citizen of the world, and a writer and poet in English as well as in Russian, Brodsky must miss his native city very much. His parents had no desire to leave it, though they schemed for years, unsuccessfully, to visit their son in America. As earlier citizens like Pushkin and Amsiferov demonstrate ("There is in this city the pathos of space" observed the latter) to be a Petersburger is at once to be a cosmopolitan and a passionate devotee of "Peter's creation". Pushkin's most wonderful poem, *The Bronze Horseman*, celebrates the great statue of Peter which confronts the Neva, and also tells a tragic tale of the floods to which the city is still liable, a tale of powerlessness and despair in the face of the brutal authority which the Horseman represents. The city is founded on such ambiguities, and Brodsky also remarks that it "is the city where it is somehow easier to endure loneliness than anywhere else: because the city itself is so lonely". This is the loneliness of Gogol's and of Dostoevsky's heroes.

Brodsky's own father was well aware of the ambiguity, being intensely proud of the Russian navy and its annals (Peter's Admiralty is still the largest and longest building in the world) and resigned to the fact that he had to leave the navy, and earn a precarious living as a trade photographer, because the Soviet authorities had decreed that no Jew could rise higher in the navy than the rank of Commander. Unable to be promoted, he was therefore bowlerhatted. His son shares the same ambiguous pride, as befits a Russian poet, and as also befits a poet and the son of a navy man he has a great sense of flags, their history and symbolic significance. In his essay on Byzantium he comments on the fact that the Turkish empire has always represented power as unambiguously as the Soviet state today, and that their red flag, with its white star and crescent, has a decided affinity with the Soviet red flag with its hammer and sickle, a mixture of Turkish crescent and Tsarist cross, and in terms of design surely one of the least graceful emblems ever devised. By contrast Brodsky yearns for the flag of the old Russian navy, "not because of its spectacular victories, of which there have been rather few, but because of the nobility of spirit which has informed its enterprise", inspiring long voyages of discovery and the charting of unknown seas.

> To this day, I think the country would do a hell of a lot better if it had for its national banner not that foul double-headed imperial fowl or the vaguely masonic hammer-and-sickle, but the flag of the Russian navy: our glorious, incomparably beautiful flag of St Andrew: the diagonal blue cross against a virgin-white background.

The Art of Austerity

Zbigniew Herbert, *Selected Poems*, translated by
Czeslaw Milosz and Peter Dale Scott (Manchester: Carcanet);
Report from the Besieged City, translated by
John and Bogdana Carpenter (New York: The Ecco Press)

In *The Unbearable Lightness of Being*, Milan Kundera imagines his
fiction in terms of a metaphysics of history. Since nothing repeats
itself, nothing really happens – if by "happening" we mean an
event of permanent human significance, an event which causes us
to weep or rejoice, to feel indignation and anger, as we do in
response to the things that touch us nearly in our daily lives. A
fiction can be imagined in terms of the German saying, *einmal ist
keinmal*; what takes place in it has no reality, since what happens
once has not happened at all. Hitler or Genghis Khan can kill as
many people as they want: it is merely one more for the book, and
a novelist can re-create in his own devices its lack of significance.

What about a poet? Poetry cannot sound like history. By its very
nature it cannot say *einmal ist keinmal*: if it comes anywhere near
doing this it ceases to be itself. Eliot comes dangerously near it in
The Waste Land by his use of the word "unreal", arranged in a
pattern of typographic isolation. It was modernism's gesture to
the non-event of recent events, but fortunately the rest of the poem
redeems this by its impenetrable singularity. Auden came close to
it in "Spain", which is precariously saved by the authenticity of
its parts and details, though the poem's facile proclamation of faith
would otherwise be a particularly blatant acceptance of historical
meaninglessness – meaninglessness in the form of Marxist "meaning". "Today the struggle", like *"La lutte finale"*, is an especially
insidious version of *einmal ist keinmal*.

In *The Unbearable Lightness of Being*, Kundera contrasts the state of total inner political cynicism in which people live in Eastern Europe, and which supplies the idea behind his title, with the weighty permanence of personal lives, the state of chance relations and events which has brought about commitment and finality. His doomed couple – doomed by the meaningless fact of the fiction, but also, and savingly, by the inevitabilities of any individual life – live for each other and for their dog, who dies agonizingly of cancer. Dogs embody the heaviness of being, and its inescapability, like the pebbles in a poem of Zbigniew Herbert's. Dogs are also powerless, with that powerlessness which is the true fate of the single individual. So are poems, which, as Auden said, make nothing happen. Canetti, in his aphorisms, says that as long as there is one totally powerless person left in the world "I cannot lose all hope". That is both portentous and tiresome, but it links up with Tolstoy's curious observation that freedom consists "in my not having made the laws". The English fancy they are free, said Tolstoy, with that majestic cynicism which often characterized the old man, because they have made their own laws. "But I, in Russia, am truly free, because the laws have nothing whatever to do with me."

The relevance of all this for a poet like Zbigniew Herbert is that it stands on its head the Marxian commandment that freedom is the recognition of necessity. Politics can never recognize necessity; only powerlessness can do so. The paradox today is that this most politically aware poet is also the poet whose works most absolutely reject the unbearable lightness of the political. A. Alvarez, in his introduction to the Carcanet paperback reissue of Herbert's *Selected Poems*, stresses that this poetry is "unremittingly political", but he does not seem to have asked himself why this should be so, and on what contemporary central European paradox this unremittingness is founded. Alvarez makes a ritual contrast between the poets of the West, with their "cosy, domesticated, senselessly sensible way of life in a mass democracy", creating "worlds which are autonomous, internalized, complete inside their own heads", with the stark poetry of the East which is "continually exposed to the impersonal external pressures of politics and history". But such a contrast is all but meaningless except in so far as it reflects the pleasurable sense of guilt and self-accusation which some critics and commentators always express when implying that artists who have really been up against it must be politically *dans le vrai*. All poets and their poetry are subject to the "impersonal external pressures of politics and history". The real contrast today is between those poets who have not made the laws and those who have helped to do so, or are at least conditioned to feel that they have helped, and are helping, to do so.

For the latter kind poetry can make things happen, in a modest way, like any other form of social action. The Ulster poets today write poems about the Irish situation which not only give it a new cultural status but arguably help to form new attitudes, at least among the small minority, perhaps mostly students, who read them. Such poetry is itself a form of social and political discussion, in tone sardonic and reasonable, and all the more effective in its moderate office for not claiming too much. It may be on the side of what Alvarez calls a "cosy, domesticated, senselessly sensible way of life", but it is certainly not "autonomous" and complete inside the poet's head: if it were it might, as poetry, have a greater impact. The autonomous and wholly personal idiom of Auden's early poems has, in retrospect, very much the air of belonging to a poet who has not made the laws, and who has the freedom that comes from being outside them. Yet Auden's idiom seemed precisely that of its age's political anxieties; and so today does Herbert's. Arguably the most "unremittingly" political poetry gets written by poets who are most detached, even – in the special way poets can be – indifferent. Only the powerless really reveal the nature of power; only the non-political understand the nature of politics. This is shown by one of the most "unremitting" political poems ever written – Pushkin's *The Bronze Horseman* – and also by such poems of Herbert's as "Five Men" and "Preliminary Investigation of an Angel".

"Five Men" records the execution of the men, presumably Poles, by a platoon of soldiers, presumably Germans. It refuses to be moved, or moving, and its weight falls on its own question and reply.

> what did the five talk of
> the night before the execution
>
> of prophetic dreams
> of an escapade in a brothel
> of automobile parts
> of a sea voyage
> of how when he had spades
> he ought not to have opened
> of how vodka is best
> after wine you get a headache
> of girls
> of fruit
> of life

After this the poet does not have to answer his own question.

> I did not learn this today
> I knew it before yesterday
> so why have I been writing
> unimportant poems on flowers

The question answers itself. The word "unimportant" disclaims any irony, just as the absence of punctuation – none of Herbert's poems is punctuated – turns all query into statement.

As the tone of "Five Men" resembles exactly the ending of *The Bronze Horseman*, so that of "Preliminary Investigation of an Angel" resembles the tone of Kafka. The angel sheds his angelic being as the investigation proceeds until from his hair "drops of wax run down / and shape on the floor / a simple prophecy". Angel and candle, points of lights, are intermetamorphosed, not by Kafka's nightmare but by the spoken and unspoken nature of Herbert's poetic language. Herbert's detachment is of the kind that takes a lot for granted: there is no point in going on about the nature of things. The last poem in the Carcanet selection, "Why the Classics", tacitly but significantly takes Thucydides for the poet's hero, and in a sense for his model too. In the fourth book of his account of the Peloponnesian War, Thucydides refers briefly to his own minor unsuccessful military assignment to relieve the Athenian colony of Amphipolis before the Spartan general Brasidas got there. He made a quick winter passage with his seven ships but nonetheless arrived too late – an everyday sort of setback for a commander in a war which was fought with dogged persistence rather than strategic brilliance. Herbert is interested in the perfunctoriness with which Thucydides refers to the incident, and contrasts it with the memoirs of "generals of more recent wars" who belittle their colleagues and display everything to their own advantage. The lesson is for art.

> if art for its subject
> will have a broken jar
> a small broken soul
> with a great self-pity
>
> what will remain after us
> will be like lovers' weeping
> in a small dirty hotel
> when wall-paper dawns

"Classical" is the word most often used to describe Herbert's poetry, both in Poland and among readers who know his work in the West. The word is necessarily ambiguous. T. S. Eliot often appealed to the traditions of classicism, and implied, as did Ezra Pound in his way, that his own poetry endorsed them. But the interior of Eliot's poetry is deeply personal, full of romantic secrets and intimacies. These are notably lacking in Herbert. Not that Herbert is impersonal: he presents a Horatian simplicity and openness, a temperament like that of a traveller or classical scholar. His collection of essays on European cultural sites, *Barbarian in the Garden*, contains some of the best travel writing of our time, but is almost disappointing in the way it reveals nothing about the inner life or history of the man himself. One cannot imagine him writing a love poem, or investigating his emotion with the zestful precision of a Robert Graves. His poetry reveals sharply and by contrast how much modern poetry has come to depend on versions of self-pity, and on the way it feeds and builds up the individual interior of a poet's work.

This is not all gain where Herbert is concerned. His poetry can seem flat, formulaic and predictable. Even in the crisp and impeccable translations of Czeslaw Milosz and Peter Dale Scott there is a certain sameness about the parallels along which each poem develops that may not show up in the variety and intimacy of its native tongue, where nuances of idiom and cadence would give it a specialness not available in English correspondence. As the translators point out, Herbert is not classical in the sense of using traditional metres or rhymes; his poetry is more like a spare form of conversation, obviously depending a good deal on word order and on the subtle use of cliché. Well-known poems like "Apollo and Marsyas" and "Elegy of Fortinbras" are no doubt much funnier in the original. In English they depend rather too much on the points they make. In "Apollo and Marsyas" the god of restraint, proportion and clarity, having flayed the faun and cleaned his instrument, departs along "a gravel path hedged with box", leaving his skinless victim uttering one immense howl on a single note, perhaps a new kind of "concrete" poetry. The joke, at the expense both of classicism and of pop art, has a tenderness, but in English the message arrives without the full depth of its implication. No doubt the cruelty of art – even Herbert's own art – arises from the fact that in the very act of creation it necessarily separates itself from human suffering, which cries out from the force and nature of its whole body and blood, and is thus abhorrent to the "god with nerves of artificial fibre".

The impasse left on the English page has no doubt all sorts of sly entrances and exits on the Polish one. The same is probably true of "Elegy of Fortinbras". Fortinbras explains the needs of the world to the dead Hamlet, and tells him that "the rest is not silence but belongs to me".

> I must also elaborate a better system of prisons
> since as you justly said Denmark is a prison
> I go to my affairs This night is born

a star named Hamlet We shall never meet
what I shall leave will not be worth a tragedy

On the face of it the poem has too much point to have a proper
inside territory; but the contrast between the two characters may
well have a greater significance in the original. Hamlet has understood the nature of action: he has in fact "understood", just as a
poem does, but what Fortinbras says of Hamlet – "you knew no
human thing you did not know even how to breathe" – is also true
of a poem.

A brief preliminary note by the translators is oddly defensive,
and yet makes a firm and just point:

> Control, conciseness, honesty and soberness are not always
> to be condemned, least of all when these are qualities of a
> poet who received a proper European initiation into horror
> and chaos. In these times sanity may become as much of a
> corrective to normalcy as the absurd was in an earlier era.

It is indeed a striking thing that so many European poets who when
young went through the full terror of the last war have written in
consequence a poetry of extreme simplicity and precision, avoiding
any overt expression of emotion, and setting the highest value on
the old artifices of logic and reason. Vasko Popa in Serbia was one
such, and Czeslaw Milosz is himself another. Man in extremity
does not imitate the abyss and its moppings and mowings, but
strives rather to detach himself from its absurdity. And it is a
paradox that the sort of sounds made by Marsyas proceed, in our
day and climate, not from anguish and loss of freedom and father-
land, but from the kinds of boredom and meaninglessness inherent
in the affluent society. As Milosz implies, being a Pole connects one,
in an intimacy which is almost comfortable, to the unchanging
horrors of history. The idea that we live in a very special time that
calls for a very special art would cause a Pole to smile. For him it is
always the mixture as before, so that the attitudes and practices of
classicism represent no arbitrary whim on the part of the poet, but
rather the most natural response in art to the imperatives of survival.
Herbert's poetry lives in the flow of history, and among the

artefacts of European culture, as naturally as a pebble in the bed of a stream.

Herbert's great-grandfather was English, and the bizarre coincidence of his name with that of two English poets sharpens the fact of his wholly European rather than Polish status. The family split into two branches, one Catholic and one Protestant, and Herbert's branch settled in Lvov, in the eastern marches, where Polish, Ukrainian and Jewish cultures made a richly cosmopolitan mix. The east has always been a fertile ground for Polish poetry. Mickiewicz came from Vilna, on the borders of Lithuania, as did Milosz. Herbert's mother was Armenian; his father, a professor of economics, a practising Catholic; his grandmother Orthodox. "And, all around, evidences of Hasidic culture . . . hence my syncretic religion." Herbert's cousin, son of an Austrian general on the other side of the family, was one of the thousands of Polish officers murdered by the Russians at Katyn in 1940.

Paradoxically, this almost too nutritious background has probably been instrumental in producing the austerities of Herbert's verse. Instead of submerging itself in the past and in its milieu, with all the helplessness of which some modern poetry makes a virtue, Herbert's poetry detaches itself into a thinner air, almost that dimension of logic and mathematics in which recent Polish scholarship has specialized. Many of the poems in *Report from the Besieged City* employ a persona called Mr Cogito, a not altogether serious figure (sometimes he becomes "the suckling Cogito") who devotes himself nonetheless to some highly serious and abstract questions – on eschatology, autocracy, or death – varied by encounters with a monster who cannot be seen ("the proof of the existence of the monster / is its victims") or with Maria Rasputin, the historical daughter of that Siberian shaman who exercised his influence in imperial Petersburg.

Mr Cogito "would like to remain faithful to uncertain clarity", and rejects "the artificial fires of poetry".

> the piano at the top of the alps
> played false concerts for him

he didn't appreciate labyrinths
the sphinx filled him with loathing . . .

he adored tautologies
explanations
idem per idem

that a bird is a bird
slavery means slavery
a knife is a knife
death remains death

Of course, poetry is always rejecting its own devices, and acquiring new ones in the process. But Herbert is not just saying "My mistress' eyes are nothing like the sun"; his equivalents are precise and cryptographic. The poem "September 17" refers to the precise date in 1939 when the Russians invaded eastern Poland, ten days after the German army had struck in the west. But the date is only allowed its precision in and for itself: the poem is saying the opposite of *einmal ist keinmal*, for in Poland invasion is invasion, a simple and continuous fact and, as Pushkin put it tersely, more than a hundred years earlier and from the eastern side: "The history of Poland is and ought to be a disaster."

knights sleeping in the mountains continue to sleep
so you will enter easily uninvited guest

Herbert is not in the least afraid of the kind of platitude which goes with his simple and perpetual equivalents in history and logic.

My defenceless country will admit you invader
and give you a plot of land under a willow and peace
so those who come after us will learn again
the most difficult art the forgiveness of sins

At the end of the book the title poem, "Report from the Besieged City", explores the same ground and reaches the same conclusion, a conclusion that has none of the brilliance of Milan Kundera's formulation but a great deal more good sense. Since the poet is too old to bear arms

> they graciously gave me the inferior role of chronicler
> I record I don't know for whom the history of the siege . . .
> all of this is monotonous I know it can't move anyone

Nothing can be less exciting than the history of the siege, and once again the conclusion is what anyone might have expected.

> cemeteries grow larger the number of defenders is smaller
> yet the defence continues it will continue to the end
> and if the city falls yet a single man escapes
> he will carry the City within himself on the roads of exile
> he will be the City

Both in relation to Poland and to humanity at large the meaning is as obvious as a syllogism, but it carries its obviousness with the weight and delicacy which makes Herbert so peculiar and so individual a poet.

The Times Literary Supplement, 1986